ABSENT HISTORY

The Untold Story of
Special Branch Operations in Singapore *1915 - 1942*

HORIZON BOOKS, SINGAPORE

© 2001, 2002 Ban Kah Choon

This edition published by
Horizon Books Pte Ltd
130 Killiney Road
Singapore 239561
Email: horizon@horizonbooks.com.sg

First published in 2001 by SNP Media Asia Pte Ltd

Cover Design by Cheryl Marie Song

ISBN 981-04-4788-4

Printed in Malaysia

For my wife, Helen

Acknowledgements

Absent History could not have been written without the generous help and advice from many people and organizations. My gratitude to Benny Lim, Director of the Internal Security Department, whose Department's security education and outreach programme enabled access for the project in the first place and whose advice smoothened the research as well as opened up new directions My thanks to Lin Chung Ying, Director (Projects) who suffered many a bout of writer's mania from me with stoic kindness, Cinda, Christina, Professor Lim Pin, Maureen Olivero, Christopher Yaw, Jacinta Ho, Mark Low and the many past and present officers of the Internal Security Department who have offered advice, help and friendship along the way. Finally, but not least, I would like to thank Chye Heng for the foreword. I am also grateful to Yap Hong Kuan for his reminiscences and some of the photographs.

Foreword

When Kah Choon asked me if I would write the foreword for *Absent History*, even as I was happy to oblige, the thought did occur to me that perhaps an academic rather than a retired Special Branch veteran like myself would be a more appropriate choice. But when I started reading the book, (and it makes an enjoyably good read!) it became clear to me that what he expected of me was to be essentially a real-life touchstone, a reality check. This is because, above all, what he endeavoured to capture in his book was not just the mass of facts and figures from which he re-constructed the history of the pre-war Special Branch, but a sense of the mood and political climate of the period which coloured the organisation as it evolved rapidly, shifting from a police intelligence to a security intelligence orientation.

I was struck by the recognition that much of the security threats faced by Singapore even as a colony more than half a century ago, were not radically or fundamentally different from what we face in present day Singapore. The factors of race and religion were always critical variables whether the threat be a simple matter of an imported cause spilling over to the colony from its principal arena of conflict or a grand revolutionary theory of class struggle. How potent these threats would become depended on how it played out in relation to the racial and religious segments, which made up colonial Singapore. Another perennial strand between then and now was reflected in what Rene Onraet, Director Special Branch (1925–35) wrote, "Untoward events in the Straits Settlements nearly always had an external influence". Based on knowledge and by my own personal experience, this has certainly not changed at all.

The intelligence officer must always be on the lookout for all possibilities and angles. For example, when German prisoners at the Tanglin Barracks subverted their Indian sepoy guards against their British officers and thereby helped bring about the eventual mutiny of

1915. Or when insensitive British army officers failed to take cognisance of an ethnic sensitive rumour that the Indian 5th Light Infantry Regiment in Singapore was being despatched to Turkey to fight fellow Muslims in what was basically a war between Europeans. In these instances, one can recognise why, among the text-book lessons of the craft of security and intelligence, those which must never be forgotten are not to underestimate your adversary, not to take for granted your friends and the fact that most intelligence failures did not stem from blissful ignorance of the threat or even a lack of intelligence but from a self-afflicted blindness which looks but does not see, choosing not to conceive and verify what contradicts one's conventional assumptions. In the world of the Special Branch, a closed mind is more than a moral hazard—it can sometimes be very fatal.

Kah Choon confesses that in writing this book, he has made a fascinating journey but which has saddled him at its conclusion with more questions than answers; he says "so much is still familiar but much is also no longer quite the same". He is not alone in this sentiment. There was more than the occasional moment of déjà vu for this reader. The reference to the Banishment Warrants issued against subversives and criminal elements who posed a serious threat to public order and security of the Singapore colony and the Straits Settlements stir personal recall from my early police career under the British, of scenes of people wailing and hurling obscenities at the CID building, then at Robinson Road, in protest against the banishment of their relatives.

Even though the point is not new, it was still interesting to read and trace how the struggles and campaigns of the Communist Party of Malaya after the War had its roots in the revolutions of Russia and China, how the purity of the ideological argument which inspired and gave hope to the oppressed classes in the end also created a structure like Comintern which turned doctrine into dogmatism and discipline into obedient blindness, the latter probably more than anything, made a Lai Teck possible. And in the end, as the CPM leaders themselves must admit, the failure of the revolution laid in the party's failure to genuinely turn itself (and not for the lack of trying) into a multi-racial movement to transcend its Chinese-dominated personality (which however reflected its historical sources of strength).

I believe *Absent History* is the first substantial book written about the Special Branch in Singapore, covering its work and operations both in the then colony and the rest of the Straits Settlements from its beginnings to the eve of the Second World War. While the book no doubt holds value to the student of history and politics, as well as I contend, security and intelligence professionals, it is a book intended for the lay reader for whom I am confident its narrative will prove an enjoyable and worthwhile experience.

Lim Chye Heng
Director, Internal Security Department
(1975–1982)

15 January 2001

Editor's Note:

Lim Chye Heng served 22 years of a 30-year public service career in intelligence and security work. A CID police officer from the '50s to the '60s, he served in the Special Branch under British, Malaysian and Singapore governments from 1960 to 1966. He then spent the next eight years in intelligence work in the Ministry of Defence before assuming the position of Director, Internal Security Department. He is on record as the longest serving Director of ISD, holding the critical appointment from 1975 till his retirement in 1982.

By way of an introduction …

Absent History examines the events that led to the founding of the Special Branch in 1916 and traces its subsequent development until the Second World War overtook British Malaya and Singapore. Despite the relatively short period of the history—lasting less than 30 years—these were without doubt momentous years. While it is usual to think of the First World War as a European conflict that had little real bearing on other countries, even more so a clutch of colonies nestled in an obscure corner of the East, the fact of the matter was that the War signalled a break between the 19th century and the throes of modernity. The conflict, which slaughtered the flower of European youth, was the culmination of years of jockeying for colonial and imperial power, the consequence of industrialization and the creation of weapons of mass killings as well as the assertion of conflicting systems of thought.

Britain's Asian possessions could not be insulated from these events. The First World War brought into sharp focus the challenges to the hitherto largely uncontested hegemony of British colonialism. One of the ways this came about was the increasing influx of new ideas to the colonies: religious doctrines, nascent nationalism, resistance to colonialism and alternative political/social doctrines found ready adherents and a sympathetic hearing. The complexity of this phenomenon, which the Special Branch had to grapple with, was reflected both in the variety as well as the extent of the threats the new and diverse thinking spawned. Where colonial policing had been concerned mainly with criminal activities (triads, pirates, robberies and murders) the new problems seeped deeply into religious as well as political fields, complicated further by an international dimension since the origin for such events frequently came from external developments in Asia and Europe. Responses to modernity and imperialism, the efforts by Japan to establish an imperial presence, the calls from the Middle East for a religious war and the Bolshevik revolution of 1917 in Russia all contributed to a security landscape that was at once convoluted and dense. Indeed, the 1915 mutiny of the Indian troops in Singapore bore these multiple characteristics, being the result of an explosive amalgam of German instigation, Indian nationalism, religious fundamentalism and anti-colonialism. While the mutiny never really posed much of a danger to British dominance after the first anxious days, its repercussions were momentous.

Outbreaks like the 1915 mutiny posed no immediate threat to British hegemony, which sat securely on its unrivalled military power. However, there were also those who were perspicacious enough to realize that history had taken a turn. The stage was set for the struggle of competing political and social ideals, many of which had their inspirational origins in faraway Europe or China. The strategic dimensions of colonial security had been irreversibly altered and a different response was needed to meet the threat. In the twenties, radical revolutionary uprisings occurred in many parts of Asia especially in China, French Indo-China and Indonesia. Many of these made common cause, were influenced or directed by the Communist Third International in Russia that saw colonial wars as an effective response to the threats of European war.

Moreover the human landscape of the colonies was also undergoing rapid changes during this period. Immigration swelled the population. At the turn of the century, the Chinese numbered only 800,000. By the eve of the Second World War, this had increased to 2.5 million, a third of the population of the Federated Malay States. British policies helped to further accentuate this change. The Great Depression in 1930 brought much hardship. As the number of unemployed increased, the colonial Government reduced the quota of immigrants allowed to enter Singapore. Although the number of male arrivals fell drastically, this did not decrease female arrivals, as the law did not affect them. One consequence was the increase in number of the locally born, who thought of British Malaya as their homeland. In addition, the number of Chinese who journeyed back to China was also reduced, as many were fearful that they would be refused permission to return. Those who stayed often married and settled down in Malaya and Singapore, adding to the numbers of those who had a stake in these lands.

From the beginning, the Special Branch never thought of itself as a domestic policing unit concerned only with the immediate problems of native or local origins. How else could it have been? Britain's Southeast Asian colonies were trading enclaves, open to the constant passage and transit of people, goods and ideas. These new ways of thinking, whether they be about empire or revolution, crossed barriers as distance shrank given advances in transport and communication. Singapore's rapidly developing importance as a hub of maritime trade also meant that it was exposed to the newest developments in other lands. The security threat to the region reflected the burgeoning unrest in Europe, Northeast Asia and the Eurasian heartland as communist ideology, strikes, extremist religious outlooks, pan-Asianism and nationalism struggled to gain centre stage.

The history of the Special Branch is then a complex, multi-dimensional response to all these circumstances and threats. The Branch had an often-privileged view of the unfolding events that was unique. While it no doubt represented the establishment's sense of things, at the same time the very nature of Special Branch work meant that it sought and almost always possessed a view of the other side of things, of what the potential adversary thought and believed in. Although the Branch often acted anonymously, its input into the colonial government's perspectives and responses to events was often very important and, in certain cases, decisive.

In writing this account, I feel much like a person who takes a walk down the half-lit corridors of a familiar past but armed now with an unusual map. There are many turnings and doors that beckon. Some of these doors I have knocked on and entered only to retreat, mindful of the time and commitment to remain faithful to the subject of my main narrative—the history of how the Special Branch began in Singapore and the activities, as well as the operations it engaged in. I have found it a fascinating tour, rewarding in terms of the archival materials the research threw up as well as the questions that the project raises. A challenging project should perhaps throw up more questions than the answers that it provides. If this is so, I am consoled for I have at the journey's end, more questions than when I began; so much is still familiar but much is also no longer quite the same.

I am aware that the documents I examined represent both an account of events and actions as well as their representation. History offers a certain kind of knowledge, detailing facts and occurrences, yet it is also as much about the ways these are narrated and presented to the readers. If on the one hand we gain an understanding of the socio-historical processes of the period we are examining, we ought also to appreciate the processes that lie behind that story. In trying to trace out and interpret that which is otherwise absent, we need to go beyond the immediate facts of that history, to look at the interstices, the narratives and the wider culture of that moment. And then there is another dimension, the role of the reader in bringing his own preoccupations and interests to the past. Yet all these layered perspectives would not be possible in the first place unless what is absent to view sees the light of day and is out before us again. History is a presence of what is there and available as well as what is not there, not available, forgotten, buried or silent.

Secretive by the nature of its work, self-effacing by training and operational philosophy, and bound by laws and codes of secrecy, the contributions of the Special Branch to Singapore / Malayan history often went unrecognized. The present volume is an attempt to tilt the scores somewhat; to put before the reader the drama, the history and the achievements of the Branch, the events during the 30 years from its creation to the Japanese invasion. In doing this I hope to restore some of the missing pieces or perhaps sketch the outlines of the hidden but otherwise crucial roles of the pre-War Special Branch, to coax and bring out to light some of that vital absent history.

Contents

Tales of Unrest

1915: THE CRUCIAL YEAR

On 14 February 1915, Singapore was in the midst of celebrating the Chinese New Year. The sounds of firecrackers and festive bombs filled the air. Despite the outbreak of war in Europe there was much to celebrate and a three-day holiday had been declared. Singapore was cushioned from the strife, far removed from the killing fields of France. The colony was prosperous and continued to benefit from much of the building that had made it very much a metropolitan centre of the East. Dissidence and trouble were the last things on the minds of its inhabitants, whether these be the Chinese traders or coolies engaged in festivities or the politically dominant British with their endless rounds of sports, fashionable tea and evening sundowners. The celebrations continued into the next day. Chinatown and, in particular, the New Bridge Road area were thronged with revellers. Some British ventured in their cars to see the celebrations. However, most avoided the noise, preferring the quiet of their homes in Tanglin. As it was a holiday, sporting and other leisure activities of the British residents were in full swing. Some swam, others had tea at the fashionable Raffles, Adelphi or Europa Hotels. A number, such as Major A M Thomson, were at the Padang watching a cricket match at the Singapore Cricket Club, that bastion of imperial pride. The command centre at Fort Canning, the nerve of Singapore's defence, was all but closed with only one person, Mr Blackman, a schoolteacher and telephone operator on duty. It was, as far as the authorities were concerned, no more than the usual Sunday of a prosperous, settled and orderly imperial colony fast becoming the most important port in Asia. It was, of course, 1915; the European war was entering its second bloody year. However, except for the minor incursion of the German cruiser, *Emden*, the previous November, there was little discernible trouble as far as the military was concerned.

At 3.00 p.m. of 15 February, residents in the Alexandra and Normanton areas heard rifle shots. Most dismissed these since it was hardly unusual to hear rounds going off as the army barracks were located there. Others who heard the shots mistook them for firecrackers, part of the Chinese New Year festivities. They were wrong. The shots signalled the start of an attempted mutiny by the Indian troops of the 5th Light Infantry. The British authorities did not appear to have any inkling of trouble. General Ridout, the General Officer Commanding British forces in Singapore, had just that morning inspected the troops and reported that he was favourably impressed with their turnout. Shortly after 2.00 p.m., a group of sepoys under the supervision of the Quartermaster, Hav Muhammad Yar, was loading ammunition onto a lorry at the regimental magazine. The ammunition was to be transferred to the Fort Canning ammunition dump ahead of the regiment's deployment to Hong Kong. Naik Sazawar Khan, assisted by Naik Muhammad Sadiq, with two store orderlies, Mahboub and Ali Baksh, in attendance led the working party. After having completed loading the ammunition, the men started to take on two barrels of oil. At that moment a sepoy, Ismail, from C Company, fired a shot at them. This seemed to have been the catalyst, if not the signal, for the mutiny as the men from A and B Companies of the right wing, comprising mainly Rajput Muslims, poured out onto the parade ground and seized control of the camp.

While some of the sepoys laid siege to their commanding officer, Colonel Martin, in the barracks, other sepoys set off with other objectives. One group of mutineers rushed to the nearby internment camp at the Tanglin Barracks to free the German prisoners, expecting them to join in the general uprising. A larger group moved towards the city, some four miles away. These went towards the Sepoy Lines area emerging in the New Bridge Road area with the General Hospital to their right. As the first reports of the mutiny reached the authorities there was still skepticism. Quite a few thought that it was merely one or two Indians who had gone amok. They were soon proved rudely wrong as the first reports of European casualties, the targets of the Indian mutineers, came in. At 4.30 p.m., General Ridout informed the Governor, Sir Arthur Young, at Government House that a mutiny had broken out among the men of the 5th Light Infantry.

Despite the immediate steps that the Governor took in asking for help from nearby naval forces, the mutiny was clearly an unpleasant surprise to the British in their sunny, cosmopolitan and rich haven in the tropics. The mutiny was a watershed in the way the British would regard and respond to threats to the internal security of their Malayan colonies. It was a loss of innocence, alerting the British to the fact that Singapore, their prized island possession, had become a crossroad where revolutionary ideas and political sedition found fertile ground for the breeding of militant radicalism. The War Office gave its considered view of this in September 1915, noting in a memorandum to the Colonial Office that:

> there is no doubt that Singapore, from its geographical position, was the stopping place of any rank seditionists, whose names have since been brought to light in trials in India. The place was a depository at one time, before the War and subsequently for a time, for seditious literature.[1]

Many serving officers in the colony even at the start of 1915 would have regarded this view as alarmist. Certainly, at the beginning of the 20th century, the British would appear to have little, if any, reason to be concerned about their tropical possessions in Southeast Asia. The Straits Settlements comprising Malacca, Penang and Singapore were developing quickly into significant hubs of the British Empire's trade. In particular, Singapore was showing all the signs of its prosperity as it evolved into a thriving, cosmopolitan city. There was cause for equal satisfaction with the Malay states. Sir John Anderson, Governor of the Straits Settlements and High Commissioner of the Federated Malay States (FMS), was full of praise for the progress in the FMS. Large tracts of land had been brought under commercial cultivation or were being mined for minerals. Roads and railways linked key towns together to the ports of Singapore and Penang, generating a steady flow of revenue and personal wealth. Law and order was firmly established, a reliable police force was in place and the British flag flew unchallenged on the key waterways that controlled the flow of ships and immigrants. Better still there appeared to be little that could challenge the supremacy of British power. Despite the occasional riot by Chinese secret societies there were, to Sir John Anderson's mind, the obvious advantages of civilization that British rule had brought to all. Malaya had more than all the

> usual adjuncts of administration and comforts and amenities of civilization than any of the Crown Colonies in the Empire.[2]

If this sounded somewhat fulsome, many of the British planters and traders would have regarded it as well justified.

The land and their lives were as close to paradise as many of them could have wished for. The country was, of course, hot, humid and sticky, far removed from the fashion or cultural bazaars of London, Paris and Berlin. However, once you accepted the distance there were all kinds of advantages. The Malayan peninsula was not a cruel place. Frank Swettenham, another governor of the Straits Settlements, wrote nostalgically of how often his mind returned to

> the narrow land that lies between two storm-swept seas, itself more free from violent convulsions than almost any other. There is perpetual summer; no volcanoes, no earthquakes, no cyclones. Even the violence of the monsoons that lash the China Sea and the Indian Ocean into periodical fury, is largely spent before it reaches the unprotected seaboards of the richly dowered peninsula.[3]

British paramountcy and the invincibility of British arms upon which all this rested was unchallenged. This important and comforting assurance was always a ready reminder to any dissident behind the obvious gloss of progress, prosperity, material wealth, trading dominance, exclusively white clubs and colonial pomp. A few defence planners suspected that this power was a fragile illusion that had yet to be put to the test. The Achilles' heel of colonial defence came from the increasing dependence upon native troops. Like the Romans, the British Empire had expanded until it needed mercenary troops to police its long and distant frontiers. In Southeast Asia and China, as in India itself, Indian troops were widely used to garrison imperial outposts and fight various colonial wars. Like all mercenary troops, as the Romans found out, unfailing reliability of these troops to the Crown could not be guaranteed. Besides, there was always the memory of the Indian Mutiny in 1857 to bring back to mind the consequences of what might happen if native troops got the better of their British masters.

A reminder of this vulnerability shocked the complacency of the British community in Singapore on 15 February, the second day of the Chinese New Year when elements of the 5th Light Infantry mutinied in its Alexandra Road barracks. The 5th Light Infantry was the main garrison unit defending Singapore even though it was in the process of being reassigned to Hong Kong. The first thought that came to many in the colony was that this was a replay of the dreaded events of the Indian Mutiny. Compared with the Indian Mutiny though the number of human lives lost was relatively low. Even then some 40 were killed. The uprising itself was soon put down; it was over in less than a week, suppressed by a mixed force of allied troops that responded to the colony's call for help. However, the trauma of the event was felt in all its severity. It also had a lasting impact on the development of internal security in the colony. *Blackwood's Magazine* carried a report by a woman observer that managed to evoke for us the terror and desperation of those days:

> I never felt more frightened in my life; my knees seemed to be giving way, and I kept saying to myself, "Keep your head, keep your head." ...

> The Indian Mutiny flashed into my mind, also the fact that we had no white troops. L was splendid, so cool and collected, but his face was as white as death. I knew he felt pretty desperate ...[4]

This mutiny was all the more dangerous as it coincided with plans by the Germans with whom the British were at war to undermine the British Empire by fomenting unrest among its native subjects through appealing to their religious sentiments. One aim of the mutineers of the 5th Light Infantry was to free the German prisoners of war held in the nearby detention camp. Together with these trained military men, the Indian sepoys intended to seize control of the island.

The British should have known that the peaceful harmony of their colony was deceptive. Even before Britain entered the European war in August 1914 the Germans were already sowing dissension among the Turks and other Middle Eastern peoples. There was also the increasing violence of the pan-Indian nationalists, especially the militant Ghadr (Mutiny) movement. Indian political agitators sought to spread their message of resistance to colonialism among the Indian troops who provided a supply of trained fighters. When the European war broke out, a popular strategy was to attack the British for sending Indian troops to fight what was essentially a European war. Ghadr agents also subverted morale by discouraging Muslim troops from fighting with Turkey, an Islamic nation. At the crossroads of commerce and sea traffic, Singapore was a key hub where agents, provocateurs and spies passed or stopped to recruit sympathizers. Its strategic position also made it an important node through which these varying ideas competed and contested for supremacy. Singapore as the first port of call for travellers, immigrants and traders of all descriptions and pretensions, the gateway to the Malayan interior, was inevitably at the front of this invisible ideological war of intelligence, subversion and espionage.

In the early years of the 20th century, the internal security of British Malaya and the Straits Settlements was threatened by the very reasons that had led to the rapid development of the Straits Settlements. As trading and commercial centres, the FMS and the Straits Settlements were often exposed to all the currents of competing ideologies and politics that jostled for dominance. Many international currents of intrigue and alternative politics came together in Singapore, an important crossroad of Asian trade. Singapore, thus, attracted a host of often-unwelcome guests who were putting into operation the orders of distant governments or organizations. The basic or *ur*-text of the security threat to Singapore came into prominence in this way. The threat to Singapore was external, emanating from outside agencies with the agenda of displacing British colonial power. On the other hand, the British security agencies made it their primary business to detect, monitor and neutralize these efforts. For them the threat to the internal security of Singapore (as well as of Malaya) was from without. Events and ideas that had their origins far away from the island invariably affected the colony. This belief became the standard operating doctrine guiding the various security organizations set up by the British to protect their paramountcy.

One consequence of these events was the formation of the Special Branch, which was to play an increasingly important role in the security of Singapore. The necessity for a group of men trained in the arcane arts of internal security such as intelligence gathering, the monitoring of suspects, counter-espionage and the running of agents was recognized almost immediately after the 1915 mutiny. From such a small beginning the Special Branch grew into an efficient force that successfully thwarted repeated attempts from groups out to challenge and displace the British. The highpoint of the Branch's activities must be the successful infiltration of its main adversary, the Malayan Communist Party. By 1935, the Branch was so much in control that it was routinely reading the top secret documents of the MCP, arresting nearly all its top officials and, in a coup that must surely rank as one of the most significant in intelligence work, manoeuvred one of its agents to the top post as secretary-general of the Malayan Communist Party.

The mutiny of the 5th Light Infantry of the British Indian Army in Singapore brought all the weaknesses of colonial defence into unwelcome focus. Indian soldiers had come to play a strong military role in the strategy of the Empire. They had become increasingly necessary to the defence of the Indian subcontinent; their hitherto unquestioned loyalty had meant that they were also a ready source of recruits in the various colonial wars. Indian troops had taken part in the suppression of the Boxer rebellion and had also just recently been deployed in the autumn 1914 occupation of German possessions in the port city of Tsingtao in China. In Malaya Indians—mainly Sikhs, Pathans and Punjabis—formed the colony's first and best-organized local regiment, the Malay States Guides (MSG). In terms of firepower and training the MSG was on par with British units and certainly superior to the small 391-men force of the Johore Military Forces or the even more poorly trained part-time units such as the Singapore Volunteer Force that constituted the reserve defence for British Malaya. Indians were also well represented in the Straits Settlements' police force. There was, in Malaya, a strong Sikh contingent of 220 men (out of 1,420 men) which was often deployed for anti-rioting activities. This contingent was also the best trained of the police units.

Even more worrying was that the mutiny of the 5th Light Infantry was not an isolated event. The first two years of the First World War, which tested Britain sorely, saw not one but three episodes in Malaya where the might and prestige of the British Empire were challenged. The 1915 mutiny was preceded by an equally serious act of rebellion when the MSG in 1914 refused to serve overseas. Delicate handling resulted in a negotiated settlement. However, this could not disguise the blot on British prestige. In particular, the outright refusal to carry out an order threatened the perennial tenuous relationship between the colonial masters and the increasing army of mercenaries needed to police the Empire. A third spot of trouble soon occurred. Almost before the sounds of the firing squad executing the 47 mutineers of the 5th Light Infantry had time to fade, Langham-Carter, the British Adviser to the Sultan of Kelantan, telegraphed Singapore in April 1915 about a serious uprising that had broken out in the Pasir Puteh district of the state. While the Kelantan trouble is usually seen as a separate event— a specifically 'Malayan' problem—the beginnings of armed resistance and nationalist dissatisfaction with British rule among the indigenous Malays had most certainly emerged. Indeed, throughout much of the first decade of the 20th century parts of the northern states, especially Kedah, were gripped by so-called 'bandit' troubles. While not directly a challenge to British rule, rural unrest, nonetheless, signalled a major fault line in the colonial society that sustained imperialism. It is possible to argue that the 'bandit' problems reflected social unhappiness with the reforms that British colonial planners were forcing upon the existing social and political structures.

The 15 February mutiny in 1915 was part of a larger wave of unrest that rippled through British possessions in Asia. The immediate events and shape of the mutiny are too well known to need much discussion[5]. However, the mutiny clearly tested the colony's response to internal security at a time when it was least prepared. It would be wrong though to say that the authorities were caught entirely by surprise. The interesting thing from our perspective is that intelligence monitoring and espionage were already at work. The British were aware that the Indian troops were the target of political agents of the Ghadr Party that advocated disobedience and armed action against colonialism. British intelligence was already actively monitoring them and the Colonial Office in London was certainly aware of the inspiring force and organization behind such agitation. Perhaps, it was more of the failure to take advantage of or to disseminate such intelligence that led to the British being caught unawares when the uprising actually occurred. In the event, the British did not hesitate to redress this slip, taking vigorous steps to create a broad and effective intelligence system in the years after.

The 5th Light Infantry was a veteran of colonial wars. Its roll of battle honours included Arakan, Afghanistan, Ghunze and Kandahar in 1842 as well as Kabul, Moodkee, Ferozeshah and Sobroan in 1857. The regiment also took part in the Third Burmese War of 1885–87 that ended in the annexation of Burma as well as in the Second Afghan War of 1879–80. It could therefore be regarded in every sense of the word as a trusted unit competently successful in frontier wars and colonial policing duties. The 5th Light Infantry originally comprised two battalions, one raised at Fategarh, the other at Cawnpore. Its various titles are themselves a historical record of the shifting vicissitudes of the Indian army. First called the 2nd Battalion 21st Regiment Native Infantry, it became the 42nd Native Infantry in 1824 and then a Light Infantry in 1843. After the Indian Mutiny, the 42nd Native Infantry was designated as the 5th Bengal Native (Light) Infantry in 1861. In 1885, the word *native* was dropped and the regiment took its name as the 5th Light Infantry in 1902 after the army reforms. The 5th Light Infantry was, therefore, a proud regiment with a string of victories behind its name. Perhaps it was its battle honours that made it one of the leading choices for garrison duties in an important port of the Empire. On 26 March 1914, the regiment left Nowgong in the Indian central provinces for Singapore, its first overseas posting.

Much has been written of the unhappiness the troops endured in their new garrison duties. Despite the reputation of Singapore as a land of milk and honey for European residents, the island was an alien landscape in many ways to the men of the 5th Light Infantry. Among other complaints were those of their rations. Goat and goat's milk, important parts of their staple diet, were hard to come by. The men had to make do with the more expensive chicken meat for their protein. To the high cost of living was added the poor indecisive leadership of the officers. These led to a gradual loss of morale and a loosening of discipline. There was dissension and disagreement between the new commanding officer, Lieutenant-Colonel Edward Victor Martin, who had just assumed his duties in 1913, and a number of senior officers. Not only was the chain of command somewhat in disarray, leadership was also ineffective. Lieutenant-Colonel Martin was to bear the brunt of the blame—a file note on the subsequent Court of Inquiry into the mutiny condemns him as a "hopeless CO" (Harper and Miller, 1984, p. 226). However, the military command as a whole must share the fault since it was not alert to the possibility of trouble despite the presence of obvious signs. What intelligence coverage available was not collocated; certainly no appropriate threat assessment was made or an alert scenario (the point at which an intelligence officer would regard as potentially dangerous) studied. It was not that information was entirely absent. There was certainly intelligence monitoring not just of seditionist elements but also of elements in the 5th Light Infantry suspected to be open to subversion. This must suggest that the unit had been identified somewhere by someone as being a possible source of trouble. With the outbreak of war, postal censorship had been stepped up. The authorities were aware of extremist sentiments from their reading of the mail. In addition some surveillance of local dissidents was also carried out. Unfortunately, these efforts were not sustained. To make matters worse, information was usually controlled by the security service in India so that much of it was not available to local planners. The British were especially interested in the activities of Muslim religious teachers or *imam* who were being watched. Yet nothing was really done; the colonial administration at Fort Canning maintained its rather nonchalant attitude that sedition had little to do with internal security. If there were any problems with the 5th Light Infantry, they argued that these were largely issues of poor discipline that could be sorted out with proper military leadership.

This muddled state of affairs was reflected in the rambling, unfocused findings of the subsequent Court of Inquiry held to look into the reasons for the mutiny. Despite an exhaustive investigation that ran into some 400 printed pages of oral evidence, written statements and other details, the Inquiry leant towards the somewhat lame and incredulous explanation that poor discipline was primarily responsible for the outbreak of trouble:

> the British officers were at sixes and sevens. The Indian officers
> of the right (or mutinous) wing were divided up into two camps.
>
> (Sareen, 1995, p. 38)

Of course, the report does mention contributory causes since these became glaringly obvious in the course of the investigation. These larger issues were expressed, or 'fudged' being the better term, as

> the sowing and growth of fanatical ideas which were carefully
> planted and fostered by cunning agencies.
>
> (Sareen, 1995, pp. 38–39)

In his discussion of the report, Sareen concludes that:

> it appears from the evidence available that the Court of Inquiry was more concerned with the question of quick punishment of the mutineers than to find out the real cause of the mutiny. The court could never think that the sepoys rose against the authorities due to national awakening or as a result of the dissatisfaction with the system under which they were working.
>
> (Sareen, 1995, p. 18)

Yet evidence emerges from the Inquiry itself as well as other sources that the mutiny had a radically political and religious dimension. The 1915 mutiny was not just a spot of unrest among garrison troops dissatisfied with their cantonment duties. It fitted into a larger context of political agitation and manoeuvring that brought together German efforts at subversion and Ghadr attempts at fomenting agitation. Ideas of nationhood, resistance and national independence were swirling among the Indians at this time. Many Muslims were uneasy about the war with Turkey. For many Muslim troops, war with Turkey was unpopular and, arguably heretical, since a *fatwa* from the Turkish ruler had called for a holy war against the British.

The General Officer in Charge of Singapore, General Ridout, had informed Lieutenant-Colonel Martin as early as 27 January 1915 that the 5th Light Infantry would be moved to garrison duties in Hong Kong. As Harper and Miller underline, this would, in effect, deprive an important strategic colony of the only regular battalion of troops at a time when the Empire was at war:

> A possible reason was given in the Singapore Government's review of the affairs of the colony for 1915 when, in dealing with the mutiny, it said, 'Rumours of disaffection (within the regiment) no doubt influenced the military authorities in their decision to remove the regiment to another station.'
>
> (Harper and Miller, 1984, p. 31)

That Ridout chose to take the risk suggests that he, at least, was convinced that the 5th Light Infantry should be moved out of Singapore, taking it even further away from India, the fountain of its unrest. It seems likely that by 27 January 1915 when the decision was made, Singapore was already alerted to the disaffection within the regiment. In fact, Ridout's decision to redeploy the regiment out of Singapore follows a pattern the British had been using to solve the issue of likely unrest. When the regiment was sent to Singapore in 1914, the aim could have been to break its links with subversive forces. In posting the regiment to Hong Kong—and this, we must remember, was done within less than a year of their arrival in Singapore—a similar solution was being employed. The regiment was this time sent even further away from India, the focus of any likely revolutionary sentiment. In the same way, the 130 Baluchi, an Indian regiment, had been similarly transferred to Burma in November 1914, thereby avoiding the possible "revolt of the regiment" (Kuwajima, 1991, p. 35) that had come under strong

Ghadr influence. Such redeployment of troops out of India appeared to be carried out for reasons of the internal security of the subcontinent without much thought for the actual situation of the colonies they were being posted to.

With the benefit of hindsight, it was rather unwise to send the 5th Light Infantry to Singapore. The Malayan colonies had a substantial Indian population by 1914:

> In the Federated Malay States, the estimated number was 172,000; in the Straits Settlements, 82,000 and in the Unfederated Malay States, 13,000, making a total of 270,000.
>
> (Khoo, 1975, p. 2)

Indians were found in every sector of the commercial and administrative lives of the colonies. Moreover, the positions of the colonies as transit points for trade and passengers meant that current news, political ideas and religious doctrines could find their way easily to the population. This was the case with the militant doctrines of Indian nationalists as it would be with communist ideals in the next decade.

To make matters worse the deployment of the 5th Light Infantry was handled in a typically colonial manner. The news of its posting to Hong Kong was conveyed in a cursory, offhand manner without an attempt to set the troops' minds at ease. Soon a rumour swept through the wholly Muslim regiment that they were being sent to fight Turkey. Despite some efforts by a few English officers to convince the sepoys that their destination was Hong Kong, the damage had been done. Rumours continued to spread throughout the regiment. Even as the Commanding Officer, Lieutenant-Colonel Martin, announced to the regiment that their deployment on 16 January was for Hong Kong, agitators like Chistie Khan, subsequently identified as a ringleader, spread mischief among the sepoys, convincing many that it was actually Turkey they were sailing for and that the British wanted them to fight against their Muslim brothers. Some of the British officers were sensitive to this religious dimension. At the Inquiry, Captain Lionel Ball, the double company commander, stated his firm opinion:

> that the mutiny was engineered on religious grounds.
>
> (Sareen, 1995, p. 419)

Pressed for his reasons by the Court, which in any case went on to ignore them, Ball maintained that religion was the common factor used by the mutineers to identify themselves. Thus when the sepoys broke into the internment compound holding the Germans the first thing they did was to question the prisoners, "You Mohammedans?"

The mutiny broke out on 15 February at 2.00 p.m. with the first shot fired by sepoy Ismail Khan. This was apparently the signal for the right wing of the 5th Light Infantry, made up of Rajputs, to begin the uprising. After looting the magazine of its small arms ammunition the mutineers soon moved beyond the camp. However, the mutineers did not appear to know quite what to do once they had met their initial objectives. The general consensus among writers who have studied the 1915 mutiny is that the lack of concrete aims led to the rapid disintegration of the mutiny after the initial success. Within two days, by 17 February, the "mutinous right wing had become a scattered, leaderless rabble" (Harper and Miller, 1984, p. 172). In fact, most of the casualties inflicted by the Indian troops occurred in this early period. All in all, some 40 Europeans, Chinese and Malays were killed and wounded between 15 and 17 February. The number of casualties tailed off after that and did not amount to anything significant in the following days. In his sermon reported in *The Straits Times* of 4 March 1915, the Bishop of Singapore gave thanks for the narrow escape of the colony. Like many he attributed this to:

> the lack of a prepared plan of actions amongst the mutineers. Had they been ready with some definite plan of attack on Singapore at the beginning of the outbreak how many of us would be alive now? Scarcely any, as far as we can judge. So it was lack of preparation on their part which lost advantage to them.
>
> (Sareen, 1995, p. 838)

It was this absence of a rigorously pursued strategy rather than any competent moves by the authorities that prevented the mutineers from making headway and a more severe situation from developing.

However, this did not mean that there were no plans at all. It was comforting to the British to feel that the mutiny had something of the nature of instant combustion, that is, it happened almost by itself. This 'explanation' effectively prevented any further discussion of the more complex reasons that could have triggered off an incident like the 1915 mutiny. But there was, on reflection, a strong possibility that plans were already in place to foment trouble. The initial stages of the mutiny suggest that the troops knew what their key objectives were. This aspect was downplayed in keeping with the official and public view that the mutiny was nothing more than a breakdown of discipline. The actions of the mutineers on that first afternoon suggest that they did want to achieve specific goals. Ismail Khan, who fired a round at a party of soldiers loading ammunition for Fort Canning could have felt that news of the mutiny had leaked out and suspected that the British were removing the ammunition to prevent it from falling into the hands of the Indians.

Having seized the ammunition (itself, a significant act that immediately suggests that some planning had been done), the mutineers set off in three columns. One party of some 80 sepoys led by Havildar Ibrahim headed for the German prisoners of war camp two miles away. They hoped to free and to get the Germans to join them in the general uprising. This aim was, however, frustrated as the prisoners, perhaps with a clearer understanding of the military situation, opted to throw in their lot with the British. The Germans were more terrified of the mutineers' intentions, preferring the relative safety of their detention cells. A second party of mutineers moved towards the Sepoy Lines, eventually penetrating the Central Police Station. The intention here appeared to be to head for the commercial and civic district. However, intentions are not good enough in war or mutiny. Stripped of any clearly discernible strategic objectives once they had made their first move, the sepoys soon concerned themselves with the killing of any British they happened to meet. A third group numbering 100 to 150 sepoys proceeded to the Band barrack in Alexandra Road. There, having murdered the CO, Captain Maclean, they forced arms upon the Malay States Guides, urging them to join in the uprising. The effort failed. As with the Germans, the appeal fell on deaf ears. Many of the Guides did not respond. Instead they wandered around aimlessly in disconsolate groups until they were rounded up and confined to their barracks.

***

Let us put all this into perspective from an internal security point of view. The British administration had fewer than 600 men to quell the mutiny. On the morning of 15 February, the military forces in Singapore consisted of the following:

1. The 5th Light Infantry stationed at Alexandra Barracks — 9 British officers, 818 officers and men (Indians)

2. The mountain battery section of the Malay States stationed at Alexandra Barracks — 1 British officer, 97 officers and men (Indians)

3. A detachment of the 36th Sikhs quartered   60 men (Indians)
   at Tanglin Barracks awaiting the arrival
   of the regiment from Hong Kong for
   deployment elsewhere

4. The Royal Garrison Artillery and Royal   7 officers and
   Engineers stationed at Pulau Brani and   231 men (Europeans)
   Blakang Mati   3 officers and
                                                115 men (Indians)

5. The Malay States Volunteer Rifles   4 officers and 81 men
   undergoing a month's training at   (Europeans)
   Normanton Camp[6]

Across the straits was the small detachment of the Johore Military Force. Besides the Indian troops only the Johore Military Force, the handful of British artillerymen and the 85 sailors from *HMS Cadmus* had proper military training. The Malay States Volunteers hardly had any training. The left wing of the 5th Light Infantry had not joined in the rebellion but could not be used to suppress the mutiny as their loyalty was suspect. In fact, the men from the left wing were disarmed at the first opportunity for fear they would be tempted to join their colleagues. Against the British were ranged the 300 sepoys from the double companies of the right wing of the 5th Light Infantry. In fact, the final round-up of the mutineers netted more than 600 men as a number of the Malay States Guides were also detained. In addition, there was also the fear that if the mutiny were to spread beyond Singapore, there could be real trouble from the 800 Malay States Guides. The situation was desperate enough on the first day. In the first push of the mutiny, the 5th Light Infantry not only set upon the detention barracks, attacked the quarters of the British soldiers, came within reach of the strategic docks as well as the Central Police Station but were also poised near the downtown civic areas like Commercial Square and the Town Hall.

The threat was, thus, in the initial stages frighteningly real, exacerbated by the lack of personnel familiar with internal security or military matters. There were many volunteers pressed into service by the urgency of the situation who did not know how to mount a proper patrol or even one end of the rifle from the other. So desperate was the situation that the British even signed up the Japanese as special constables forming a 190-strong Giyotai or Volunteer Corps. The Japanese, on their part, extracted the promise from the British to reimburse their daily meals and necessary expenses. In the first hours of the mutiny, the Singapore authorities also sent out a general call for help from allied ships in the region. The Japanese also responded to Admiral Martyn Jerram's request for help, despatching first the *Otawa* and then the *Tsushima*. Together with the French cruiser, the *Montcalm* and the Russian *Oriel*, they landed sufficient marines to help suppress the mutiny. By the time the six companies of the 4th Shropshire Light Infantry arrived from Burma all was, as the Governor put it, well in hand. If the naval ships had not been near Singapore and the mutineers had been bolder in their plans this outcome would have been very much in doubt.

Much has been made of the presence of the German prisoners in the Tanglin Barracks. After the *Emden* raid, all Germans in Malaya and Singapore had been detained. Those in Singapore were kept in the Tanglin Barracks. These were a mixed bag comprising mainly traders and other legitimate businessmen. It was suspected though that some were spies. In addition, the crew of *Emden* were also kept as prisoners of war in the same barracks. Certainly they played a prominent part in the plans of the mutineers as one of the first acts of the rebels from the 5th Light Infantry was to take control of the barracks. It turned out that the Germans did not choose to be active partners of the mutineers. Still the Germans did attempt to subvert the morale of their guards. Prisoners like Naval Oberleutnant Julius Lauterbach of *Emden* attempted to spread anti-British propaganda among the sepoys guarding them. Lauterbach, as the most senior officer present among the prisoners, was the de facto chief in the camp. It would, indeed, have been surprising if these prisoners had not tried to subvert the appetite for war among the Indians given the general drift of German military rhetoric and strategy towards Turkey and the other Islamic states. What is, however, surprising is the astonishing lapse of security as well as poor judgement on the part of the authorities to have the 5th Light Infantry guard the Germans for so long. The British military authorities appear to have put little weight on the possibility of German propaganda on the Indians. It was not until 14 February, the eve of the mutiny, that the Volunteers and the Johore Military Force replaced the 5th Light Infantry in its internment duties. Lauterbach in his memoirs claimed considerable credit for the weakening of the sepoys' morale. However, how much this actually contributed to the mutiny is unclear. There were British officers who felt that subversion by the Germans could not be dismissed. Asked for his opinion of the reasons behind the mutiny, Major William Cotton, second in command of the 5th Light Infantry, stated firmly his belief that German propaganda was responsible:

> In the first place sedition fostered by the Germans as a nation and the Turks; secondly, I consider the Malay States Guides refusing to go on service had a great deal to do with the mutiny. It had a very bad effect on the men and made their minds ripe for joining in any outbreak.
>
> (Sareen, 1995, p. 400)

However, here, as elsewhere, the Court of Inquiry dismissed this possibility, preferring to take the view that:

> any German collusion was confined to a select few who probably fostered mutinous ideas amongst their late guard, composed of Indian officers and men of the 5th Light Infantry, to their own individual advantage.
>
> (Sareen, 1995, p. 41)

This, if anything, is disingenuous. Since when has any military action not been led by 'individuals'? In any case, it would have been too much to expect the mixed bag of German and Austrian military officers, naval officers from *Emden* and its escort officers as well as traders and other civilians to act concertedly. One of the chief suspects for spreading propaganda, Herr Diehn, was a prominent businessman. Despite admitting that Diehn was a principal German agent actively working against British interests in Sumatra and India, General Ridout again chose to gloss over the question of German influence on the mutiny. As in the case of other plausible reasons, Ridout resorted to the convenient excuse that there was no definite material evidence of German intentions. Of course, short of catching one of the Germans with a code book or other evidence there would indeed be no real evidence.

This belief in the benign disinterestedness of the Germans completely ignores what actually happened. With the first sign of unrest, 17 of the prisoners including Lauterbach and Diehn seized the opportunity presented by the confusion to escape from the internment camp. In fact, Lauterbach had since early January been digging a tunnel to effect a breakout of the detention camp. He claimed later in his memoirs that this tunnel was nearly completed when the mutiny broke out. The timing of the mutiny, therefore, appeared to have caught the prisoners by surprise. To that extent there was indeed no invisible German hand behind the troubles. However, it is another thing to ignore the considerable propaganda the Germans were spreading to their guards. It was also self-interest that made the Germans decide not to throw in their lot with the sepoys. Diehn, one of the key German leaders, knew fully well that resistance was not likely to last long. The Indians were not likely to continue holding the upper hand for long once British and allied reinforcements reached Singapore by sea. Consequently he went out of his way to ensure that the Germans would not be caught in the crossfire. The Germans offered no help to the mutineers. Harper and Miller argued that since Indian troops "operate well only under the orders of Europeans" (Harper and Miller, 1984, p. 71), this refusal of the German officers to take part in the mutiny contributed substantially to its failure.

The assertion that without European leadership the sepoys amounted to nothing much is, however, not only debatable but also suggestive of the racial prejudice typical of colonials. Leave the natives alone, so the argument goes, and all their plans will surely collapse into disarray. In a way this common prejudice lies behind the oft-repeated view that the sepoys had no plans. Extend this further and we come to the comforting explanation that the mutiny was essentially a consequence of the breakdown of discipline. Yet in their hearts those at the highest echelons of the colony's administration knew otherwise. Both the Governor, Sir Arthur Young, and the GOC, General Ridout, realized the serious political implications of this mutiny. Certainly, London did not regard the matter complacently. The then Permanent Secretary to the Colonial Office, Sir John Anderson, did not mince his words when he gave his comments on the findings of the Court of Inquiry:

> The regiment knew that England and Germany were at war and it was only natural that they should expect the Germans to take advantage of their liberty and arms that they offered.
>
> (Harper and Miller, 1984, p. 227)

No intelligence, or for that matter military personnel, would disagree with this cautionary note which was a criticism of the way the authorities in Singapore had been so lax about basic security. It was surely essential precaution to separate the disaffected 5th Light Infantry from the German prisoners as soon as information on seditionist tendencies became available.

The dismissive complacency that kept insisting the mutineers had no firm plans was also not correct. While there was no specific plan as such, there was certainly agreement among the militants in the 5th Light Infantry that some steps were necessary. Indeed, once the first shot was fired and trouble broke out we can see a strong indication of a common course of action. In quick succession, the sepoys seized the ammunition, freed the one group of trained military men likely to join in the mutiny (the Germans), tried to coerce the disaffected Malay States Guides into a common cause against the British and showed up the powerlessness of the British masters by slaughtering them. While murder is certainly repugnant, the use of terror for political ends is too well known for us not to recognize it in the actions of the sepoys. The 5th Light Infantry did not run amok shooting all and sundry; they chose their victims, picking out only the British. There was certainly a definite set of common intentions even if there was no plan. When the events were examined later, the authorities realized the mutiny had revealed all too clearly the serious threats to the internal security of Singapore. In particular, political sedition and revolutionary agitation had emerged as the key dangers they had to deal with. Their views on internal security had to undergo a fundamental change.

The mutiny of 1915 was, therefore, an ominous sign of things to come with regard to the stability of British colonial power. If the sepoys had seized Singapore even for a short while, the repercussions would indeed have been serious. Not only would a treasured colony be lost but the overall internal security of many of the Malayan states would also be affected. In addition, the anti-colonial movement in India would have drawn fresh inspiration and be further emboldened by this success. It is therefore not surprising that despite the careful efforts to downplay the significance of the 1915 mutiny, much soul-searching regarding the security of the colonies went on for some time. The colonial administration believed that stern retribution was necessary in order to send a signal to any others that might be contemplating similar actions. Punishment was swift and harsh. Many of the mutineers were condemned to death or lengthy hard labour. The execution of the mutineers outside Outram Prison was arranged before the largest possible crowd. It was meant to be a spectacular display of British power and might.

A watershed had been crossed. Singapore was no longer just a pleasant commercial port associated with easy, complacent colonial living. It was no longer insulated from the larger political events and ideas that were making radical inroads into all areas of life. The authorities woke up to the fact that their beautiful colony was in the cauldron of politics, revolution and radical ideology that was affecting Asia as much as the world. The threat would come increasingly from political infiltration and subversion and not just from military attacks. This would be so even if there was little doubt that British dominance would be re-established once sufficient forces were marshalled. Control was imposed on the news while public proclamations downplayed the seriousness of the situation, preventing further panic. An official communiqué by W H Lee-Warner, Private Secretary to the Governor, on the first day of the mutiny referred to a "riot" rather than a mutiny. It was the earliest example, though not the last, of press censorship and counter propaganda being employed deliberately in the colony. Meanwhile in London, the official announcements mirrored the propaganda by referring to the "jealousy and dissatisfaction" among the Indian troops leading to a "serious riot" and "disturbance". Lord Crewe, Secretary of State for India, in his statement to the House of Lords hastened to assure the members that "the violence was rather of the nature of a regimental riot than of anything which could possibly be described as a mutiny" (Sareen, 1995, p. 768). In the best tradition of spin doctors, Lord Crewe went on to provide his own interpretation of the events to members of the House:

> I am anxious for the house to understand that the disturbance undoubtedly was of a purely local and special character connected with regimental matters, and the sort of colour which in some quarters was endeavoured to be put upon it—the suggestion that it was of the nature of a racial or religious uprising against the British Government—is in no way sustained by the circumstances.
>
> (Sareen, 1995, pp. 768–769)

Lord Crewe was clearly eager that too much should not be read into the situation. He was careful to raise the pertinent point—that perhaps the mutiny had its origins in racial or religious problems—so that he could dismiss it as an improbability. Within a few days the local authorities had restored order and could set about proffering their own views about the mutiny. By 22 February, the outcome was put beyond doubt by the arrival of six companies of the 4th Shropshire Light Infantry (Territorials) deployed from Rangoon on the *S.S. Edavan*. In his communiqué of 22 February, the Governor adopted a sterner tone, promising a summary court-martial of the mutineers. All that was left with was to remind the world that any attempt to challenge British might would meet with an unfortunate and painful end.

Lord Crewe's careful comments actually serve to alert us to those very issues he had been trying to sideline. The main concern of the authorities was with the consequences that would result from the collapse of the vaunted idea of British superiority. That superiority was based on the perception of its invincibility. This had from the start been reinforced by carefully cultivated assumptions of superiority in the areas of science, manners, language, culture and civilization. Once that invincibility was lost these interrelated assumptions would also be undermined. In addition, colonial paramountcy and military power would be undermined. Hitherto, challenges to this paramountcy had come from outside the colonies, essentially from the naval and military forces of competing European nations. Now the British realized that the threat was as likely to be from within their colonies. In particular, ideology presented an even greater challenge. The 1915 mutiny was a turning point in the way the British looked at security in the Malayan colonies. Political intelligence, espionage monitoring and surveillance of potential subversives took on increasing significance. After 1915, intelligence became a systematic and necessary part of its security. If anything, 1915 reminded those responsible for the Empire that Singapore (and by extension, the Malayan territories) was part of an increasingly complex and interrelated web of politics, religion and espionage that had the domination of Asia as its prize. The British understood that any effort to displace their rule would be played out in the domains of ideas, knowledge and beliefs. After all, their Empire had been built on similar tactics that espoused the superiority of Western ideas in the areas of race, religion and knowledge.

The various efforts by London and the colonial administration to dispel fears of a wider, more sinister plot behind the 1915 mutiny did not always find unquestioning acceptance. For one, the *New York Times* in a commentary despatched from Singapore on 8 March severely questioned the official view:

> The failure on the part of the authorities to give a more intelligent and detailed explanation of the situation in Singapore is a vivid indication of the significance and importance with which they attach to it—an indication of their unwillingness to allow a true account of the affair to reach other British possessions, where it might be acted upon as a precedent by the native population.
>
> Contrary to the mass of information offered for public consumption, India and Burma have been the scene of grave disturbance ever since the entrance of Turkey into the theatre of hostilities, and the knowledge of the happenings in Singapore, it is feared would act as a spark to the already-laid fuse of riot and rebellion.
>
> (Sareen, 1995, p. 769)

In fact, many in Singapore realized that things could have turned out very badly. As Harper and Miller underline in their book, "The British community knew that it had had a narrow escape and that only luck had prevented a catastrophe" (Harper and Miller, 1984, p. 233). Those who lived through the crisis felt almost instinctively that the mutiny was not an isolated event but part of a larger series of events that had overturned their complacency with British rule over the subject races.

The Governor, Sir Arthur Young, himself wrote that it was too easy to blame the handful of German internees for instigating the mutiny:

> Much as I should like to think that the mutiny was due to their machinations only I am afraid that it is due to something much more serious.
>
> (Sareen, 1995, p. 712)

Like a good civil servant, Young did not specify what that "something much more serious" could be although we can make a fairly good guess. Others were not willing to be so circumspect. Indeed, R C D Bradley, British Adviser to the State of Johore in 1933 and an eyewitness to the events, made no bones about what he thought the mutiny represented. In his account of the mutiny, he emphasized that for him:

> the real facts of the case, which in a similar manner, but on a much smaller scale, of course, recall similar tragic events that occurred at Meerut, Delhi, Kanpur and Seetapur during the great Indian Mutiny of 1857.
>
> (Sareen, 1995, p. 782)

In an even more vehement note to a fellow officer, Major Lugard, Bradley not only re-emphasized this similarity with the Indian Mutiny but also underlined his fear that the uprising would lead to a racial war against the British. 1915 was for many like Bradley an ominous replay of the horrifying incidents like the Cawnpore Massacre in the Indian Mutiny of 1857–58. In that earlier and more devastating mutiny loyalty was shown to be superficial, regimental honours made irrelevant, racial and religious hatreds spilled out into the open and British military power tottered on the brink of disaster. These were Bradley's and every colonial's nightmare, which explains the somewhat hysterical nature of Bradley's note to Lugard:

> The men of the 5th Native Light Infantry were described as being Punjabi Mohammedans. They were nothing of the sort. They were Hindustani Mohammedans, birds of an entirely different species, indeed of the same breed exactly that was the worst for cruelties to our women and children during the great mutiny of 1857.
>
> (Sareen, 1995, p. 782)

The events in 1915 brought to the surface this almost primeval fear of being racially engulfed and destroyed by the native population. To make matters worse, and this cannot be over-emphasized, Singapore was at that time the only place in Asia where a mutiny that challenged British dominance occurred. If it had succeeded or dragged on in any way, the flames of revolt could easily have spread throughout the Asian colonies.

Such a conflagration was what military and intelligence planners of the German High Command had hoped for and tried to capitalize on. Upon the outbreak of the First World War, Kaiser Wilhelm of Germany made it a priority to ignite the discontent among the native subjects of the British Empire. An important means towards this was to work upon and whip up religious sentiments among the Muslims. This was in keeping with German plans to provoke the Ottoman Empire and other powers in Middle and Central Asia into a *jihad* or holy war against Britain:

> Our consul and agents must inflame the entire Muslim world against this hateful, lying and unscrupulous nation.
>
> (Hopkirk, 1994, p. 1)

Singapore was, of course, merely a small part of these plans to subvert the British Empire. The prize for Germany was always the Middle East and India, in particular. However, as it turned out the 5th Light Infantry was a ready-made target of discontented troops. Events showed that the internal security of Singapore could not be separated from these machinations taking place in far-off German war rooms, Turkey or the United States. After 1915 it became a central tenet of internal security planners that seditious actions were nearly always the result of external machinations. While this gave focus to Special Branch actions, it also led to an inability and unwillingness to recognize that political discontent could just as well arise from local unhappiness.

The perception of German involvement in the 1915 mutiny in Singapore was further emphasized by the rising tide of militant nationalism which posed an increasingly serious challenge to British imperial pretensions. Starting as dissatisfaction with racial and economic prejudices, its adherents soon broadened their aims to include the formation of a nationalist, religious and political front that would sweep aside colonial domination. One important centre of these developments in the anti-colonial movement was India. In 1909 Vinayak Savarkar's *The Indian War of Independence* had reinterpreted the Indian Mutiny of 1857 in such radically revolutionary terms that it was left out of the catalogue of the British Museum Library to prevent unauthorized reading. This explosive book argued that the "Great Mutiny" was an act of armed resistance against an imperialist power bent upon subjugating India. Savarkar inspired many like Har Dayal, a brilliant organizer who gave up his education at Oxford University, to follow his footsteps. Drawing upon the disaffection of the many thousands of Sikh immigrants, Har Dayal together with revolutionaries like Sohan Singh Bhakna founded the Hindi Association of the Pacific Coast in Portland, USA, in May 1913 (Kuwajima, 1991, p. 29). Within a few years this association became even more militant, evolving into the Ghadr (Mutiny or Revolutionary) Party with adherents in North America, Burma, China, Malaya and Japan. The main aim of the Ghadr Party rapidly hardened into the overthrow of British rule by any, including violent, means.

The growth of the Ghadr in America was phenomenal. Within a year of its founding a stream of adherents, mainly Sikhs, had been recruited. These, according to Ghadr's aims, were to be sent home to Indian Punjab to foment unrest with the aim of creating an independent homeland. These Ghadr members were instructed in the classic doctrines of guerrilla war. Some weapons would be provided initially; however, they were to attack police stations, seizing whatever weapons they could find. They were also to start revolutionary work among the people, robbing the rich, supporting the poor and attacking the white colonizers. While Ghadr started first as a reformist party fighting for the rights of landless peasants and exploited workers and campaigning mainly against economic and social discrimination, it very rapidly became a magnet drawing together those with revolutionary ideals. Soon, the thrust of Ghadr went beyond the local emancipation of Punjab or the agitation for land reform. Ghadr rapidly took on a pan-Indian dimension that sought to free India from the colonial yoke. By December 1914, Ghadr had already established links with the Hindu revolutionaries in Bengal, led by committed leaders such as Rash Behari Bose. Of even greater concern to the British authorities was that Ghadr had by 1914 also forged a common cause with disaffected Muslims who saw the British war against Turkey as an attack against the Islamic faith. Through its newsletter Ghadr spread its message of militant resistance to overseas Indians. Reflecting this wider constituency the newsletter was by 1914 printed in four dialects. In addition to Urdu and Gurmuki, the original dialects, the Ghadr newsletter also appeared in Gujerati and Punjabi. The British closely monitored the issues, which were distributed to Hong Kong, the Netherlands East Indies and China.

By this time German intelligence, well aware of the opportunities of adding to the unrest, had made contact with and promised aid of various kinds to the militant Ghadr. For the Germans, this was an unparalleled chance to instigate unrest in the British colonies as well as to realize the grand plan of the Kaiser to forge a united front with Islamic countries. To Ghadr it was all the same, whether the aid came from Germany or someone else, as long as it went towards helping to overthrow British rule. The Turks too saw similar advantages in such an alliance. A common platform was thus made possible. In December 1914, British postal censors intercepted a seditious letter from the Netherlands East Indies addressed to an Indian in Pahang. After listing British misdeeds against Turkey including the failure to keep promises made at the beginning of the Balkans war, the wresting of lands under Islamic control from their rightful rulers and the detention of battleships which had already been paid for by Turkey, the letter exhorted its readers to rise against British imperialism:

> Now what should Indians do? First of all they should collectively tell the British (1) to recognize Turkey's possession of Egypt and (2) to hand over to Turkey the battleships which if done would put an end to any further trouble between the English and the Turks. But if England would not do so, then O Hindus and O Mohammedans, draw your swords and the English out of India. Thus you will free yourselves and by weakening in this manner the English Empire you will save weak Asiatic countries from being trampled upon. Rise, for this is the time to rise.[7]

The same sentiments had been expressed in a Ghadr newsletter intercepted in March 1914. On this stage German spies, Ghadr revolutionaries and Islamic agitators attempted to act out a common script. It would, thus, be wrong to see only a German hand in all the troubles that followed. The situation had become more serious as it was rapidly answering the 'homegrown' dissatisfaction of the Indians. It had become less of German machinations of anti-colonialism than a response from the Indian colonies themselves. Thus in 1915, even when promised German help of weapons did not materialize, the revolutionaries decided at a secret meeting in Lahore to press ahead with the planned uprising on 21 February 1915. In the projected uprising, the appeal to a larger pan-Indian sentiment was underlined by the three colours that made up the proposed national flag of the new—and free—India. Each of the major ethnic groups was represented by one colour of the flag—red for the Hindus, yellow for the Sikhs and green for the Muslims. It was also decided that the call for an uprising should be spread among the overseas Indian communities so that they could rise in support if they wanted to. Singapore as the leading transit point and port of call for many Indians was clearly an important target. It would be a real blow to the British if the colony were seized. In addition to the pan-Indian appeal, the rapid spread of the Ghadr Party, its doctrines and militancy can be traced to the hard work and magnetic appeal of Har Dayal. It was recognition of his abilities rather than any outright murderous acts that led William Hopkinson, a former Indian police officer, to describe the Har Dayal he was shadowing in San Francisco as "the most dangerous" of the Indian extremists.

Although the Governor of India, Sir Michael O'Dwyer, downplayed the overall seriousness of the uprising, the security implications were real enough. Among other things, the racial overtone seen in the uprising's slogan, "Maro Ferrangi Ko" or "Kill the English", could have escalated rapidly to an all-out attack against white men and women. In Singapore, the mutineers waylaid white men, asking them if they were "Inglees". Harper and Miller emphasized that this anti-British aim was the most obviously prominent characteristic among the mutineers:

> it was difficult to place any principle or plan on the conduct of the mutineers in general, except for one absolute fact: the majority of them were clearly not interested in molesting Asians or Europeans other than the British.
>
> (Harper and Miller, 1984, pp. 81–82)

The implication is clear: the killing of the British could easily become a rallying cry for the wider Asian alliance of the colonized races. The spectre of such an Asian 'united front' would have been very frightening. It was, for instance, known that the avowed aim of the Indian nationalists was to seek a common cause with the Chinese. In later years Indian nationalists formed common fronts with the Bolsheviks and the Japanese. The Indian National Army fought against the allied forces in the Second World War. Its platform was freedom for India as well as resistance to colonial exploitation. A poem in *Ghadar Ki Gunj*, a revolutionary newsletter, exhorted its readers:

> O Brother, do not fight in the war against the Chinese. Beware of the enemy. He should not deceptively instigate you to fight your Chinese brothers. The enemy splits brothers and makes them kill each other. The people of Hind, China and Turkey are real brothers. The enemy should not be allowed to besmirch their brotherhood.
>
> (Josh, 1977, p. 193)

If an Indian-Chinese alliance were dismissed as being far-fetched in the early years of the century, the avowal of brotherhood with Turkey was definitely a cause for concern. A hostile Turkey meant the weakening of the flanks of the Balkans, the soft underbelly of Europe, as Winston Churchill had put it so graphically. A pan-Islamic movement was even worse since it could set the whole Middle East and the Indian continent ablaze. This possibility was not so fanciful since the Sultan of Turkey had just declared a holy war against Britain in a *fatwa* in November 1914.

As R C D Bradley had pointed out, in what must have been full knowledge of the implications, the mutineers were "Hindustani Mohammedans". Lord Kitchener himself had expressed the view that the 5th Light Infantry was "too Mohamedan (sic) for service in Egypt" (quoted by Brigadier-General Ridout in Sareen, 1995, p. 691). He had reason for such concern since active service against Turkey was decidedly unpopular with Muslim troops. The outbreak of war with Turkey fanned rumours that Indian troops were being earmarked for a transfer to the Middle East. Such rumours were rampant both among the Malay States Guides and the 5th Light Infantry. There were also those in Singapore who were ready to take advantage of the strong feelings among the Muslim soldiers to further their cause. Kassim Ali Mansur, a wealthy Indian-Muslim merchant from Surat, was so pro-Turkish that he acted as a conduit for some men in the Malay States Guides who wanted to pass a letter to the Turkish consul, Ahmad Muallah Daud, in Rangoon. This letter which was intercepted by the British intelligence in Burma declared that the soldiers were prepared to fight for Turkey and requested for a warship to carry them to the front. In retrospect, the request has an astonishing naivete about it, suggesting an unthinking, emotional outburst rather than a carefully plotted venture. Still, it was wartime and to the British authorities this was regarded as treason to the Crown. It was also known that Kassim was well regarded by the men of the 5th Light Infantry, some of whom visited his home frequently. On 23 January 1915, Kassim was arrested and charged with espionage. The arrest document stated that he had behaved in a treasonous manner and had given information to the enemy. The fact that there were 10 charges underlined the very thorough monitoring of his activities. Indeed, the British had been keeping him under close observation for some time, contradicting thereby the view that the authorities were ignorant of the threat by religious elements. Kassim's arrest added considerably to the unhappiness and agitation of the 5th Light Infantry, especially among those sepoys he was friendly with.

Kassim was not the only agent working against British interests. In fact, intelligence reports identified one Nur Alam Shah as the more dangerous among those spreading seditious anti-British propaganda. Nur Alam Shah was an *imam* at a mosque in Kampong Java Road, a mosque well attended by men from the 5th Light Infantry. Described as "a man of about fifty years of age ... (with) a short grey beard" (Sareen, 1995, p. 617), Nur Alam Shah was also an active Indian Muslim nationalist linked to a revolutionary party, most likely Ghadr.

> As to the man, Nur Alam Shah, it would appear that he belonged to the Revolutionary Party, and had been left behind by parties returning to India to collect funds for the cause.
>
> (Sareen, 1995, p. 699)

His activities were viewed with enough suspicion to have his movements closely monitored. At the subsequent Court of Inquiry into the 1915 mutiny, two reports by agents R__ and G___ were made available to the proceedings. In addition to being fascinating reading, the documents confirmed the presence of secret service agents, informers and other signs of active intelligence gathering. Among the earliest documented accounts of internal security in Singapore, the reports peel back the cloak of secrecy, allowing us to see into the concerns and methods of the colonial masters.

An agent from the authorities who had infiltrated into the ranks of the conspirators described Nur Alam Shah in a report as "a very seditious and fanatical man. He is always talking sedition against the British Government. He preaches fanatical doctrines daily" (Sareen, 1995, p. 616). It was also reported that Nur Alam Shah encouraged speculation among the sepoys that German warships would be arriving to invade Singapore soon. The report goes on to provide a list of his honorific titles: *Pirji, Sainji* and *Baji,* indicating that the British agents had got close to their target. The second report provides even more details, filling in the blanks as it were: "He is known as *Baiji* by Punjabis and *Shahsahib* by Bengalis. The Malays call him *Habit* ... He (Nur Alam Shah) is styled a *Pir* or holy man" (Sareen, 1995, p. 617). As is usual with such reports, the account of his activities came with the agent's comments. The agent reported that he had heard Nur Alam Shah advising soldiers not to fight for the British but to instead take part in the mutiny. The agent also reported on his contacts, providing a list of people who came into frequent contact with the *imam.* Some of these, like Kramat Ali, did not go on to feature in the mutiny. Others like Jemadar (sic) Chistie Khan came to be regarded as ringleaders of the mutiny. While it is usual to challenge such intelligence reports as unreliable or paranoid, their truth in this instance is supported by the testimony of Indian officers in open court. Subedar-Major Khan Mohamed Khan recalled how sepoy Manowar Ali in an obvious reference to the war with Turkey would "ask a blessing for the success of the armies of the faithful" (Sareen, 1995, p. 20) at Friday prayers in the mosque. The Subedar-Major had thought it serious enough to report the incident to his CO. Even more ominous was the confession of sepoy Jellah Khan, reported by Arthur Young, that the troops had been told:

> "that although they had fought previously against Moslems, the Malvi (sic) told them from Mosque this was unlike, as fighting against head of religion the Sultan at Stambul. Stated also how Germans are allies of Turk the Moslem Indians in France though they may not fight against us they will not fight for us in Asia. We get letters from Indian and know feelings."[8]

Young was no doubt referring to the interception of seditious letters as a result of the postal censorship that was in force in the Malayan colonies at the outbreak of hostilities in Europe. However, it is interesting that Nur Alam Shah was never put on trial despite the weight of evidence. Instead, he was detained and deported on a banishment warrant. Clearly the British did not want to stir up further trouble among their Muslim subjects.

One cannot help feeling, though, that these were not the only agents, or reports submitted. There must have been others, whose activities in the usual manner of intelligence agencies could have been regarded as too sensitive to be revealed. There were references to other British intelligence agents operating in Singapore at this time. In their book on the mutiny, Harper and Miller give us an account of how:

> One night, Cotton sent for Ball and both met a secret service agent who had been sent from India with orders to move among the men of the battalion. He spoke of a general reluctance among the troops to going to Egypt to fight the Turks, and he also added that Chistie Khan was "leading the sepoys to protest against going to Egypt".
>
> (Harper and Miller, 1984, p. 32)

Major William Cotton was the second in command of the 5th Light Infantry while Captain Lionel Ball, as we know, was the double company commander. This must call into question the often repeated view that the mutiny caught everyone by surprise. In a separate incident that came to light subsequently it was noted that General Ridout had planted a secret agent in the Alexandra Barracks. In a dreadful bungle, this agent was arrested by the police while trying to report to the authorities at Fort Canning on news of a possible uprising. As General Ridout ruefully admitted:

> Unfortunately my agent, a Punjabi, was arrested on suspicion on the evening of the 15th, and thus the information never reached me.
>
> (Sareen, 1995, p. 695)

Clearly, it was not the local police that had planted the spy. In this case, it was either the military or, more likely, the Indian colonial administration office that inserted and ran such an agent. Despite clear proof that he must have some knowledge of the impending mutiny, General Ridout had, of course, every reason to stress his ignorance of the trouble at the Court of Inquiry. By doing so he would effectively escape censure for not alerting the authorities or being on top of the situation. This explains General Ridout's claim:

> In short no breath of seditious intent had reached me, and there was nothing to show that the men were discontented, and no report of any internal trouble whatever had reached me from any source.
>
> (Sareen, 1995, p. 695)

While not engaged in a cover-up, General Ridout was certainly not letting on everything that he knew. Given the various intelligence reports floating around regarding the activities of Nur Alam Shah and the general morale of the 5th Light Infantry, the lack of any suitable precautions is indeed astonishing. If, however, we argue that no intelligence was available then we will see a failure in the coverage of potentially volatile troops. Either way the final impression is not a favourable one. My own feeling is that there was at the very least a failure to recognize both the relevance of intelligence gathering and the need for adequate interpretation of security matters. This was, however, to be a lesson General Ridout would not forget easily as his subsequent contributions to internal security show.

***

Intelligence analysis is often a painstaking and careful piecing together of disparate and apparently inconsequential or irrelevant information so that a sensible picture emerges. The nature of subversion and espionage means that the adversary is not likely to announce its intentions directly or clearly. It will often seek to conceal its tracks, use cutouts to deflect attention from the real objectives and present a number of different layers of 'truth' to prevent or obstruct discovery. The emphasis of the Special Branch or any organization engaged in internal security is different from that of military intelligence. The latter's task 'ends', its goal achieved when it uncovers the plan of an impending attack, the threatening units and the enemy's objectives. Even if the enemy uses subterfuge, disinformation and deception, these are linked to specific military goals and targets. Once the military intelligence identifies them, the game is up and the chase over for the moment. This is not the case with an organization like the Special Branch.

An enemy spy may be arrested, his networks uncovered, cell members arrested, and his aims identified. However, this in no way means the end of the hostile power's determination to continue with hostile infiltration or subversion. Agents are not 'ends' in themselves, they are for the most part eminently expendable. So one agent that is arrested does not mean the end of further efforts. Indeed, no espionage agency is likely to put all its eggs in one basket depending upon only one agent no matter how successful he is. Very often different agents work simultaneously to penetrate the same target without knowledge of each other's existence. Thus uncovering one agent is usually not the end of the matter. All it reveals is that the enemy has an interest in a certain area. There can also be more than one reason for a spy's arrest. Perhaps this is the result of competent investigation. At other times it can be fortuitous chance, the sheer incompetence of the spy or even a deliberate ploy by his controllers to throw him to the enemy. This meant that, for the Special Branch, the game never ends and a high element of uncertainty is always present. The intelligence war is a secret war that is unending. The picture is seldom, if not ever, complete and assessment and action must be made on elliptical or partial and uncertain perspectives. There was one aspect that the Special Branch officer can be certain, however, and that is once an enemy decides to mount an operation, the loss of one or two spies will not deter him.

A very special characteristic of the Special Branch that shapes its work is that its concerns are above all political. In a sense, the Branch enforces or polices the boundaries of political security of a government. In this way, the Branch reflects, through its concerns, the character of a government in power. While it may be a mirror, even if sometimes obliquely, few governments are prepared to acknowledge openly the effective actions of the Special Branch. These actions often demonstrate the threats that a government is prepared or not prepared to accept and its threshold of risk in a particular political context or reality. The Branch's role, at any particular time, reveals what stand the ruling elite or the government takes, on the balance of competing considerations as the permissible level and political challenge, in open or secret forms, by indigenous or external sources, or both. When that balance is crossed the Branch swings into action. This political security dimension means that the Special Branch officer often needs to wear different lenses and approach cases with different mindsets from that of the military intelligence officer. The intelligence failure in the 1915 mutiny makes these distinctions obvious. Many of the available intelligence reports were not analysed in the context of local events, instead they were sent to the political intelligence officers operating out of India. Rarely was there an agent that reported directly to the Singapore authorities.

Both the 1915 mutiny and the unrest that coincidentally happened in the northern Malay states emphasized the urgent necessity to create an organization that could enforce the British political and ideological outlook in these colonies. That outlook was simple enough, determined by the overriding need to maintain British paramountcy in matters of trade. Whether it was the Branch seeking out attempts to destabilize the social structures, challenges to British dominance, the infiltration of agitators, formations of political cells or the smuggling of arms, the overriding aim was the same: nothing that could conceivably upset the fundamental reason for British presence in Southeast Asia was to be permitted. As long as this was not disturbed or challenged, the British were prepared to tolerate and be open minded to all views. The moment any ideas or actions impacted trading dominance, the British used all necessary means against the offenders. Thus in the twenties, the Special Branch accepted the presence of a number of Indonesian communists in Singapore despite its active crackdown of Chinese communists as the Indonesians were not engaged in activities that threatened British interests. For a number of years, radicals like Darsono, Baars, Samaoen and even Tan Malaka passed through or stayed in Singapore without interference from the Branch. Active action was taken against the Chinese communists as they wanted to displace British rule. As long as British paramountcy was not disturbed the Special Branch had no interest. In areas of immigration, counter-espionage, anti-communist, or even the monitoring of religious extremists, the key criterion was the likely impact these had upon the health of British investments. The Special Branch that was created reflected this central platform and the political agenda of imperial rule. Every action was contingent on ensuring the essential stability that would allow the British to milk the wealth of their colonies. This brutally simple purposefulness was the abiding strength of the British colonial administration and its institutions. The Special Branch's aims were direct; it knew with unhesitating conviction what it should do and went about the task with full vigour.

The 1915 mutiny followed by an unexpectedly severe outbreak of trouble in northern Malaya served to throw into sharp relief the following aspects relevant to the security of Singapore:

1. There was no sense of internal security. The Governor's and the military's attention were turned firmly outwards. At best it was to meet the likelihood of an attack by the German East Asiatic squadron. How this could be translated into any actual threat to the colonies without a strong German expeditionary force was never addressed. The threat was, in any case, conceived to be essentially naval; that is, the disruption of sea lanes, though in the one instance when that happened, the German raider *Emden* thought it best not to put the defences of the fortified Singapore base to the test.

2. What interest there was in internal security was that of a complacent colonizing power. This becomes clear if we compare the immediate and over-response of the authorities to the Pasir Puteh troubles. Peasant uprising and banditry were threats and events that an occupying colonial power recognized immediately and knew how to deal with. Infiltration and subversion on the other hand were political issues that were at this time alien to a colonial occupying force. In the early years of the 20th century, the British in Malaya were not ready to recognize the corrosive damage of subversive ideas.

3. The British did not realize that future threats would be increasingly ideological and political. In the past they had thought in terms of protecting their possessions from other marauding European powers or, at best, the occasional pirate attack or some local resistance. In addition, for a considerable period they continued to conceive of security in terms of traditional colonial policing, which meant putting down native wars and troubles. Hence they failed in the lead-up to 1915 to anticipate the dangers of German propaganda, of Ghadr ideology or the pro-Turkish feelings among the Muslim troops in their employ.

4. One glaring weakness was that there did not seem to be inter-agency liaison among the army, navy, foreign office, political intelligence or the police. Not only was the security of Singapore very much with the Indian office but also since the 5th Light Infantry was an Indian regiment the question of its morale and fighting effectiveness was under the purview of the Indian Secret Service. Although Sir Charles

Cleveland ably led the Service, its distance meant that crucial information was often delayed. Indian secret service agents were operating in Singapore but more often than not they reported directly to India, only briefing the Singapore military on 'specific' issues. In any case, there was no Singapore equivalent for them to liaise with. As the case of the Malay States Guides serves to show, there was no exchange of information even between the local bodies such as the FMS and the Straits Settlements. On the day of the mutiny, the Inspector General of Police, Captain Chancellor, was not informed until 4.45 p.m., by which time his police had already engaged the sepoys. The IGP was quite rightly so furious at this failure to alert him at the earliest opportunity and to provide him with essential information regarding the deteriorating situation at Alexandra Barracks that he subsequently lodged a vigorous protest with the Governor.

5. The most serious aspect from the internal security point of view was the failure to identify or 'sniff' out any likely threats from the disaffected troops. There was no tripwire, no alarm that went off when the danger signals reached an alarming level. In fact, it would seem that the authorities had no idea what constituted a truly alarming development. Few officers, especially those in critical and close touch with the ground, had any opinion at the Inquiry on the likelihood of a plot or offered any views about a suspicious pattern of events that was occurring. In fact, in reading the official reports we feel that such views were dismissed as speculations. Moreover these speculations were not encouraged since it was not politically correct to link military affairs with political or religious matters. Consequently, the discussion of such matters as poor discipline, insubordination or morale in relation to political developments was limited or avoided altogether.

6. There was no collation and hence no evaluation of the various pieces of information that were floating around despite the official denials. Put another way there was no chance of any event being identified as 'significant', let alone being further investigated. The colonial administration ignored all the early signals of a possible outbreak of antiwar and anti-British feelings, as well as the impending signs of trouble in the barracks such as insubordination and the loss of control. These were simply not collated into an overall analysis that would serve to show an escalating momentum.

These weaknesses were endemic within the existing colonial policing system. Similar signs of trouble that led to the earlier mutiny of the Malay States Guides in December 1914, barely two months before the 5th Light Infantry went on its rampage, confirmed the glaring flaws in the security system. Official accounts of the 1914 incident downplayed its significance. It was described as insubordination rather than the mutinous act that it certainly was. Yet what else could it be? At the outbreak of the First World War, the Malay States Guides were sent first to Singapore and then selected for service in East Africa. All seemed to be well until notice was given to the regiment that they would be serving overseas. In an extraordinary gesture, the Guides refused to obey the deployment order. Major-General Reade, the then General Officer Commanding, had received an anonymous letter in December 1914 declaring that the troops would not fight in any territory other than what they had been contracted for, that is the Malay States and the Straits Settlements:

> As our brethren who have been shot in the Komagata Maru case have troubled and grieved us, some of us have lost dear brothers and other blood-relations, we can never forget the kindness of the Indian Government (British) for the shooting and slaughtering of the dead who lost their living in Canada from which country they were expelled, and were not allowed to land and return, but the Indian Government again taking the poor dead as seditious people did not allow them to land at their own home even. When we have no right to walk freely on our own land then what do you want from us in other countries? As we are butchered in our own country we cannot expect better treatment in other countries, therefore we strongly tell you that we will not go to other countries to fight except those mentioned in our agreement sheets.[9]

The colonial administration chose not to see this as a mutiny. Lieutenant-Colonel Lees, the commanding officer of the Guides, reported that this did not represent the feelings of his men, even going as far as to suggest that the letter was written by someone outside the unit. In fact, the British knew that discontent was rife. They were aware that three men, Jemadar Sher Zaman, Jemadar Vilayat Shah and Havildar Sunder had been persuading the Punjabi sepoys of No. III Double Company stationed at Belakang Mati to join in the refusal to be deployed overseas. It is significant that Lees changed his story somewhat after the 1915 mutiny in Singapore. In an account of the Malay States Guides submitted to the Governor in July 1915, Lees admitted:

On 4 December (1914) they refused to go to East Africa and on 5, 6 and 7 December they were in a dangerous state.[10]

This is an extraordinary revelation for it underlines how inflammable the situation was. If this alarming refusal of the Malay States Guides is regarded as a mutiny then the British army faced two mutinies in less than three months in one of their richest colonial possessions. Such a rejection of military orders constituted, at the very least, grave insubordination if not mutinous behaviour. The fact that troops were here bargaining with their commanders suggests a loss of moral control by those in charge. It says a lot of the weak bargaining position of the British when they gave in to the demands of the Malay States Guides. It was agreed that the unit would not be sent overseas but withdrawn to Taiping in Perak except for its Mountain Battery which was to continue with its garrison duties in Singapore.

Publicly, the military authorities denied the political significance of this unexpected behaviour. As was the case with the 5th Light Infantry, a number of reasons were proffered which effectively fudged the real issue. The result was that no firm conclusion was reached regarding the reasons for the misconduct. It was claimed, for example, that the Guides refused to be posted to East Africa because they were frightened. The question of their being disaffected, so it was argued, did not therefore arise. Another reason—typically colonial—was that the troopers did not want to be taken from their proclivity for money-lending activities, which it was suggested the Sikhs were prone to. In any case, it was further argued, the whole incident grew out of the misplaced patriotism of a new subedar-major (equivalent to a lieutenant). It seems that in his enthusiasm on hearing that war had broken out, he had hastened to Lieutenant-Colonel Lees, the commanding officer of the unit, and suggested that the Guides be sent to serve on the western front. Reacting to this misinformed enthusiasm, the CO put the Guides on alert for war duties. Of course this is not true. When has strategic planning ever been based entirely on a junior officer's suggestion?

The plausible reasons were nearer to hand and were acknowledged in the Court of Inquiry set up to scrutinize the conduct of the Guides. The members of the Inquiry fell back on the familiar reasons which had to do substantially with the spread of anti-British sentiments among the Indians by the Ghadr Party. The war with Turkey was also unpopular, in particular among the Muslims who were responsive to the calls to defend their faith. Alun Jones noted that these intertwined issues were central to the Malay States Guides' refusal to serve in East Africa:

The most significant cause of discontent, and certainly of one of much import to the government, was the Court's suggestion that 'general seditious agitation, intrigues of enemy agents (and the) religious influence of Turkey … may have affected the situation.'

(Jones, 1971, p. 43)

Almost as soon as the Court of Inquiry had completed its findings by 14 January 1915, the authorities arrested Kassim Ali Mansur on 23 January. Mansur, we would recall, had passed on a letter from some men in the Malay States Guides to the Turkish consul in Rangoon. The letter intercepted by the British had asked for a Turkish warship to ferry the dissidents to fight against the British in the Middle East on 23 January. The police felt that he played a significant part in the discontent. Mansur was also well known to a number of the men of the 5th Light Infantry as he used to invite them to his rubber estate in Pasir Panjang for weekend sojourns. Given the connection, it is all the more surprising that it was not until 13 February that the 5th Light Infantry was relieved of its guard duties of the German prisoners of war. Someone had finally woken to the fact that the Germans could also be spreading disaffection. By then, whatever damage was possible had already been done. In fact, this delay meant that contact between the Indian troops and the German prisoners they were guarding was not broken off until just two days before the mutiny broke out. This is a clear failure to heed a basic dictum of internal security.

Paradoxically, it was with internal security in mind that the British deployed the Malay States Guides back to the Malay States. The decision to send the Guides back to their cantonment in Perak was, as with the case of the deployment of the 5th Light Infantry to Hong Kong, to isolate the troops from the sources of ideological infection. It was thought that the Guides when back in Taiping, Perak would be less likely to be exposed to Ghadr propaganda. Here the British miscalculated the prevalence of Ghadr support although it was indeed fortunate, given the subsequent events in Singapore, that the Guides were sent upcountry. Ghadr's reach was in Perak as well. When the train carrying the Guides pulled into Ipoh station, an enthusiastic crowd of Sikhs was on hand to welcome the troops whom they greeted as heroes who had tweaked the British lion's whiskers. Charles Hannigan, a police officer who was at the station, expressed his uneasiness when he observed the rapturous welcome given to the returning troops. There is more than an accidental link between the behaviour of the Guides and the mutiny of the 5th Light Infantry. Their actions signalled a shared dislike of the war, the same sentiments for Ghadr ideology and a sense of communal brotherhood. Like it or not, the Malay States Guides had achieved a political victory (very much like a trade union that had won concessions from an unsympathetic employer) although, of course, its military career was to all purposes finished after that.

In October 1915, the Malay States Guides were finally sent to Aden where they acquitted themselves well in the fighting. However, imperial memory is long and unforgiving. In a memorandum on "The Situation in Singapore" dated 22 February, Arthur Young had noted:

> As to the future treatment of the Guides, in 1915, the HQ recommended (with the concurrence of the GOC) that they would be disbanded by a process of attrition, i.e. by allowing the men to retire at once with pensions or gratuities on generous terms subsequently compulsorily retiring men when desirable. In this tel. (conversation) he recommends that any who wish should be allowed to resign and that there should be no more recruiting.[11]

The overriding concern was reliability and in 1919 the Guides were finally disbanded. British military authorities had reason to suspect that the refusal of the Guides had an impact upon the 5th Light Infantry. It is likely that the sentiments revealed in the anonymous letter to the then GOC Major-General Reade were common knowledge to troops serving in such proximity to each other. Guides and sepoys would have, in any case, attended the same social and religious functions where such sentiments could be easily heard and were, indeed, expressed.

The letter to Major-General Reade had been very specifically political in its appeal to the Guides. Here in condensed form was a collage of nationalist resentment, economic unhappiness, and social discontent with colonial prejudice that could easily serve as a platform for any revolutionary, anti-imperialist movement. Interestingly enough, the letter made a specific reference to the ill-fated voyage in April 1914 of the *Komagata Maru* which was transporting Sikh immigrants to Vancouver. The incident was widely talked about in Singapore especially as Gurdit Singh, who chartered and financed the venture, was a prominent Singapore merchant. Gurdit Singh's aim was to ferry landless Sikh immigrants to a better life in the Canadian west coast. However, the ship was refused permission to dock in Vancouver as the immigrants were said to be Ghadr militants and revolutionaries. They were summarily sent back to India. Many Indians read this as racial prejudice and a 'whites-only' immigration policy. The *Komagata Maru* passed through Singapore on its way back. The incident could not have failed to attract attention and sympathy among the large Indian population in the colony. Certainly, it is foolish to expect that the Guides or the 5th Light Infantry would not be aware of this.

For some six months the *Komagata Maru* was a floating display of white prejudice towards Sikh immigrants. It also acted as a focal point for the various Indian communities that rallied to the aid of the unfortunate passengers in those ports the ship called at: Hong Kong, Vancouver, Kobe and, finally, Budge Budge in India. Although the ship was not allowed to dock in Singapore, a good indication of the Colonial Office's awareness of its political impact, the Indian community was certainly aware of its presence. Also local Indians could not have been ignorant of the killing of 18 Sikhs in Budge Budge, India by the 2nd Battalion of the Royal Fusileers while trying to stop a procession to a temple. It is just too naive to assume that there would not have been a network of information among Singapore Indians through which news from 'home' was spread by word of mouth. Worse, the tendency to exaggerate or add on to such was always present. Although postal censorship was in force many letters were carried by travellers or through private means. There was simply no way of stopping news, especially that on the *Komagata Maru*.

There is strong evidence that such resentment and revolutionary rhetoric had become common knowledge of the serving Indian sepoys whether they were with the Guides or the 5th Light Infantry. Lieutenant Morrison, a medical officer, was particularly struck by the changed attitude of the soldiers. His uneasiness grew when he associated this with the troubles that had affected the Malay States Guides:

> About November I noticed a distinct change in the tone of the men and I think my attention was really drawn to this by the Malay States Guides' trouble making me more observant and less trustful. I then watched the men closely and I came to the conclusion that they were becoming very casual in their attitude to British officers.
>
> (Sareen, 1995, p. 543)

Officers like Captain Lionel Ball who was in charge of the right wing of the 5th Light Infantry had also reported that the men were less respectful. Lieutenant Morrison also noted that Sub-Assistant Surgeon Bell had overheard the men talking seditiously on Pulau Brani:

> Why should we fight for England and be killed in Europe when we are only paid half a coolie's wage and our wives and children will be left to starve on?
>
> (Sareen, 1995, p. 544)

Here the general feelings of unhappiness had crystallized into a definite resentment of the economic and social exploitation by the colonial masters. It is hard not to see here a shared perception of colonial arrogance that Ghadr and other nationalist movements such as Bose's Bengali party were trying to mobilize.

***

Like the 5th Light Infantry, the Malay States Guides had an impeccable background of colonial policing and imperial duties. Their refusal to serve was, therefore, all the more striking. Tracing their proud history to the beginnings of British intervention in the Malay States, the Guides were the first local regiment led by British officers and were trained for internal security duties. In July 1873, the Mentri of Perak had employed Tristram Charles Sawyer Speedy, then Assistant Superintendent of Police in Penang, to raise a force to pacify the rich tin-mining district of Larut. As for most colonial policing needs, Speedy turned to India for recruits, raising a unit of 110 sepoys from Punjab. Arming his men with some Krupps cannons that he had bought, Speedy named his unit "The Perak Armed Police". Its main duty was to ensure the security and peace of the Larut tin mines. Speedy's career illustrates the crucial but often understated link between arms and British presence. Not only did his mercenaries suppress the gang wars in Larut but he was also, to all intents and purposes, the local British representative. Not surprisingly, Speedy was the first official to be appointed under the Residential system that followed from the Pangkor Engagement of January 1874. It was, of course, the Pangkor meeting that opened the way for active British intervention. In that sense, Speedy's armed troops prefigured the format of colonial advance, which went hand in hand with policing duties.

While Speedy was not a good administrator he was a first-class soldier and adventurer. Under him, not surprisingly, The Perak Armed Police prospered. When it was decided that a local regiment should be raised in order to deal with internal troubles (that is, handle internal security), The Perak Armed Police formed its nucleus together with other Sikhs recruited from the police units of Perak, Selangor and Pahang. This first local regiment raised in 1896 by Lieutenant-Colonel R S Frowd of The Perak Armed Police was named the Malay States Guides with its base in Taiping. It was essentially a mercenary force engaged in frontier and internal policing duties owing loyalty not to the state of Perak but to the Crown. There is no difference between the Guides and the myriad of colonial units that were engaged in defending

British imperial interests and borders. Its British masters would have regarded its breach of loyalty as all the more disturbing since it called into question the whole nature of the tenuous relationship between auxiliary native forces and their colonial masters. The great Indian Mutiny had not only threatened the British with murder in their beds but the unravelling of their control and command systems which were needed to keep the empire docile. The Guides it was feared were repeating this tragedy.

It is, therefore, all the more surprising that the implications of the Guides' refusal to serve overseas were not examined in detail until after the mutiny of the 5th Light Infantry issued a salutary reminder of the links! If the authorities had been more alert they would have realized that many of the elements in the 1915 mutiny were already present in the case of the Malay States Guides. Increasingly militant nationalism, religious fervour, resentment over economic exploitation and awareness of their status as a social underclass fuelled the unhappiness of the sepoys. These sentiments lie behind issues as diverse as the formation of the Ghadr Party, the revisionist account of the Indian mutiny, the call to revolution, as well as the refusal to fight what was regarded as essentially a European war that was against the *fatwa* of the Turks.

Given these larger considerations, internal security could no longer be limited to the narrow confines of a colony or its immediate hinterland. Global events and, more importantly, ideas emanating from far away came to play a dominating role. This would be even more so for areas that are meeting points or crossroads whether by history or geography. The influences that worked on the pressure points of the sepoys' imagination came from Vancouver, San Francisco, India, China, Japan, Germany and the Middle East. On the other hand, British responses were traditional and slow, rooted in 19th century ideas of colonial security. The British were not even forward-looking. Their usual response to threats was to isolate them, send away the problem in other words. Thus, the Malay States Guides were sent back to their cantonment in Taiping on the assumption that this would reduce the malign influence of subversive contact. Similarly, the 5th Light Infantry was reassigned to garrison duties in Hong Kong, moving it further away from India and the Middle East. Other British methods reinforce this effort to insulate their colonies from change: censorship, quarantine (such as when the *Komagata Maru* was refused permission to dock) and deportation. However, given the porous nature of immigrant society, the permeable discourse of trading ports with the vast number of ships that call at the Straits Settlements it is unlikely that such efforts to isolate the troops were ever remotely successful. Ironically by being sent to guard the

German prisoners the sepoys came into close contact with those very subversive ideas they were to be protected from!

In many ways, British security planners were ill prepared in the early years of the 20th century to meet the challenges of ideological subversion and the competition of ideas in their far flung dominions. The assumptions of superiority had always aided colonial rule. Faced now with competing alternatives to these the British were slow to respond. Their ideals and models of civilization, work and progress had underpinned Western expansion for many years even if they lay on very shaky foundations. In the crucial areas of technology, military science and social planning, the early industrialization of the West gave their colonial emissaries unparalleled power and belief in the good they were bringing. Now that very same supremacy was unravelling, being challenged both from within itself by the contradictions of its society as well as by those countries that had escaped its clutches. Militant nationalism was not the only challenge. The rising 'red' tide of Bolshevism was essentially a reaction against the over dependence on technology that had distorted Western life. Its most enthusiastic proponents in spreading this message to the rest of the world were Europeans—Russians, French, Germans, English and Dutch. These were people within the system of capitalism itself. On the borders of the Western technological empire, revitalized Islam, Confucianism and Hinduism were showing signs that they were not prepared to accept European ascendancy at face value. Japan put forward its own version of racial supremacy that had been the exclusive preserve of the whites. In the early years of the new century, intense international rivalry was increasingly driven by ideological competition. Ideas agitated the hitherto docile colonial populations and fought for their allegiances. Offering alternative ways of social, economic, cultural and political organization, questioning the purposes of life and labour and promising different meanings of life, these new attitudes made rapid inroads into the colonies.

It would be incorrect to suggest that these issues only affected the security of colonies. What was happening during these years was a worldwide upheaval in which social and class structures were questioned and overturned, political hierarchies usurped and comfortable ideas thrown out. Given these conditions it was not surprising that revolutionary doctrines found many recruits. Both in Europe and the United States the state elite and ruling class faced with such challenges responded by heightening political surveillance. The operations of the Special Branch and its sister organizations like MI5, Military Intelligence and the Naval Intelligence Department showed continuous preoccupation from 1915 onwards with the subversive dangers of revolutionary doctrines of various kinds. Whether these be anarchism, the free Ireland opposition to Home Rule, the Fenian bombings, Bolshevism, the suffragettes, radical trade unionism, subversive pamphlets or even pornography the British establishment felt these as dangerous threats to its way of life. The First World War brought the dangers even closer home but was itself only part of an escalating pattern of violence. This is not the place to discuss the history of the Special Branch in detail. However, the development of intelligence and counter-espionage agencies in the colonies clearly cannot be separated from events in the British colonies and Europe. When the European war broke out in 1914, British intelligence agencies closely monitored both the espionage activities of German spies as well as their sympathizers (including fellow travellers, trade unionists, anarchists and aliens) who could weaken morale and the war effort. The war accelerated the expansion of intelligence personnel who were needed not just to track agents but to monitor the more elusive dimensions of subversive ideology. This growth was truly phenomenal:

> By the time of the armistice in November 1918 the Special Branch was 700 strong, compared with 70 in the summer of 1914, and MI5 had 844 officers compared with around a dozen. Their budget increased in proportion. To supplement their efforts there was a staff of 1,453 men and women intercepting and censoring letters at the Post Office, and others to do the same with telegrams.
>
> (Porter, 1989, p. 135)

The expansion was precisely in those areas of ideology and subversive politics that were now first priority. There is justification for this even if it also reflects war paranoia. Spies no longer worked just for material gain or patriotism. They reflected the complexity of the age by their ideological and religious motivations. Conviction, beliefs, religion, disaffections and other psychological motivations now matter as much as rewards.

The mutinies in Singapore were, in this sense, not unique. They mirrored the larger preoccupations and impulses of the age. They were also precursors, early warning signs, as it were of things to come: Bolshevism, anti-colonialism, nationalism and religion that would compete for the hearts and minds of the colonized people. If the events in 1914 and 1915 showed that the colonial administration was still ill prepared to counter subversion the situation was, on the other hand, not entirely discouraging. The British were lucky to have in Malaya a group of intrepid men sensitive to the new situation. Serving officers—whether military or police—often displayed a keen curiosity (what has been called a "CID curiosity") regarding behaviour, action and motives that proved useful in their work. Monitoring and surveillance were already being practised. Postal censorship was also in place. Infiltration into potentially anti-British organizations was carried out. Coverage of morale, political activities and unfriendly behaviour were also attempted although to a limited extent. There was also a quarantine system that denied access to those regarded as politically undesirable. Finally the draconian banishment warrant gave the authorities a potent weapon to deport those they felt were unfriendly to British interests. What was glaringly absent was the proper use of information. The problem was not so much the lack of information but the examination, evaluation and understanding of it. There was no organization within Singapore and the Malay States to process the data that came in. Little or almost no collation took place, no threat evaluation was made and, more importantly, no central authority was there to make decisions on these matters. Hence information often took the form of impressions (with no efforts at confirmation), reports after an event (no real time processing) or general observations (no specific checklist on what evidence to look for). Having said all this, it should also be pointed out that the existence of some structure, even if admittedly limited, allowed the colonial government to expand the coverage decisively and rapidly when the need was recognized.

The mentality of the colonial administrators remained the stumbling block. Most of the time security was conceived of in terms of policing unruly elements such as secret societies or bandits. Otherwise it was native unrest or frontier turbulence at the edges of British colonial power that occupied attention. So the aim was policing criminal or piratical elements for most of the time. No doubt this reflected the colonialist outlook that insisted on reading or describing any resistance as criminal. While this attitude is hardly conducive to an internal security that should be concerned more and more with the political dimension, the saving grace is that the British had a very clear idea as to what security was. Security, whether it be external or internal, was single-mindedly focused on the protection and preservation of the paramount position of the British so that they would be free to extract the wealth of the land. Internal security was to ensure the least disturbance to British trade, manufacture, plantation and commercial interests so that maximum advantages will be given to its nationals and subjects. The full force of the security apparatus would be deployed against those who sought to upset, displace, or worst, replace British interests. As far as the British were concerned there was a direct relationship between territory (imperial possessions) and wealth (colonial exploitation). This was what the Malay States Guides were raised for: to ensure a peaceful environment for the businesses of the tin mines and rubber plantations. This aim, as we have seen, backfired on the British. When the decision was made to send the Guides overseas, the sepoys argued that it was not in their contract and terms of service to be deployed overseas; in other words, they were strictly an internal security force that was used for policing and colonial duties. Anything more was unacceptable.

The British were fully aware of this and had set up their police forces accordingly. There was really little danger to their Malayan possessions from an external threat. Even during the war, German naval raiders were at best spoilers; they disrupted trade but posed no danger as an occupying force. The other naval force likely to be unfriendly was Japan but the Third Anglo-Japanese Alliance had taken care of that to some extent. In any case, as long as Japan's immediate attention was fixed on China she would not be interested in Southeast Asia. The Malayan peninsula was in an enviable position, safe from any direct predators. To the east laid the South China Seas and friendly French colonies. The Dutch were neutral but had a joint interest in ensuring colonial peace so they could be trusted to cooperate in the weeding out of subversive elements. It was a role that Britain herself had played at the height of the anarchist movement in Europe. Playing host, then, to a steady stream of anarchists, Britain developed a comprehensive security apparatus to keep tabs on its guests, feeding information on their movements to friendly overseas governments. If there was any danger to Southeast Asia it would come from India itself as one declared objective of its increasingly militant nationalist movements was to undermine the stability of British possessions. However, even here the British felt they had some advantages. Since the 19th century, the India Office had its own intelligence system which was bolstered in 1909 when an Indian section was formed in the UK Special Branch.

If political security was a weakness the same could not be said for colonial policing. Here the British excelled as the trouble that followed the 1915 mutiny showed. If we examine the response to the Kelantan uprising in Pasir Puteh in April 1915 (barely two months after the mutiny), we will soon realize how swiftly and decisively the reaction could be when the threat was recognizably colonial, that is an outbreak of disaffected natives threatening British rule. Coming as it did so soon after the February mutiny of the 5th Light Infantry, the Kelantan outbreak sent alarm bells going off in the Straits Settlements. It could not be written off as merely another riot or a small outbreak of unhappy Malay peasants. The British recognized almost immediately the implications: at the very least it threatened a breakdown of law and order which could spread to the other states; at the worst, it was another challenge to British authority. There was also the hidden hand hypothesis: Kelantan was Malay and devoutly Muslim. Could the war with Turkey and the *fatwa* from its sultan have provoked the revolt? Could sympathy with Germany have fuelled the boldness of the rebels? If nothing else the Pasir Puteh uprising was thought to have the backing of members of the royal family. Could this lead to a conflagration of populist revolt? The importance of the Pasir Puteh uprising in the history of Kelantan is that it:

> was indeed the last attempt by certain members of the royalty to reverse the direction by which change was occurring in the state. It must be noted that earlier, during the period of the Graham administration, their traditional powers had been eroded almost completely as far as matters of justice and finance were concerned.
>
> (Talib, 1995, pp. 134–135)

So the dissatisfaction was as much political as it had to do with tax revenues and land issues. In fact, under the colonial regime it was not possible to separate economic and social issues from the political dimensions. They were all caught in a complex array of its ideology.

In late April 1915, an uprising occurred in the district of Pasir Puteh in the northern state of Kelantan. Pasir Puteh was a coastal area sharing a border with Trengganu. It was one of the two rural districts of Kelantan (Ulu Kelantan being the other), lying in the southeastern part of the state. It took its name from a small town a few miles up the Semerak River, the only river of size in the district:

> Pasir Puteh is about 30 miles from Kota Bahru, the capital. An earth road has been made from Kota Bahru as far as Gunong about half the distance, and is for light motor traffic in dry weather. The remainder of the journey has to be made across the padi-fields, which are a sheet of water in the wet season. The only other communication between Kota Bahru and Pasir Puteh is the sea. There are no telegraphs or telephones in the district.[12]

The state of Kelantan itself was then very sparsely populated. The 1911 census showed 286,751 residents. However, although remote, Pasir Puteh was of some importance as an imperial post. The district was one of those that had been given a definite 'British' administrative stamp both in terms of police posts and a District Office because its proximity to Trengganu made it ideal as a customs post to prevent the smuggling of cattle and other things. It was also part of the buffer with Siam, the neighbouring country to the north, which until recently claimed control over substantial parts of northern and eastern Malaya. Pasir Puteh was, bearing in mind the population of Kelantan, densely settled with 25,523 residents. Its revenue was, however, not very much, amounting to $24,000 and this came from padi, coconuts and cattle. There were few European (that is to say, British) estates in the district and on the whole British presence was limited. Pasir Puteh had three police stations and a District Office headed by a Singapore Malay, Abdul Latif. The proposed Gunong Road to Kota Bahru was as yet half completed and the area was relatively isolated with the sea being the best link to the outside world.

When news of the outbreak reached Singapore, William Maxwell, the Acting Colonial Secretary to the government of the Straits Settlements, was sent to review the situation. In his report he put forward a number of concerns as well as expressed his fears of a likely connection with the Singapore mutiny. Perhaps it was because Maxwell had also written the preliminary report on the 1915 mutiny that his comments read like a replay of the events behind that event. He drew attention to the effects the 5th Light Infantry had on the morale of the natives but also warned that Turkish and Indian sedition had damaged the loyalty of the subjects. German propaganda had convinced many that the British were losing the war in Europe. Moreover, British prestige had taken such a beating as a result of the mutiny that the Kelantan natives were emboldened to try their luck at a revolt. Maxwell's report is important for the amount of attention he gives to the subversive potential of ideas and psychological attitudes. One can well believe that he must have learnt from the lessons of the 5th Light Infantry. His findings are worth quoting at length for the careful way he emphasizes the impact of ideological subversion. We cannot help in reading Maxwell's report but feel that for the first time we are seeing an intelligence evaluation that is subtly aware of the fuller dimensions of a security threat:

> Though there is nothing to show that any German, Turkish or Indian seditionist influence … the Kelantan people have for some months past undoubtedly believe that Great Britain was being defeated in the European war. When the Singapore mutiny took place in February … wild stories spread through the State of the massacres of Europeans and the successes of the mutineers. It was commonly believed that all the European troops

and all British battleships had left the East for Europe. So firmly did the Kelantan Malays believe in British impotence in the Straits Settlements that, when the British men-of-war were on their way to Kelantan, the news was received with incredibility even in the highest circles.

In the opinion of the British Adviser, His Highness the Sultan has, ever since the Singapore mutiny, believed that the downfall of the British Empire was at hand. A marked change has been noted in his attitude and unwonted opposition and difficulties have been experienced by the British Adviser within the last two months .... It is not that His Highness has anything to do with the outbreak. All that is meant is that his behaviour reflected the opinion which he shared with other people in the country .... Since the Singapore mutiny the Kelantan Malays, as a whole, have been far less respectful to Europeans, and have in many cases tended to adopt an insolent and truculent manner.[13]

There cannot be a clearer expression of the fear of the British that their authority was slipping away and of their concern that subversive influences had turned hitherto docile natives into potential revolutionaries. The tone of Maxwell's letter is also significant for the emphasis he placed on the effects of belief and propaganda. For him, this 'invisible' dimension was more dangerous than any crime or violence. Maxwell realized that losing control of the assumptions (and he was aware that they were just that) of British superiority would destroy the myth of colonial invincibility. It was, therefore, not surprising that the British were excessively overactive and righteously savage.

The uprising itself did not constitute much of a direct threat. Alun Jones suggested that the rebel forces could have numbered about 5,000 men although for the most part these were scattered about the state. At one of the more serious scenes of violence, which saw the burning and sacking of the Pasir Puteh District Office and some adjoining bungalows, there were only about 200 active participants. The outbreak was marked by skirmishes using the hit-and-run tactics denying the British the open pitched battles. Unused to these proto-guerrilla tactics, the British officers felt justified in loudly denouncing the fighting spirit of the Kelantanese. Yet the speed of British reaction suggests that they were worried. Within a fortnight of the British Adviser, Langham-Carter, informing Singapore that an *emeute* had broken at Pasir Puteh, a substantial force had been despatched. Once again *HMS Cadmus*, whose sailors had rendered sterling service during the Singapore mutiny, sailed into battle. By 5 May, it had landed a 239-strong contingent of British troops from the Royal Garrison Artillery, Royal Engineers and the King's Shropshire Infantry as well as 20 men of the Malay constabulary of the

Singapore Volunteer Force in Tumpat, Kelantan. Within a few days, on 12 May, the *SS Calypso* landed a force of 250 men of Malay States Guides in Kota Bahru to join the British troops.

The 'rebels' were wise not to meet the British troops head on. By the early years of the 20th century, the British had perfected the weapons and tactics of colonial wars. The range and killing efficiency of machine guns, rifles and naval cannons were far in excess of anything that the ragged bunch of rebels with their spears, parangs and sickles possessed. There could not be any doubt as to the outcome. The one time the rebels sought to meet the British in a regular pitched battle ended in disaster. On 23 May, the British fought a pitched battle with a group of about 50 to 60 armed Malays led by Engku Besar, To' Janggutt, Penghulu Adam, Che' Ishkak and Haji Said. Despite his claims to invincibility, To' Janggutt was shot and killed. With that and the arrival of more troops the uprising was effectively checked.

Although the majority of the rebels dispersed after this pitched fight, which clearly demonstrated the superiority of British military power, some persisted in their efforts. Engku Besar, Haji Said and a Che' Sikak fled into Ulu Kelantan where they resorted to guerrilla-like resistance for some time. It is also worth noting that the list of rebels included a headman (Penghulu Adam), a scion of the previous dynasty of rulers that had administered the district (Engku Besar), and three religious teachers among whom was To' Janggutt (whose real name was Haji Mat Hassan). These eminent local personalities do not suggest that the revolt was merely an uprising of dissatisfied peasants. Rather, the troubles at Pasir Puteh appear to have enjoyed widespread support both from the common folk (the *ra'ayat*) and the political and religious leadership. Despite such support, the overwhelming firepower of the British soon turned the tide. By August 1915 the uprising had been crushed and the Malay States Guides withdrawn.

It was difficult for the British to identify the specific reasons for the Pasir Puteh uprising. However, a closer examination suggests that some of the contradictions of British colonial policy in 19th century Malaya may have contributed in no small way. These exacerbated the unrest in the state leading to the breakdown of internal security. The incident was neither a "spontaneous combustion" nor the result of provocation. Rather, it showed the convergence of festering unhappiness and resentment. Confirmation of this lies in the very amorphous nature of the rebellion; a number of incidents broke out simultaneously in the district. This showed either very careful orchestration by a central organization, or a populist outburst. Many factors appeared to be at work with a whole range of issues coming to the fore once the revolt had taken place. Yet amidst this polyphony of dissension there were **some** dominant notes which conveyed the unhappiness of the Kelantan ruling house and the population over the behaviour of the British.

The various reports filtering up to the British administration gave different explanations of the uprising. The Governor, Sir Arthur Young, held the Adviser to the Sultan of Kelantan, Langham-Carter, in some suspicion. It was suggested that his poor abilities contributed to the outbreak. Another widely held belief which came out after the preliminary investigations suggested that the introduction of a new land tax to replace the existing produce tax had created considerable unhappiness among the people. On 1 January 1915, a land tax was introduced. A fixed sum was collected for each acre of land. Thus, first-class land would be taxed at $1.00 to $1.20 per acre every year while second-class land would be taxed at 80 cents. For third-class land, the tax would be 60 cents and 40 cents for fourth-class land. It was thought that the farmers were unhappy, as the new law would tax them by acreage rather than the amount of produce. The scheme was nevertheless implemented as it made revenue collection easier and more predictable from year to year. This **could** conceivably have made the farmers resentful except that as W A Graham pointed out, padi land had been taxed by acreage from the turn of the century (Graham, 1908, p. 74). Langham-Carter also felt that the new tax had nothing to do with the uprising. Taking a diametrically opposite view from Maxwell, Langham-Carter wrote: "I say that the land tax had nothing to do with the uprising."[14]

Perhaps this should be taken with a pinch of salt since any mishandling of the land tax implied the incompetence of Langham-Carter himself. The Governor was, however, more prepared to believe George Maxwell, the Acting Colonial Secretary, who argued that the Adviser, Langham-Carter, had mishandled the introduction of the land tax. According to Maxwell, the new land laws were not properly explained to the people. However, other reports suggest other possible causes including palace intrigue against the British. One of the leaders of the uprising, Engku Besar, was the grandson of Ungku Seliah or Tengku Sri Mah who had some claims to a dynasty that was independent of the Sultan at Kota Bahru. When he was alive, Ungku Seliah paid only lip service to the Raja of Kelantan, ruling Pasir Puteh as if it were his own territory. Perhaps Engku Besar was out to reclaim what he felt was his own piece of land. Another intriguing and this time more worrying possibility was that the palace had a hand behind the uprising. Captain R J Farrer of the Singapore Volunteer Force who served as an intelligence officer of the expeditionary force reported that the people of Pasir

Puteh themselves believed that: "if some big people did not acquiesce, this could never have happened."[15]

The British received news that tacit support came from palace officials including the Tengku Besar and the Tengku Bendahara, both uncles to the Sultan and who were also in control of the State Council. The Sultan himself was disaffected as British interference had crippled his hereditary powers. The Sultan, on hearing of the uprising, had sent out a call under his traditional rights of *kerah*, corvee labour, to raise troops. This was apparently to defend himself against the rebels but the British viewed his action with considerable suspicion. There were some in the British camp who felt that the Sultan was preparing for a general uprising led by the palace. Moreover the troops would be used or dispersed after the uprising posed some trouble to the British.

While the land laws were not directly responsible for the uprising they were perhaps, as Arthur Young put it, the last straw in a long chain of events that had seen the steady erosion of palace power and encroachment by the British. There was a lot of resentment over the somewhat unscrupulous methods used by W A Graham, while acting as the Siamese adviser to the government of Kelantan, and of the Duff Development Company to promote British commercial interests and political control. Pasir Puteh was, in this context, a 'hot' spot where issues of national pride, royal privileges, unpopular taxes and colonial exploitation came together to create a dangerous situation. Perhaps Arthur Young sums up all these conflicting possibilities best:

There has been for some time a feeling of dissatisfaction, traces of which have been discernible even in the Palace, with the state of things in which the native Kelantanese gets little or no share of the spoils. Further the war has decreased the earnings of the raiats. The price of copra, one of their staples, has fallen, and their earning power by honest work has been greatly reduced through the closing down of various coconut estates owned by Europeans. In addition to this the padi crop has proved a comparative failure in the Pasir Puteh district. My own impression to this effect gathered from the evidence of the straw in the fields was confirmed without suggestion on my part in all quarters. It was therefore to be anticipated that the collection of revenue would prove difficult this year.

In these circumstances the threatened enforcement of the new Land Rules ... proved to be the last straw. There can be no question that the fixed land rents will increase the total payable by those already paying taxes, and will also bring on the rent rolls of names of a number of people of position who have hitherto evaded payment of any tax.[16]

In addition, the increasingly visible signs of British control—the police stations and the District Office—were obviously an unwelcomed and constant reminder of the loss of status and power. There could also be the suspicion that the new land tax was a prelude to the encroachment of British estates into an area where locals had hitherto owned and cultivated the land. Abdul Latif, a Singapore Malay, who headed the District Office, was disliked as much for his harshly insensitive methods as, one suspects, for being a foreign representative of the British. In fact the District Office was targeted early in the uprising and sacked before being set on fire.

There were also rumours and propaganda being circulated in Kelantan about the impending defeat of the British by the Germans as well as news of the *jihad* or holy war that Turkey had declared against the infidel British. The sepoy mutiny in Singapore had shown that seditious rumours could not be taken lightly as they could provide the spark to ignite existing resentments. Maxwell, for one, as we have seen was convinced of the dangers of such activities. He had pointed out that the Kelantan Malays were convinced that Britain was losing the war with Germany. Moreover the February mutiny in Singapore had made many think that the British would not be able to send troops to other troubled areas in the peninsula. Such is the persuasive power of rumours that to repeat Maxwell's point:

> When the Singapore mutiny took place in February, wild stories spread through the State of the massacre of Europeans and the successes of the mutineers. It was commonly believed that all the European troops and all the British battleships had left the East for Europe. So firmly did the Kelantanese believe in British impotence in the Straits Settlements that, when the British Man-of-War were on their way to Kelantan, the news was received with incredulity even in the highest circles; and the arrival of Colonel Brownlow's force and of *HMS Cadmus* created a feeling almost approaching bewilderment.[17]

The rapid, and to some observers excessive, deployment of British and ancillary troops like the Malay States Guides was obviously a showing of the flag. It was a reminder to the Kelantan rebels of imperial power as well as an attempt to crush the rebellion quickly.

It is revealing when we look at these two events in 1915 together rather than as isolated separate occurrences. The punishments handed out by the British are an indication of their fears and anger. British reaction ranged from the harsh to the savage. Colonial history often treats these incidents separately as if they were merely local events. Yet a very noticeable common thread of frustration and resistance to British rule, of efforts at some kind of nationalist response, of awakenings to religious and pan-racial movements runs through them. It was inevitable: Asia could not be insulated from the War and the stirring events sweeping the world. It is true that colonies like Singapore had little to fear from the War itself. Even the German cruiser, *Emden*, thought it best not to test the labour defences of Singapore. It sailed past Singapore and was sunk off the Cocos Islands in November 1914 after some desultory success. However, the War brought people, culture, religion and politics within Asia into contact. Through the entreport of Singapore new ideas and inspirations passed into the consciousness of the native subjects:

> People of Asia experienced the first mutual contact on a large scale as a result of the First World War. Singapore was distant from the war front in Europe. But, the Indian Mutiny and anti-Japanese boycott movement provided its residents a chance to realize that they were living in a part of the world which was seriously affected by the war.
>
> (Kuwajima, 1991, p. 121)

Kuwajima's comments are indeed thought-provoking as they draw attention to the sea change that was taking place throughout Asia that would bring people and politics into violent collision. Situated at the crossroads of Asia, the free port and gateway to Malaya became inextricably linked to the larger currents of ideology and beliefs.

The British authorities reacted with haste, some would say excessive haste, to the 1915 mutiny in Singapore. The first summary court martial into the mutiny was held on 23 February, barely eight days after its outbreak. Two men were found guilty and sentenced to death. The names of these first two to be shot were never revealed but a contemporary report in *The Japan Times* provides a description of their execution:

> The Asahi Correspondent writes from Singapore that two ringleaders of the mutinous Indian soldiers were executed in the open grounds behind the Banda prison on February 23.
>
> The event brought crowds of spectators to the place from the city, among whom an Occidental girl in her teens was the most conspicuous. After they had waited for some time, a British officer made his appearance and read aloud the sentence before the motley audience. The gist of it was that one of the two killed a citizen at the outbreak of the mutiny, while the other killed or wounded more than ten persons, and that they were therefore to be shot.
>
> (*The Japan Times*, 19 March 1915 in Sareen, 1995, p. 844)

The proclamation signed by Lieutenant-Colonel A B Garnett was translated into Chinese, Malay and other languages. The firing party of 10 Scottish soldiers next drew up and, at a command, shots rang out.

However, by now the British were sensitive to the political complications of the mutiny especially in the eyes of the Muslims. British intelligence soon picked up a rumour that was spreading among the Muslims that this court martial and the execution would set the pattern for future trials. The fates of the other mutineers were to be decided in secret and they would all be hastily shot, so the rumour went. In response to such disquiet the Governor decided that the trials would be in an open court. When the trials resumed on 1 March the public were admitted. Although 202 sepoys from the 5th Light Infantry and 11 Malay States Guides were put on trial, in the end, 47 from the 5th Light Infantry were executed: two Indian officers, six Havildars and 39 rank and file. The rest were sentenced to hard labour imprisonment of one to seven years. A total of 212 men received punishment.

After the initial fear, the shock of the mutiny set in, affecting the tone of the local press which, no doubt, reflected public sentiments. Where *The Straits Times* had reported five public executions on 22 March, it soon used harsher terms seen in the headline "Execution of Twenty-Two Renegades" a few days later:

> The sentences of the court-martial on the batch of 47 mutineers of the 5th Light Infantry were promulgated in public yesterday afternoon outside the walls of Singapore prison and, in the case of those who were condemned to death and sentences were executed on stage. An enormous crowd, reliably estimated to number more than 15,000 people, was packed on the slopes of Sepoy Line looking down on the scene. The square as before was composed of regulars, local volunteers and Shropshire under the command of Colonel Derrick of the S.V.C. The firing party consisted of men from the various companies of S.V.C. under Capt. Tongue and Lieuts. Blair and Hay.
>
> (*The Straits Times*, 26 March 1915)

Throughout April the executions continued until all 47 had been dealt with. The British were determined to make their point—that mutiny and treason would be dealt with harshly.

The point was stressed over and over again before a large crowd of spectators who came to see the executions outside the Outram Prison. The irony could not have been lost on those who stood on the slopes of the Sepoy Line to gain a better view of the shootings. The spectacle— for what else could it be—reminded them that disobedience to British rule would be punished severely. However, the executions did not go off with the military smoothness that had been hoped for. Terror, hopelessness and despair marked some of the shootings:

> It became apparent that some of the prisoners could not stand the strain. One man started to cry out and this affected the others. In a few minutes the line was swaying and praying and shouting.
>
> (Harper and Miller, 1984, p. 202)

The aiming was sometimes not accurate and it needed another volley to complete the job. British wardens with revolvers despatched those who were still alive. In one case, Lance Naik Fazil, who had been wounded, was bound to a chair and shot in the prison compound. The final act occurred at the end of April when Kassim Ali Mansur who had forwarded the sepoys' letter to the Turkish Consul in Rangoon was arraigned before the Supreme Court and sentenced to death by hanging on 3 May. His execution was carried out on 31 May at Pearl's Hill prison.

These executions were but the immediate consequences of the mutiny. Both the regiments involved were to bear forever their dishonour and betrayal of the British colonial cause. The 5th Light Infantry was shipped out of Singapore on 3 July 1915 for the Cameroons in West Africa where they fought against the German colonial army. At the end of the year they were redeployed to German East Africa fighting in what became known as Tanzania. Still later, at the end of 1917, the 5th Light Infantry found themselves in Aden, this time with the Malay States Guides fighting the Turks. Records showed that the 5th Light Infantry acquitted themselves well in these difficult campaigns. At the end of the war they were returned to India where, four years later, the regiment was disbanded as part of the reorganizing of the Indian army. Much the same fate befell the Malay States Guides. The Guides were deployed for a while in Kelantan to suppress the To' Janggutt uprising at Pasir Puteh before going overseas to fight in Aden in October 1915. As with the 5th Light Infantry, the Malay States Guides were disbanded in 1919 "ostensibly because the government considered the regiment too expensive to maintain" (Harper and Miller, 1984, p. 243).

If the British reacted with harsh severity to the mutineers, they exhibited a streak of savagery in the punishment of To' Janggutt. The forcefulness of British reaction with the memory of the Singapore mutiny fresh in their minds was to be expected. They were clearly not going to be satisfied with the mere triumph of British military might. A more severe demonstration of imperial displeasure had to be arranged.

To' Janggutt who had inspired his followers with claims that he was invulnerable provided the perfect illustration to remind the natives of British anger. Despite his claims, To' Janggutt was clearly not immune to bullets since he was shot and killed at the encounter with British forces on 23 May. The British set out to make an example of him. As the population watched:

> the authorities crucified his body head downwards on the far bank of the Kelantan river. There it was left for several days, a gruesome exhibition of the fate waiting all who dared to take up arms against the government.
>
> (Jones, 1970, p. 69)

No doubt, one intention was to show that the rebel was not invulnerable and that he was a very dead man indeed. The other intention was to teach an object lesson in terror. This is very much in keeping with colonial practices that were carried out from Africa to China throughout the 19th century.

However, the British soon stopped these purges, as they were counterproductive. The point having been made they preferred to use well-tested procedures of administration to control security. In Singapore the mutiny was followed by an increased emphasis on intelligence which led to the formation of the Criminal Intelligence Department (in effect, the Special Branch) in 1919. Other institutions to provide feedback and monitor the ground were also created. In the wake of German efforts to manipulate Islamic sentiments, there was a need to maintain constant knowledge as well as appropriate contact with local religious leaders. As Talib pointed out:

> In 1915, after the successful suppression of the Tok Janggutt Uprising, the Majlis Ugamam dan Isti' adat Melayu was formed. This Council for Religious and Malay Customs ... formed ..."a body to which resort (could) be had for advice in all matters affecting the customs of the country." The Majlis also performed other duties, besides being an organ through which the government was able to consolidate its hold over the state.
>
> (Talib, 1995, p. 124)

The security of Singapore at the strategic end of the Straits waterway and as a crucial garrison centre for Malaya was further enhanced by the passing of the "Reserve Force and Civil Guard Ordinance" in August 1915 by the legislative council. This was the first Act passed in a British colony imposing compulsory military service on all male subjects between 15 and 55 years of age who were not in the armed forces, volunteers or police. Simultaneously a Reserve force in the Volunteer Corps was created for fit men over 40 years of age. The history of these legislative and other measures taken in response to security is a fertile area for research. However, these examples should serve to demonstrate how seriously the British came to view internal security after 1915.

The colonies also gained from the experiences in political intelligence and espionage that the War forced upon the British. The huge expansion of British intelligence between 1914 and 1918 reflected an ever more sophisticated and comprehensive awareness of the need for high-grade information. Obviously this had an impact upon the colonies. The methods and organization developed in England soon found their way to the imperial possessions. However, the traffic was not entirely one way. The colonies were an ideal testing and recruiting ground for the Special Branch and MI5. Procedures of censorship, immigration control, surveillance and interrogation could be freely tested in the colonies since their use, unlike in England, would not spark off a wave of protest. Many senior staff of the British intelligence including directors of key organizations like MI5 learnt their trade as it were while in the colonial police force combating secret societies, illegal political organizations and other undesirables. From the start there had always been a deep and complex relationship between the intelligence agencies 'at home' and those in the dominions. The web-like image of British intelligence with a centre controlling events and manipulating each and every distant 'station' in faraway colonies is simply not true. In fact, the very nature of intelligence agencies would make such absolute control impossible as operations often were run on a need-to-know basis. Operational control was often kept secret at the local level to prevent leakage. Identities of field agents or informers were protected. They were known only to their local handlers to prevent their 'covers' from being blown. The attitude of the civil service in Whitehall, including its intelligence chiefs, is also relevant. These chiefs often found it convenient not to know too much about what was happening in the field. The ultimate defence in any political fiasco involving a botched operation was, of course, to claim ignorance of a rogue agent acting on his/her own initiative!

1915 was a crucial test of British preparedness in combating infiltration and subversion. The colony had weathered the storm more by good fortune than design. A combination of poor strategy on the part of the mutineers, the quick arrival of allied troops, the geography of the land which gave advantage to naval forces and superior firepower crushed the various efforts. Yet for all that it was a remarkable year: two mutinies by serving regiments with proud battle records and an uprising from disaffected subjects. These cannot be written off as mere occurrences. The authorities realized that the threat scenario had changed. It would be politics and the competition over ideas that would determine who remained paramount in Malaya. Their response was to form the Special Branch.

Notes

1. C.O. 273/435, War Office to Colonial Office, 28 September 1915.

2. PP Cd. 2777 (1906). Anderson to Colonial Office 6 September 1905 enclosing Annual Reports FMS 1904.

3. Frank Swettenham, "A Love Philtre", *A Nocturne and Other Malayan Stories and Sketches*, Kuala Lumpur, Oxford University Press, 1993, p. 190.

4. Anonymous, "A Lady's Experiences in the Singapore Mutiny", *Blackwood's Magazine*, CXCVIII, 1915, p. 782.

5. The standard work on the mutiny remains R W E Harper and Harry Miller, *Singapore Mutiny*, Singapore, Oxford University Press, 1984. However, a richly alternative viewpoint that situates the 1915 mutiny as part of the larger resistance to British colonialism can be found in the works of Sho Kuwajima.

6. Account compiled by W G Maxwell, Adviser to the Kedah Government, 25 February 1915, C.O. 273/420.

7. C.O. 273/431, Foreign Office to Colonial Office, 26 July 1915.

8. Cited in Arthur Young to the Secretary of State for the Colonies, 20 February 1915, C.O. 273/420.

9. From India Office to Colonial Office, 5 February 1915, C.O. 273/433.

10. Lieutenant-Colonel Lees, "Short History of the Malay States Guides", 15 July 1915 in Arthur Young to A Bonar Law, 23 July 1915, C.O. 273/427.

11. Arthur Young, "The Situation in Singapore", hand-written notes, 22 February 1915, C.O. 273/420.

12. Arthur Young to A Bonar Law, 2 June 1915, C.O. 273/426.

13. Confidential report of 1 June 1915 by W G Maxwell, Ag Secretary to the High Commissioner. Enclosure in Arthur Young to A Bonar Law, 2 June 1915, C.O. 273/426.

14. Langham-Carter, Memorandum on Maxwell's Official Narrative of the Outbreak in Kelantan, 12 July 1915. Enclosure in Arthur Young to A Bonar Law, 20 July 1915, C.O. 273/427.

15. R J Farrer in his 31 May 1915 confidential report. Enclosure in Arthur Young to A Bonar Law, 20 July 1915, C.O. 27/427.

16. Arthur Young to A Bonar Law, 20 July 1915, C.O. 273/427.

17. Confidential report of 1 June 1915 by W G Maxwell, Ag Secretary to the High Commissioner. Enclosure in Arthur Young to A Bonar Law, 2 June 1915, C.O. 273/426.

Forging the Defence

THE EARLY YEARS OF THE SPECIAL BRANCH

The events of 1915 had the immediate consequence of alerting the British authorities to the nature of the threats facing their Malayan colonies in the increasingly uncertain world of the 20th century. These clearly lay in the western regions. Whether it be Punjabi Ghadr extremists, Hindustani nationalists or pan-Islamic efforts at undermining British imperialism the danger was ever present. To make matters worse, Germany was active in the Central Asian and Afghan provinces bordering India. Her agents stirred up unrest and sowed dissension in the hope of creating a conflagration of British interests.

Despite its deceptive air of prosperity and calm, the 1920s were challenging times for the Special Branch. It faced not just attempted assassinations, bombings, trade boycotts and riots but also the beginnings of revolutionary movements that attempted to bring the Chinese and the colonized people together in a common platform against their British masters. The Kuomintang had become increasingly radical under the influence of groups such as syndicated anarchists who made their way to Malaya in the First World War. By 1923 the Special Branch was reporting on the work of communist agitators in Kuala Lumpur. The 1920s were therefore the years in which the political discourse of the Malayan peninsula became radicalized with competing alternatives.

The wave of unrest in 1915 also revealed that future threats would increasingly be ideological. Competing systems of beliefs, alternative ideals of life and differing systems of social organization would rock the colonies. Religion, politics and nationalism would compete for the hearts and minds of the subject population. It would be ideas that would move men and women to action, willing them to challenge the hitherto unquestioned dominance of imperial might. After 1915 it became obvious that while Britain was militarily all-powerful, not all issues could be settled through force. The internal dimensions of political infiltration and ideological subversion within her colonies assume ever-greater significance. These fuelled nationalist unrest, peasant uprisings and political radicalism that confronted the British administration with very different problems from the past when they were pacifying pirates or fighting the triads.

The British soon realized that, given the geography and economy of their Malayan possessions, security could never be a local matter. It had from the start to involve all the dimensions of intelligence gathering including detection or the forward collection of information, its collation and interpretation in a regional, if not international, context. Singapore would always be exposed to the winds of wars and conflicts even if these were far away in India or even Europe. The trouble might be local but its origin was in nearly every instance elsewhere.

Immediately after the events of 1915, the government realized that a professional intelligence service was necessary to the security of the colonies. The very different threat scenario could not be contained or handled by the police force or even the detective bureau. Specialists who could understand the hidden dimensions of events trace their origins and follow through with the meanings they often hint at were needed. Unlike the police, an intelligence organization took a longer, more patient view of things, often spending much time monitoring a suspect whom they might not even arrest. The aim was not merely to close a case but to track down the perpetrators behind the scene. Such an agency had to be aware of global events and not be excessively preoccupied with matters of everyday policing.

Given these operational needs it was almost inevitable that there would be some difficulty finding a suitable administrative cover for the nascent intelligence service which the Singapore authorities had set up. Initially the agency was placed with the military. Before long it was housed with the police. There were compelling reasons for this. The British realized from their colonial operations nearer home—in Northern Ireland—that political intelligence often needed entirely different skills and methods from the military. While not strictly in the domain of police work, political intelligence, where the enemy was likely to be located among civilians, needed powers to enable detection, control and arrest. These the military did not have and could only possess if it imposed martial law. It was for this reason that the Special Branch of the London Metropolitan Police, as it came to be called in 1887, was formed to deal with the Fenian bombing campaign in the home counties. The authorities felt that they needed entirely different procedures to deal with the unrest.

It would be wrong to assume that it was entirely a one-way street, that it was all a matter of England sending out security experts to the colonial police. Unlike other branches of administration, security was very much homegrown. The nub of the matter was that security needed an intuitive feel of the pulse of local events and actors upon which assessment and judgement is measured. This was one area that could not be managed from an office in London. Indeed, often it was the other way around; many who occupied key positions in intelligence in England learnt their trade in the colonies. A moment's reflection would show how useful colonial policing was to these officers. It was in the colonies that the whole spectrum of countermeasures was often in use. Police intelligence in the colonies routinely involved the screening and detection of immigrants and transit passengers who made their way through their ports. Singapore was a prime example. The island served as a gateway to the Malay States and through it a steady stream of transit passengers and goods passed. The screening and detection of undesirables was obviously necessary. Moreover, these elements frequently hid among the general population, indistinguishable for the most part from the civilian population who might even be sympathetic to them. Here again the police had to develop methods of surveillance and interdiction suited to the situation. The police would need to mount frequent surveillance, screen identities and bring in suspects for interrogation to piece together information about underground elements seeking to avoid detection. And for the Colonial Office, all these conducted within the added complexity of an operating terrain of foreign language or languages and cultures. Often these suspects would appear to be innocent since no enemy agent was likely to draw attention to his activities. The crime would be discovered only as a result of the investigation, making the procedure significantly different from police work.

Many of the methods employed by the Special Branch would not have found acceptance in England. But in the colonies the subject population was in no position to offer any protest. The procedures the Special Branch used in England were honed to perfection in their colonies. For example, the Irish problem which England faced was in essence a colonial problem where a colonial police had to maintain order through the control of an unsympathetic population.

The colonies were also fertile grounds for infiltration and agitation. There was already unhappiness among the subject population who resented their inferior status and restricted economic opportunities. Such a situation would attract the unwelcome attention of the enemies of the British. Moreover, the many contending ideas of this period—anarcho-syndicalism, fascism, communism, nationalism, religious idealism, pan-Asianism—had found ready adherents among the colonized. The first half of the 20th century was a time when beliefs and convictions were overturning social and political systems, creating a wave of unrest throughout the world. A radicalization of life, culture and politics took place and altered the discourses of the society, dislocating the hitherto well-defined relationship between the ruler and the subject. Many were attracted to the revolutionary rhetoric and ethics that permeated contemporary culture. The authorities had to build up the necessary expertise and mechanisms to counter these threats to the hitherto undisturbed well-being of their colonial enterprises.

India was one of the more fertile grounds for the training of intelligence operatives in Asia and Africa. The Indian Political Office and the Criminal Intelligence Department provided some of the key officers to the Special Branch and MI5. Sir Basil Thomson, who ran the Special Branch in England from 1913 to 1921, had served in the colonial police forces of Fiji, Tonga and New Guinea. So good was he at his job, which included breaking the back of industrial action and the 'red' menace, that from 1919 to 1921 he was made Director of Intelligence of the Special Branch. He was intelligence supremo of England.

Colonial policing saw some of the most efficient uses of then available technology to control crime and subversion. Sir Edward Henry who had served in the Indian Civil Service developed a simple system of classifying fingerprints which helped in the work of law enforcement agencies. These new techniques were introduced rapidly into the colonies. Within three years of Scotland Yard opening its fingerprinting bureau in 1901, W L Conlay of the Malayan police was visiting London to study the procedure. Conlay refined and improved the fingerprinting method, introducing his modifications to the Malayan police upon his return. The effectiveness of Conlay's improvements may be seen from the prints held at the Central Registry in Kuala Lumpur which grew from 7,751 in 1906 to 203,075 in 1927. The photographing and indexing of suspects were also methodically carried out. The British showed that they were not averse to learning. The police were always experimenting and were open to new techniques that improved their work. Alec Dixon recounts how his chief, Superintendent Henderson of the Detective Bureau, reorganized the fingerprinting department following a visit to the French *Surete* (Dixon, 1935, p. 76).

Not surprisingly when the need was felt for a competent intelligence officer to monitor events in Southeast Asia the ideal person was found among the colonial police rather than in England. It was the India Office that provided the right man: David Petrie, a young officer with the Punjab Police and Criminal Intelligence Department. A Scot born in Aberdeen, Petrie was with the Indian Police from 1900 to 1936. He was appointed Assistant Director, Criminal Intelligence, to the Government of India before rising, in due course, to be Director of the Intelligence Bureau of India. Even as early as November 1915 as recognition of his success and the value of his work, Petrie was appointed Indian Intelligence Officer for the Far East. Among his first duties was to visit Southeast Asia to "develop the organization and system" (C.O. 273/434) of the proposed intelligence unit in Singapore. Petrie (or Sir David Petrie, as he became) went on to head MI5 and the Security Service DI5 from 1940 to 1945, a crucial period for England (Bunyan,

1976, p. 193). He was handpicked by Winston Churchill to revitalize Britain's war-time security. While his position in India corresponded with what today in intelligence circles would be called a Station Chief, he should in many ways be regarded as the first director of the Special Branch in the Straits Settlements. Certainly his primary task of building up the system would earn him the title of the founder of the Branch. In any case, it was clear that the history of sustained and organized intelligence work begins with the unit set up by Petrie.

Petrie's recommendation to set up a separate unit focusing on intelligence was the right move. It showed that he had identified the problem correctly. The mutiny and other events in 1915 did not indicate the failure of intelligence but an **absence** of it. There was simply no procedures, no organization, and, even more worrying, no awareness of the magnitude of problems that subversion could pose. Whatever bits and pieces were known about the mutineers could not pass as intelligence since these were neither processed nor collated. On 4 May 1916 Arthur Young, the Governor of the Straits Settlements, wrote formally to A Bonar Law of the Colonial Office with the proposal to set up the unit:

> I have the honour to apply for your approval of the creation of the Criminal Intelligence, and Criminal Investigation, Departments in the Straits Settlements Police Force ...
>
> (C.O. 274/441, Young to A Bonar Law, 4 May 1916)

In recommending two separate departments, Young and Petrie showed that they were aware of the fundamental differences between intelligence and regular police work. The distinction was made very clear in a subsequent paragraph that also spelt out the charter of the future Special Branch:

> It is proposed to follow the system in force in India, and to arrange that the Criminal Intelligence Department shall devote itself fully mainly to work in connection with sedition, with the operation of spies and political agents and political information generally, whilst also specializing (as in India) to a certain extent upon organized crime, such as the activities of a gang of coiners. Criminal Investigation, on the other hand, is concerned only with the ordinary offences against the law.
>
> (C.O. 273/441, Young to A Bonar Law, 4 May 1916)

The Criminal Intelligence Department was formally established at the end of 1918.

In his letter, Arthur Young took the chance to acknowledge the pivotal role that Petrie had played in these recommendations:

The events which followed the outbreak of war showed that not only was a Criminal Investigation Department needed, but that a Criminal Intelligence Department (which was wholly wanting) was also essential. The present proposals have been drawn up by Captain A R Chancellor, Inspector General of Police, and are made in the light of the experience of the past year in dealing with the activities of enemy agents: they have been referred to, and concurred by Mr D Petrie, CIE, a Deputy Director of the Criminal Intelligence in the Indian Police Service, who has been visiting the colony upon duty.

(C.O. 273/441, 4 May 1916)

Among other things, Petrie ensured that the new Criminal Intelligence Department would be left alone to function in its designated sphere of work without interference from the military or the police establishments. The Governor also took up Petrie's advice on the areas that the Criminal Intelligence Department should focus. The CID, Petrie had advised, should concentrate its monitoring on the Indians, the Chinese and the Japanese. Given the threats posed by Ghadr the immediate task was to recruit suitable Indian officers to staff the section. It was proposed to create three appointments for northern Indians recruited from the Indian Police. In recommending the creation of the Chinese and Japanese sections, Petrie showed that he was already aware of the likely dangers to come from the Far East. The Governor asked for a substantial increase in the police budget to go towards the secret intelligence expenditure.

Events continued to unfold even as the British authorities were assigning men and building up their resources to correct the defects in their internal security and intelligence architecture. Increasingly, the new developments threw into sharp relief how complex the business of intelligence was. Larger, more dangerous currents were swirling throughout Asia. Even if it were the wish of most in the Straits Settlements to be left alone to get on with the business of making money, the turbulence would sooner or later affect them. In 1915 a plot that showed how international the context of espionage had become came to the attention of the Singapore authorities. The plot had its inception in Europe and America, came to a climax in Batavia and was aimed at creating a bloodbath in Calcutta, India. Nothing could illustrate more the importance in those years of the Straits Settlements as transit points for the increasing crowd of businessmen, adventurers, spies, political agents, and gunrunners than this episode. In this case, enemy espionage services took advantage of the relatively benign security of the hitherto neutral United States and the East Indies territories of the Netherlands to launch their subversion against India. At the crossroads of these transit routes Singapore was inevitably a part of the network of these agents. As their detection was vital to the security of the region Singapore emerged rapidly as the hub of counter-espionage work in Southeast Asia. In this incident the Germans were behind the machinations of various agents.

Even before the sepoy mutiny of 1915 in Singapore Sir Charles Cleveland, head of the Indian security service had been convinced of the likely troubles that Punjabi and Hindustani extremists could cause. Cleveland was also convinced that Singapore was but a means to strike at the British in India. While the island had suffered the first shock at the hands of the extremists, the real target of these agitators remained unchanged. It was no less than the dismantling of British rule in India. These schemes found ready support from the German Kaiser as well as the German external intelligence agencies. It was after all part of the German war plans to instigate native dissidents against the British colonies. Thus they had supported Turkey's call for a *jihad* that would galvanize the Middle East against the British. If India and, perhaps its neighbouring territory, Burma could be similarly thrown into disarray so much the better.

In early 1915 the Germans began using their secret service funds to purchase substantial amounts of guns and other weapons to support these dissidents. As an indication, Kuwajima notes that Papen and Hans Tauscher had assembled by the first week of December 1914, 8,080 Spring field carbines, 410 Hotchkiss cartridges, 500 cartridge belts, 500 Colt revolvers with 100,000 cartridges and 250 Mauser pistols with ammunition (Kuwajima, 1988, p. 37). The weapons were intended for use by Indian extremists to effect an uprising in Calcutta and other parts of India. An elaborate plan was conceived to smuggle the guns and ammunition into India. One batch of guns that was bought in the United States was loaded on board the schooner, *Annie Larson*. At a remote part of the Mexican coast *Annie Larson* would transfer her cargo to a tanker, *Maverick*, that would sail across the Pacific to the Netherlands East Indies with the cargo. The guns would then be loaded onto smaller vessels that would cross the Indian Ocean for Calcutta. At the end of this convoluted voyage across half the world the weapons would be delivered to a dummy company, an import export firm, named Harry and Sons. It was hoped that the elaborate scheme would throw the authorities off the scent.

This was but one part of the rather elaborate effort by the Germans to ship arms into India. The whole venture was in fact rather extensive. Guns had also been purchased in Thailand for smuggling into Burma where a simultaneous uprising had been planned. In addition the

German consul in the Philippines had purchased 5,000 rifles and 500 revolvers. Accompanied by two weapons instructors these were loaded onto a motor-schooner, *Harry S*, which would make its way across the Indonesian islands to Burma.

There can be no doubt that a bloodbath would have occurred if these weapons had reached their destinations. In 1914, Sikhs tried to disembark from the *Komagata Maru* at Budge Budge Harbour, Calcutta. The 2ⁿᵈ Battalion of the Royal Fusileers had to enforce order as a melee began. The situation rapidly got out of control; shots were fired, killing 18 Sikhs and wounding 25 others. A European police officer, a head constable and two spectators were also killed. British intelligence knew that the potential for violence was always present (Singh, 1966, pp. 33–34).

It was lucky then that the guns never reached their destinations. The plot was uncovered when a German officer in disguise was detained in June 1915 while passing through Singapore (Hopkirk, 1994, p. 188). In his possession were documents, a map of Bengal with markings that suggested landing sites, as well as a codebook. Vincent Kraft's arrest was not the result of a stroke of fortune as British counter-espionage agents had been watching his movements for some time in Batavia. The British, not wishing to expose their sources, did little to correct the impression that it was the Dutch authorities that had provided the tip-off.

During his interrogation Kraft, confronted by the weight of evidence, was 'turned' by the British who not only got him to confess but also to act as their agent. Petrie must almost certainly have been present during the interrogation. Kraft turned out to be a goldmine of information providing details not only of German plans in the Netherlands East Indies (NEI) but also the impending 15 December uprising planned for the Indian subcontinent. It is a testimony to the skill of his British interrogators that Kraft not only spilt the beans but also agreed to act as a double agent. He returned to the NEI and provided high-grade intelligence about German plans.

Suitably armed with Kraft's information, the British acted with characteristically efficient ruthlessness. The engines of *Harry S* conveniently broke down, forcing the ship to dock in a Celebes port for repairs. There she was boarded and searched by the Dutch customs which proceeded to seize the arms on board. Another ship that had been sailing for Thailand with a shipment of weapons apparently went down with all hands in a typhoon. It has always been suspected that this was something more than an act of nature. Just before 15 December, the date set for the uprising, the British conducted raids in Calcutta and Burma, detaining over 300 suspects. Pressure was also put on the Thais to raid and close down the training camps that the extremists had established on their side of the border. In another move, US customs authorities boarded *Annie Larson* and seized her cargo on 29 June.

When all is said and done this must surely count as a very significant intelligence coup for the fledgling British security services in Southeast Asia. Unlike the Singapore mutiny of 1915 where information was either ignored or misinterpreted and proper intelligence evaluation absent, the British during this time monitored, detected and turned the danger to their advantage. With one strike they crippled not only the German intelligence network in Southeast Asia but dealt a body blow to plans by the Indian nationalists to challenge British rule. British concern with the German plot could also have been instrumental in their decision to deploy the 5th Light Infantry in Kelantan since this effectively removed the sepoys from any likelihood of seditious rumours about impending events. Certainly the swiftness and severity of British response to the Kelantan uprising would suggest that they were intent on sending out a strong signal to any likely dissidents.

This was not the entire extent of the British hand. While even authorities like Hopkirk continue to believe that it was the Dutch who tipped the British off (Hopkirk, 1994, p. 188) the truth is even more startling. The British had for some time been privy to German plans in the NEI and their Consul-General in Batavia, W R D Beckett, had in place an extensive network of informers and agents watching the situation. They even had a double agent known by the code name "Oren", born of a Swedish mother and a German father, working under deep cover within the European business community of the NEI. Not surprisingly, Beckett could write with complete authority and conviction on these developments to the Batavia government. His memorandum indicated that it was he and not the Dutch authorities in Batavia who was in possession of the facts. Of course, it was also an indirect admission that the British were running a full-scale espionage operation in the Dutch territories:

> These suspicious movements connected with munitions of war by vessels which appeared to have the Netherlands East Indies as their base and the activities of certain Germans within the Netherlands East Indies which pointed to a knowledge on their part of these movements have led to a world wide investigation by the authorities of his Brittanic Majesty's Government. (These) investigations have resulted in the discovery of a deep laid scheme organized by the German Government and to be carried

out by agents to spread sedition, revolution and unrest in British India
and Netherlands Indies.

> (C.O. 273/473, Grey to A Bonar Law, 20 November 1915, enc.
> Memorandum by W R D Beckett)

This was but one of the precursors to a closer working relationship in
security between the British and the Dutch. Events in the following
decades such as the rise of communism and of the militant Islamic
movement would bring about even closer links between the different
colonial regimes. The British watched developments in the NEI carefully
as the Straits Settlements were but a day's sail to parts of the Dutch
territory.

The British decision to start a professional intelligence agency in
Singapore could not have been taken under more propitious
circumstances. The Kraft episode provided additional compelling
proof, if any were still needed, that Petrie's recommendation to set up
a Criminal Intelligence Department should go ahead. Indeed, by the
end of the War the basic organization was present. The sympathetic
ears it gained from the highest leaders of the colony helped the work of
the fledgling department. Petrie's work was made very much easier by
the support of Brigadier-General (and subsequently Major-General)
Howard Ridout who became General Officer Commanding, Singapore,
in 1915. Having learnt a bitter lesson from the 1915 mutiny on the need
for timely intelligence, Ridout was all in favour of the new department.
During the early years of the Branch when it had considerable financial
constraints, Ridout allowed a German bank draft of 100,000 pounds
that had been seized by intelligence to be used for Special Branch
activities[1]. The money went into the secret vote that was used to pay
agents and purchase information throughout Southeast Asia.

Right from the start, as Ridout's financial support underlined, it was
agreed that the Special Branch would deal with political subversion
and not routine police work. The point was made by Turnbull:

> A Special Branch was created in 1919 to deal specifically with political
> subversion ...
>
> (Turnbull, 1997, p. 131)

Properly speaking, this agency in Singapore should be distinguished
from the Special Branch that existed in England. In practice the Straits
agency combined the duties and powers of what in England were
divided between the Special Branch and MI5. The Singapore Branch
did not just confine its activities to local political security issues but

often extended its counter-espionage operations overseas when the need arose. Thus in the follow-up to the case of Kraft and the German instigators the British ran operations in Batavia. Among the reasons for its many later successes was this amalgamation of viewpoints that gave the Singapore department the necessary width of perspective that was essential in counter-espionage and anti-subversive operations. The department had, in other words, two eyes rather than one to detect the enemy.

In contrast the overlapping responsibilities of the Special Branch and MI5 in England often brought about tensions and made for an uneasy relationship. The Special Branch was the older organization, founded in the 1880s to deal with Fenian bombings arising from the Irish unrest. MI5 came into being only on 28 August 1909 when the Committee for Imperial Defence decided, in the face of the approaching war with Germany, to give a formal status to one of its sub-committees that was in charge of internal security, censorship and the protection of British ports and harbours. Under the leadership of its first director, Sir (at that time, Captain) Vernon Kell, MI5 grew rapidly. Its duties were substantially similar to those of the Special Branch although its interest in industrial and trade union matters was not of significance to MI5. The efforts to redress this duplication of duties when Basil Thomson was made Director of Intelligence from 1919 to 1921 did not work. The Special Branch, exercising police powers, continued to be a part of the Criminal Investigation Department under the operational control of the Metropolitan Police while MI5 focused on the non-executive roles of intelligence collection and analysis and became independent, reporting to the Cabinet:

> From then on MI5 was the key agency concerned with counter-espionage; the Special Branch's role was limited to helping in the final stages of an investigation, making the arrest, and appearing in court.
>
> (Bunyan, 1976, p. 155)

This is not the place to go into the organizational history of these various and competing agencies in England except to note that the Singapore Special Branch had the advantages of both. The Criminal Intelligence Department was engaged in counter-espionage as much as it was in the arrest and detention of spies.

While the Singapore Criminal Intelligence Department may resemble MI5, it also had, nonetheless, all the advantages of operational powers of the police force. During this early period, there were suggestions that the new agency be civilian in orientation, that is completely cut off from its police affiliations. One such proposal which luckily came to nothing was put forward in 1919 by W˙ H Lee Warner working then for the Far Eastern Section of the British secret service. Essentially his plan would have led to the establishment of a Civil Intelligence Bureau. This suggestion was turned down as it was realized that the Special Branch would lose its edge of having both police powers of arrest and detention as well as intelligence capabilities.

***

The Special Branch in Singapore had a modest beginning when formed in late 1918 as the Criminal Intelligence Department of the Straits Settlements Police. In fact, the CID was effectively the Special Branch and dealt from the start with political rather than criminal matters. However the detective bureaus and the Criminal Investigation departments of the different settlements handled criminal matters. Although Young had recommended that G G Seth, a Class IV officer and the Deputy Public Prosecutor, as the first director of the Criminal Intelligence Department this was not taken up. Instead V G Savi, who later became Chief Constable of Fife, was appointed the first Director of the Special Branch. Rene Onraet was the second Director serving for ten years until his promotion to Inspector General of Police of the Straits Settlements in 1935. Onraet credits Savi with much good work in laying down a strong foundation for the Branch:

> A good policeman and a linguist, speaking Malay, Fukien Chinese, Hindustani and Punjabi, Savi laid the foundations of the department on sound lines ...
>
> (Onraet, n.d., p. 82)

However, much of the credit must be given to Onraet. Under his directorship, the Branch clearly identified threats that it should focus on and went about establishing the sections and training of the manpower for these. The Branch was very good at its work, and until the Japanese Occupation, kept the situation well under control. Onraet was one of those gifted individuals who had an almost instinctive sense of what was crucial as well as single mindedness of purpose in attaining his objectives. In his writings, Onraet was always reminding his readers of the 'special' duties of his department. Though the Special Branch worked under cover and in plain clothes it did not mean that they were doing the same job as the detectives:

The Detective Bureau must not be confused with the Special Branch which only concerned itself with political security. The Detective Bureau investigated all serious crime.

(Onraet, n.d., p. 80)

Elsewhere, Onraet provided significant details of the Branch's work during the period, pointing out its extensive interest in all matters that affected the security of the land:

In addition to security work against political movements and suspects the Special Branch concentrated on all racial, religious and social activities, and kept an eye on the trend in neighbouring countries.

(Onraet, n.d., p. 82)

This is possibly one of the best and most forthright statements of the duties of the Special Branch from an 'open' (overt) source. From this we can see that the Branch was concerned not just with political matters but a whole range of events in the racial, religious and social domains as well. In addition, the Branch kept an eye on those developments in nearby countries that could spell trouble for the British. This meant active exchanges of information as well as joint operations. For Onraet, security was necessary to the functioning of good government as well as the continuation of trade. These were the two key areas that he felt should not be compromised. The whole basis of British presence would disappear if they were undermined.

Another of Onraet's contribution is that he spelt out objectively the central doctrine of the Special Branch work in Singapore. The Branch's fundamental task was to defend the peninsula from the infection of radical ideas that would stir up its population. He argued that the local population would not be likely to give trouble if they were left to themselves. To him sedition and insurrection always had a hidden, foreign hand. These revolutionary impulses that came from overseas (first Germany, then the Middle East and India and then Russia and China followed by Japan) had to be identified and erased. The context that the Special Branch operated in must clearly therefore be international; it should not concern itself with the drudgery of everyday policing. To him the identification and exposure of this hidden hand was crucial. Above all else Onraet felt—and this gave the necessary muscularity and conviction to his work—that untoward events in the Straits Settlements nearly always had an external influence:

> One point must be stressed. From the very outset, subversive activities in
> Malaya were always due to outside influence.
>
> (Onraet, n.d., p. 109)

It is of course possible to argue that he was merely an apologist for
colonialism, advocating the suppression of every indication of dissent
in British territories. Certainly his emphasis on the external hand in
sedition allowed Onraet an easy explanation about the various
expressions and manifestations of discontent in the colony. These could
be blamed on radicals trying to export their revolutionary actions to an
otherwise harmonious Malaya. Any unhappiness was seen as the
machinations of unfriendly outside forces. According to this justification,
most people in Malaya would be happy to accept colonial rule provided
they were left alone and could be insulated from external subversion.
The task of the authorities was to screen out such infections, if that is
the right term to use although the metaphor is illustrative, so that life
carried on undisturbed. If that failed and the weed somehow managed
to take root then it should be vigorously pulled out. Not surprisingly,
one of the most frequent weapons used by the Branch was the arrest of
a person under a banishment warrant that gave the authorities power
to send the person away from Malaya and bar his re-entry. Disregarding
a banishment warrant by sneaking back to the colonies would bring
about severe punishment, usually hard labour with many years of
imprisonment.

This is, of course, one aspect of the ideology of imperialism that
permeated much of Western thought in the late 19th and early 20th
centuries. Onraet was correct in his analysis of how British power
should be defended and its paramountcy ensured. Throughout the
years till the Second World War there were indeed many outside
attempts to influence and to shape events in Malaya and the Straits
Settlements. The Ghadr insurrection in 1915 was one example while
the Kraft case was another. Whatever it was, Onraet's conviction gave
him the certainty to define clearly such threats to the superiority of
British hegemony. It was this certainty that gave the British security
apparatus and, we may, add the colonial authorities their sense of
mission and the purposeful patience with which they went about their
business. Of course, this certainty could also blind the officials, making
them arrogant and self-serving, intent on maintaining their regime at
whatever cost.

We should not forget Onraet's many contributions to the operational
side of the Special Branch. In 1934 he started the Japanese section,
realizing the militaristic ambitions of Japan. Even when he became the

Inspector General of Police in 1936, Onraet was still keeping an eye on the Special Branch. In 1936 he identified and arranged the transfer to Singapore of Major K S Morgan as the first head of the Japanese section in the Branch. Onraet was also instrumental in the negotiations with the French *Surete* that led to the recruitment of Loi Teck as an agent against the Malayan Communist Party. After the war, Onraet returned to Malaya in 1946 and for a short while was Police Adviser. In that position he reformed the Special Branch that went on to play a crucial role in the twelve-year war against the communists.

Throughout these early years of the 20th century it was the Special Branch that led in the day-to-day affairs affecting political security in the Straits Settlements and Malaya. From time to time there were suggestions to merge the Branch with other agencies to create bigger and presumably more effective departments. However, none of these really worked as the Branch's knowledge and expertise were second to none. For a time in the 1920s, following a suggestion from London, a centralized intelligence bureau was formed to increase the effectiveness of the different intelligence agencies including the Special Branch and Naval Intelligence. Functioning somewhat like a Joint Intelligence Group, the Malayan Political Intelligence Bureau set up in 1922 did not have much direct control in the day-to-day running of counter-espionage which was where the effectiveness of an intelligence agency should lie. The Bureau with A S Jelf as its first Director was, to put it bluntly, more of a clearinghouse that facilitated exchanges of information between Singapore, London, Hong Kong, India, Batavia and other stations. In matters of political espionage there was no doubt that the Special Branch which significantly continued to be operational remained the senior service. In any case, under-funded and inadequately staffed, the Bureau despite its grand title was in no position to deter espionage or subversion even of the most amateurish kind. In 1930, the Bureau was abolished and replaced by the more appropriately named Malayan Political Advisory Committee. One thing that did come out of all this was the *Malayan Political Intelligence Journal* which was classified 'secret'. In his advisory report recommending the creation of the Bureau, C G Denham of the Indian Police also recommended that there be published "at frequent intervals an Abstract of Intelligence" (C.O. 537/904: Guillemard to Churchill, 18 October 1921 with Denham's memorandum as enclosure).

Perhaps these efforts at reorganization reflected the winds of change that were passing not just through colonial empires but even Europe and America. New and better-organized enemies were making appearances accompanied by attractive revolutionary programmes. The

1917 October Revolution in Russia had spread the communist message throughout Europe, giving hope to its revolutionaries. A wave of apparently sympathetic strikes gripped Europe:

> In 1918 there were 1,252 strikes with the loss of 6 million working days, and in 1919 more than 1,400 strikes and the loss of 34 million working days (involving two and a half million workers).
>
> (Bunyan, 1976, p. 117)

In January 1917 a revolutionary uprising broke out in Finland that led to civil war. In the middle of the decade the General Strike broke out in England. It must have seemed to the Special Branch that an irresistible tidal wave of popular uprisings and strikes was on the way. Nearer to the Straits Settlements equally gripping changes were taking place in China. These were potentially more dangerous as they affected the loyalties of the Chinese workers so essential to the maintenance of commerce in the colonies.

Throughout much of the 19th century, the Manchurian (Qing) Dynasty had been undergoing a slow process of internal decay exacerbated by external aggression. While there were efforts to reform the government, the loss of political legitimacy also provided the opportunity to those who wanted to wrest power from the Manchurians. Using the slogan, "Oppose the Qing, restore the Ming" the triads took an active role in these plans. Triads often formed part of the underground resistance against the Qing government. However, in the Straits Settlements their activities were regarded as more criminal than political since (and this is an interesting point) they rarely challenged British interests even if their sympathies with Chinese revolutionaries were clear. The British often tolerated the presence of triads, not moving against them unless their rioting got out of control and affected British commercial interests. It was not until 1889 when a law was passed allowing only benevolent societies to be registered that the triads were officially suppressed.

However, the unrest in China often threatened the internal security of British Malaya. It had not been unusual in the past for the increasing triad feuds in China to spill over into open clashes in the Straits Settlements. Triad members fleeing from the Manchu crackdowns often fled to Singapore. In 1908 about 350 triad members out of the 700 who had taken part in the abortive uprising in southern Yunnan sought refuge in neighbouring Indo-China. From there they were deported by the French to Singapore where they were looked after by the T'ung Meng Hui, a powerful anti-Manchurian organization. Despite signing pledges of good behaviour these men soon became such a nuisance by taking part in various fights and gang robberies that the government was forced to disperse them into the Malayan hinterland.

It was another matter altogether with Sun Yat Sen's revolutionary movement which succeeded in founding a new republic in 1912. The Kuomintang brought patriotic idealism and revolutionary fervour together, both of which were now seen as part of the anti-colonial struggle. The Chinese in Southeast Asia were swept into this turmoil. On 18 December 1912, the Singapore Communication Lodge of the Kuomintang was registered under the Societies Ordinance. Within a short while, despite the fact that the British authorities had refused to register new branches since 1913, Kuomintang branches were established in many towns in Malaya. On the whole the Kuomintang was never aggressive towards the British and not much substantial action was taken against them.

The rapid spread of communism in China was another matter. Communism with its radical politics that seeks to seize power from the capitalists or the colonialists was seen as a severe security threat. Unlike the Kuomintang, communism emphasized not only patriotic commitment to China but also revolutionary changes to society that would wrest political control from the colonial masters. If this happened the commercial interests of the British Empire would be destroyed and with them the primary strategic value of their possessions. The infighting between the Kuomintang and the communists often led to problems as violence often occurred. It was not without reason that 1928 turned out to be one of the most problematic years for British security with severe strikes, riots and bombings in Singapore. This was just one year after Chiang Kai Shek and the Kuomintang turned against the communists in their efforts to eradicate the 'red' menace. The repercussions were soon felt in Southeast Asia as the conflict resulted in an upsurge of agitation. The fact of the matter was it was not always directed at the British, for at this time the Kuomintang and the communists were just as interested in fighting each other as they were in challenging the colonials. In fact, all three parties were, to an extent, after the same prize: the control of the Malayan territories. The loyalty of the Chinese, which they competed for, was often a means to this end. It was an expression of the struggle for power that was unfolding in mainland China. Once again this emphasized that the security was often dependent upon political developments in other countries. In the case of the increasingly communist threat it was not just China but a whole network of influences and actions that came from Indo-China, the NEI, Holland itself and, of course, the newly-formed Soviet Union.

***

Many of these events are reflected in the incidents recorded in the Special Branch's files. In particular the *Straits Settlements Police Journal* (SSPJ) provides a fascinating window into these occurrences as well as into the thinking of the security agencies on the nature of the threats facing Malaya. Unlike *The Malayan Political Intelligence Journal*, the SSPJ, compiled by the Special Branch for restricted circulation to a select group of officers, was a monthly intelligence briefing that dealt with what happened on the ground. It reflected the Branch's views about the various cases that it dealt with. Through its pages we get a fascinating insight into the concerns and motivations of British security. The Special Branch had a window seat to the rapid changes that were unfolding in Malaya; its monitoring and intelligence giving it a special perspective and knowledge of events and personalities. As its title suggests the SSPJ was, above all, a police journal that focused on the operational strategies and evaluations of the Special Branch. In the early years—up to the mid-1930s—the SSPJ was more often than not comprehensive in its coverage and summary of the various cases. Right from the start, though, ongoing cases were never discussed, thus Loi Teck, a well-known agent, was hardly ever featured. From the late 1930s onwards the Branch went out of its way to conceal its agents' tracks so that their infiltration would not be revealed. At times there were signs that the Special Branch often did not wish to divulge the full extent of its knowledge. This was inevitable given that counter-espionage information is often operational, that is a source or an event would be regarded as 'live' as long as a lead was still being followed. Despite this the SSPJ remains a valuable document on the various interests of the Special Branch, its methods as well as the cases they handled.

One thing that the SSPJ reveals is that by the mid-1920s when the journal began its circulation, a highly sophisticated and extensive intelligence coverage was already in place. The material in the journal shows us how thorough and extensive the work of the Special Branch had become in its efforts to combat subversion. The Branch was involved with the monitoring and tracking of suspects, the interception of mail and other postal items, censorship of films and publications, crackdowns on suspect political, religious and other organizations, exchanges of information with similar agencies from Shanghai to India and all the routine matters of intelligence like the firearms trade, lost passports and activities of aliens residing in the Straits Settlements. The coverage was astonishingly comprehensive and says much for the dedication of the Branch given its limited manpower. It was also clear that the Branch was not just concerned with policing; it was seen as a gatekeeper, an organization that ensured the continuation of British hegemony.

In a sense the Branch had kept the vision of British Malaya clear and unblemished for its administrators.

Given all these it is not surprising that the SSPJ was distributed on a strictly need-to-know basis. In 1927, for instance, the journal was restricted to 34 readers. At the top of the list were the two key officers, the Inspector General of Police, Straits Settlements and the Commissioner of Police, Federated Malay States. In addition copies were sent to the Chief of Police Officer, Singapore, Malacca, Penang and Province Wellesley and their counterparts in the Federated Malay States (FMS) (Perak, Selangor, Negri Sembilan and Pahang). Each of the commissioners of police in the Unfederated Malay States (UMS) (Johore, Kedah, Trengganu and Kelantan) also got a copy, as did the Resident Councillors in Penang and Malacca. On the civilian side, the Secretary of Chinese Affairs in Singapore, the Secretary of Chinese Affairs for the Federated Malay States, the Secretary High Commissioner for the UMS and the Master Attendant of the Straits Settlements were on the distribution list. Looking at the list we will realize that these were the people who were crucial to the control of crime, immigration, local politics and trade.

Others on the distribution list were strictly more from the security side of things. They included the Director of Criminal Intelligence, Straits Settlements; the Director, Criminal Intelligence Branch (FMS); the Director of the Political Bureau (SS and FMS); the Staff Officer (Intelligence) of the Naval Intelligence Centre (Singapore); and the General Staff Officer, Malaya Command who was also based in Singapore. Effectively these constituted the security and intelligence apparatus then operating in the Straits Settlements and Malaya. In keeping with the network of intelligence that the British had spread throughout their dominions in the Far East the journal was also sent to the Director of Criminal Intelligence, Hong Kong (effectively, the Special Branch counterpart); the Deputy Assistant General of Police for Railways and Criminal Intelligence, Burma; the Personal Assistant to the Directorate Inspector General (DIG) of Police, Madras; the Special Assistant to the DIG of Police, Bengal; and the Deputy Inspector-General of Police, CID, Ceylon. The distribution list underlined the extensive network and exchange of information that was in place among Britain's Asian empire.

The distribution list fluctuated over the years, reflecting not just the changing dimensions of security but also the vagaries of fortune that struck some of the intelligence organizations. Thus, while by January 1930 the list had grown to 54 the Director of the Political Intelligence Bureau, SS and FMS, was left out as the Bureau itself had been abolished.

The 34 names in the 1927 distribution list were more or less the core group, others were added in response to the changing shape and needs of the security situation as new threats emerged. In 1930 increased efforts by the communist and other revolutionaries to penetrate and recruit students added the Director of Education, British Malaya to the list. His name was removed when the Branch felt that the problems had been contained. The inclusion of the Director of Education was significant. It showed that the Branch appreciated the fact that education had become a political issue. It also showed that the Branch realized that political threats could not be contained unless they were set in the context of the overall situation. For the Director of Education to take the appropriate steps he needed the widest possible view of things. By presenting him with the full picture as it were, it was hoped that he could spot (and report) on any developing threats. Such was the standard intelligence briefing in those days.

The escalating radicalism and increased threat to security from external sources in the 1930s is seen from the number of names added to the distribution list. These included the relevant officers in Scotland Yard (Special Branch); the Shanghai Municipal Police, Hong Kong, Ceylon, Madras, Rangoon, Jesselton (British North Borneo) and Kuching. The Ghadr movement had diminished in importance by this time so there was less urgency to liaise with Bengal and the Indian Police forces. The redistribution of the names showed that the Branch was preoccupied with events in China and with the Comintern. One significant name at this time was Colonel Sir V G W Kell of London SW7. He was, of course, the Director of MI5. The reporting chain for the Special Branch in Malaya had by now gone to MI5 and the Special Branch (Scotland Yard).

Special Branch had control of the SSPJ and with it the key areas of dealing with political subversion throughout this period. For instance in a departmental notice in the end of October 1927 issue of the journal, readers were informed that:

> in giving telegraphic information of the movement of individuals mentioned therein, the number should only be quoted and information must in every case be sent to the S.B. as well as to the Officer into whose district the suspect goes.
>
> (item 204, Journal, 5 October 1927)

The Special Branch clearly showed what it wanted to show. From the mid-1930s when the Branch was engaged in deep penetration and infiltration of the Malayan Communist Party reports on communist activities became bland, a clear indication that information was being withheld. Obviously, the Special Branch went out of its way to prevent their sources from being compromised. In July 1931, the journal was renamed the *Straits Settlements Police Political Intelligence Journal*. Out of this an abstract was made for the *Malayan Bulletin of Political Intelligence*. If this confirmed the focus of the SSPJ it also showed the drift towards a greater secrecy in the work of the Special Branch. Rene Onraet, who compiled the journal as DCI, SS for the Inspector General of Police, Straits Settlements provided the necessary continuity.

The Journal was not just an abstract but provided a bird's-eye view month by month of the major threats facing the Malayan colonies. Over the years the reader would have obtained a very clear sense of the trends affecting security, the likely issues that would emerge as well as the various trouble spots. The items for each year (the Journal itself initially being published on the 15th of each month) were numbered consecutively—for example, in 1927 there were 236 items. These were indexed and cross-referenced to earlier items and came with charts detailing seizures of ammunition and guns, passenger lists as well as photographs. The items also included a suspect list that requested information or arrest on sight. As an example, an item in the 1927 Journal notes the need to trace one J M L Gutierrez "reported as a bad character from Shanghai" who entered Singapore on a British passport (purpotedly issued in Hong Kong on 13 November 1925) and had since gone underground:

> This man arrived in Singapore on 31 October 1927, was permitted to land and has disappeared.

The item goes on to advise that:

> All efforts should be made to trace Gutierrez and his movements reported to this office.

It is clear from this item that by 1927 a regular exchange of information on undesirables, the regular checking of passports and their use as mechanisms of control as well as immigration checks were already in place. Information was being shared, allowing for the tracking of a suspect across borders.

In the main section of the Journal, there were reports on the monitoring and exchange of intelligence on a range of personalities, organizations, events and issues that had an impact on the political hegemony of the British. The listing out of recurring items provides a good indication of the concerns of the Straits Settlements police as well as their assessment of what they thought were the threats to the internal security of the region. One finds that they were not only watching personalities and organizations but also reporting on events, censoring material including films, seizing arms and engaging in routine intelligence exchange with other agencies. Reading the journal gives us a raw and immediate feel of the daily preoccupations of the Branch. This is a very different perspective from what we get from just looking at the organizational structure of the Branch, its different sections and personnel. Here in the Journal it is almost as if we are peering over the shoulders of the writer or the intelligence officer as he ponders and weighs his next move from the actual details before him. And in examining the profiles of the personalities which the Branch regarded as dangerous or worthy of attention we begin to see the ideology of colonialism in practice: what is worth defending, the boundaries of tolerance, and the discourses and practices. In examining the items we can see a common thread emphasizing the maintenance of the existing political hegemony as well as a well-woven tapestry that tells a magnificent story of the intrigues and plots of the period.

A simple listing of the items covered by the Special Branch, which were reported upon in 1927, included:

- Those suspected of criminal and other activities prejudicial to British interests. Through its pages parade a veritable kaleidoscope of colourful personalities that would give substance to depictions of the exoticism of the East. Pimps, gunrunners, prostitutes, conmen and even the odd princess were mentioned. For instance, we are told of L A Ogli "suspected of trafficking in women and drugs" (item 46, Journal 1927) as well as Professor H F Ward from America suspected of "anti-British propaganda" (item 43, Journal 1927).

- Known communists who were agitating for reforms, fomenting revolutions or efforts to overturn colonial rule. There were those like H J F M Sneevliet expelled from the NEI for "subversive activities and propaganda" and currently leader of the Netherlands Communist Party. Others included Tan Malaka who had gone underground but was reported to be "present in Moscow at the meeting of the Third Internationale in 1922" and Mas Marco "arrested for complicity in the recent revolts in West Java" (item 39, Journal 1927). In these we have some indication of the profile of communist subversives that Special Branch was interested in. What it also shows is the extent of communist penetration of Southeast Asia even at this stage.

- Sympathizers and fellow travellers who were on the fringes of the communist movement or were helping them in other ways. The Journal records the activities of one Haji Surati and his two sons who "harboured Javanese communists" in their homes, Abdul Ghaffar who was "flirting with the idea of communism" and one Tan Ah Yu listed as being in "communication with communists in Medan" (item 39, Journal 1927). Occasionally a more seductive figure flits across the pages: colourful Madame Stavrinaky Kiziewicz described as a "Bolshevist Spy, an adventuress and given to cheating" by the Indian Police (item 6, Journal 1927).

- The Special Branch also banned publications that carried anti-British views or inflammatory material. Obviously many of these were political but others were religious or regarded as being over zealous in their nationalist rhetoric. Proscribed publications, which were detained at the immigration points or seized when discovered included *The Canton Gazette, Sumatra bin Po, Kirpan Bahadur* and the *Akali-te-Pardesi* (item 11, Journal 1927). The nature of the Straits Settlements as trading ports meant that they were contact points open to every nuance and turn of the larger world. In the twenties a deluge of handbills, circulars and pamphlets passed through their harbours including the leftist inspired "The Movement for World Trade Union Unity" and other circulars that routinely denounced imperialism and sought to fan the flames of unrest.

- As films became more and more popular in the colonies they came in for attention too. The medium was gaining increasing prominence as a vehicle of messages to the masses and it was not uncommon for films to be banned. However, it was not just political films that the Branch was concerned with. As with its counterpart in England, the Special Branch devoted much effort to the enforcing of the laws against obscenity, pornography or 'yellow culture' (the term itself suggesting its ideological and cultural agenda). It was the official view that such "degenerate" films could weaken the resolution and backbone of the working class. The link between obscenity and sedition that the authorities insisted upon was made clear in various seizures of books including those of D H Lawrence. In the colonies censorship had the additional role of keeping out unwelcome ideas that taught nationalism and anti-colonialism. In 1927 14 films were banned. Some of these films appear pornographic (such as "Alimony", "Forbidden Cargo" or "Morals for Men" put out by the Penang Biograph Co. or the suggestive "Double Fisted" by the Australasian

Films Co. Others were clearly political such as "I Will Repay" owned by the Anglo Chinese Film Company or the "Chinese Gazette No. 1" owned by Tong Nam Film Company. Some banned films, however, came from the heartland of Western imperialism including "The Red Rider" by Universal Pictures Corp., "Way Down East" by United Artists Corp. or, quite inexplicably, "Return of Draw Egan" by Kodak Ltd (item 18, Journal 1927).

- Arms seizures were part of the routine work of the Branch. Of special interest were the arms discovered while on transit through the ports. As the German attempts to ship weapons to India in 1915 show Singapore was at the crossroads of shipping routes and would no doubt have an important part in any plot, a very thorough monitoring was maintained on arms entering Singapore or the transshipment of these to other parts of the East. In 1927 the police seized 35 pistols with 1,851 rounds in Singapore, 4 pistols in Penang and 1 revolver in Malacca. In addition, 56 pistols were found in transit through Singapore and 7 in Penang (item 17, Journal 1927).

- Immigration and travel control were particular useful to the work of the Special Branch. Passports, landing permits and travel passes allowed them to track the movement of criminals and political undesirables. An aliens register was also maintained, listing the country of each new resident in the colony. A separate register was kept for Chinese and Indians as well as British citizens. Significantly the Japanese were already being subject to close monitoring from an early period. The Journal shows that from the twenties the activities and even meetings of organizations such as the Japanese Association and its affiliate, the South Seas Colonial Association, were reported on. Clearly the Special Branch was already of the view that the Japanese posed a likely security threat to British interests in Southeast Asia. This aspect of the Branch's work became increasingly important as Japanese militarism spread in the East and soon assumed an importance second only to that of the fight against the communists. A Japanese section was formed in the Special Branch by Onraet to cover espionage and other activities. Contrary to popular belief that the British only awoke to the Japanese penetration and spying in British Malaya when it was too late, the evidence from the Special Branch shows otherwise. The Branch was certainly aware of the various Japanese attempts at subversion and espionage, whether they chose to act on it is a different matter.

- The activities of the trade unions, *kongsi*, labour guilds and even schools came under the watchful eye of the Special Branch. We may include the triads and other secret organizations here. The British made a simple distinction which shaped the focus of their intelligence effort. Matters that disturbed the internal security or public peace and which had a political purpose fell under its purview. Other matters that were criminal in nature (even if these included rioting and violence) were the concern of the police. Schools—in particular the night schools run by the Hailams—to improve the level of education and of general political awareness) were of concern. In the same way, strikes, labour unrest and civil disobedience (such as boycotts) that threatened the political hegemony of the British, seen as essential to the control of its commercial and trading interests were matters for the Special Branch.

- Knowledge was in that sense closely policed. Beginning from the *shu po seh* (reading rooms) Chinese schools were soon started to provide suitable education. Some of these were founded from public subscriptions, others in particular the nights schools were founded by Kuomintang members supported by the General Education Association. The night schools were a source of particular concern to the Branch since in addition to its stated aim of popularizing the Chinese language they were used to spread extremist and other propaganda. Despite various efforts such as the Registration of Schools Ordinance that was gazetted on 28 May 1920 the authorities were never really able to bring the night schools under their control. Often the Branch carried out raids on these schools followed by their orders for them to close. In 1921 the authorities dissolved the Straits Chinese Educational Association for not complying with the Schools Ordinance. Throughout this time the Branch continued with its pressure on the night schools. In 1926, 16 night schools were ordered to close their doors for unlawful political propaganda. Some of these were found to be branches for the factions of the Kuomintang party already under the influence of the communist ideology.

- Watchful control extended to religious movements. Pilgrimages especially to the Middle East were reported on. The journal records the sailing of the *S.S. Gorjistan* for Jeddah on 19 January 1927 with 920 pilgrims and the *S.S. Onfa* with 880 on 4 February (item 21, Journal 1927). Pan-Islamic sentiments remained a concern as these were linked to various outbreaks of peasant movements in neighbouring Java and Medan. In referring to a pamphlet entitled

"The Restoration of Islamic Unity", the Branch notes that "The pan-Islamic tone and the renewed activities of the Sarikat Islam at the commencement of the pilgrim season are noteworthy" (item 15, Journal 1928).

- Finally, the journal reveals both the extensive exchanges of information between the local authorities and their counterparts in key areas. The Branch received intelligence reports from China on the monitoring of government emissaries and officials. Visitors such as Liu Nan Fong a.k.a. Liu Thit Fu "who had been appointed by the Emigration Bureau at Peking as Special Commissioner to study conditions among overseas Chinese in British and Dutch colonies" (item 10, Journal 1927) interested the authorities.

This review of the items allows us to map out the terrain of their security concerns. It also shows us the range and extent of the interests of the Special Branch—from schools to pilgrims. Whatever details the Branch looked at, whatever issues they were monitoring, the end was never in doubt. It was, first and foremost, the maintenance of the political stability and hegemony of British rule in Malaya and the Straits Settlements. What interested the Branch were events or people that could overturn, challenge or destabilize the regime. To the Special Branch political threat was the likelihood of British paramountcy being subverted. The invisible line in the sand that defined what was politically acceptable and what was not came from this. On the other hand, we should not be blinded to the extent of the apprehension felt by the British. Throughout this period there were many attempts to subvert and undermine which kept the Branch busy. Moreover these came from all sides: Germany, the Middle East, India, the Netherlands East Indies, the French Indo-China, Russia and China.

The dangers were now multinational in scope as they were often orchestrated by organizations from many countries. There was an instinctive inclination of subversive elements towards groupings, alliances and united fronts as it was believed that these organisations would provide the most likelihood of success. The items in the SSPJ for 1927 should, therefore, not be read singly. Together they show the narrative of subversion, that is the common programme shared by different groups and the links between them. As the Kaiser of Germany realized in 1914, when he funded Ghadr and sought alliance with Turkey, the power of Britain could best be undermined through a global alliance. The strategic dominance of Britain came from its many overseas possessions. If these rose in revolt, the economic and strategic power of Britain would be seriously compromised. The increasing competition for economic dominance in Asia by the imperialist countries comprising Britain, France, the Netherlands, Japan and the United States also meant that espionage would be increasingly linked to trade and commerce. The roots of and opportunities for subversion stem from a whole variety of enterprises.

Onraet believed resolutely that internal security should not be separated from the overall social and political stability that allowed commerce to thrive. For him this was the fundamental reason for the British presence in Southeast Asia. Indeed if British dominance in trade was taken away there would be no reason for her to carry on in this part of the world. In this sense Onraet was very much the colonialist who equated internal security with the peace and stability that allowed the flourishing of trade within the colony. Onraet pointed out that the ends of policing should not be in the number of arrests or of cases investigated. Policing was to ensure the internal security of a country, allowing life to go on. Without this security, progress would be difficult to come by and the everyday rhythm of modern life impossible. His language is peppered with references to metaphors of growth, an ideal which, he argued no reasonable person would reject. Of course Onraet's notion of growth is subjective. Nonetheless, it was such an outlook that permeated the deliberations of the Special Branch:

> The real value of police work today cannot be judged altogether on the number of arrests made; nor can the test of its success be based solely on the results of investigations. A fair judgement can only be given as the achievement or otherwise of the ideals worked for are or are not carried into practical effect over a number of years. In two words this means internal security. Internal security grew with the growth of this new institution, and with its growth all the complex structure of modern life became possible—which is as it should be, for a force that provides this security for all classes represents the reasoned wish of a reason-conscious people.
>
> (Onraet, n.d., p. 72)

Onraet's statement provides us with a succinct definition of the nature of internal security as the British colonial system perceived it. At the same time, his invocation of economic and pecuniary gain appeals to the ideals of the "reason-conscious" people. Economic gains and moral aims intertwine. Commercial gains are naturalized within the larger common good of the safety "for all classes". It is easy and tempting to accuse Onraet of being disingenuous in his arguments. However, this is not the issue; Onraet really believed in the society that he was defending.

That conviction leaves us with the strong impression that he was confident and persuaded by his beliefs. He was no propagandist mouthing lines; rather he saw himself as expressing the goals of his life. Even his reminder that time has a different function where internal security is concerned ("fair judgement can only be given ...") gives an indication of the deep thought and experiences of a matured professional. It is tempting to be cynical but there is no reason to doubt that for Onraet terms like *conviction, ideals, commitment* and *purpose* drew more from moral than selfish impulses.

By understanding the ideological dimension behind the work of the Special Branch we would also comprehend some of its preoccupations, the firm decisiveness of its evaluations and the reasons it handled its agents and sources well. The Branch, and certainly Onraet, saw its task as the defence of those ideals which, rightly or wrongly, were relevant to British presence for promoting progress. The Branch's emphasis was political in so far as it upheld British hegemony. Whether it be "rumours, publications, etc., affecting the public peace" or leftist propaganda, the decision to take action was always derived from the impact that the trouble would have on the day-to-day profits which paramountcy conferred.

***

The Special Branch watched closely the various trade boycotts that Chinese organizations called to express their unhappiness with events in China. Most of these boycotts, directed at Japanese goods, led to riots and other acts of violence. It was not the disruption to trade alone that was the problem. The economic weapon was double-edged; it could always boil over into a challenge against the legitimacy and supremacy of British rule. On 19 June 1919 a Chinese boycott of Japanese goods in support of the 4th May movement in China led to a riot. A group of Chinese attacked a restaurant in Smith Street, ransacking it for Japanese produce. The disturbance soon spread to North Bridge Road and Kreta Ayer. The crowd at Kreta Ayer turned on the police who opened fire, killing two persons. As the situation worsened the Civil Guard was called out. Even then it needed the arrival of 100 sailors from *HMS Sydney* before the riot was put down. Martial law was declared on 20 June but another Chinese was killed from a bayonet wound. When calm was restored there were three dead and eight injured and the damage to goods ran to some $20,000.00. Indeed, a boycott challenged the ability of the British to provide law and order necessary for its people. If a boycott persisted for any length of time the prestige and legitimacy of the British as rulers would be affected. Moreover, some of the boycotts were even aimed at British goods, an unhealthy development of the pressure tactics of massed militancy. A report on the "anti-smoking" campaign of 1927 drew attention to the call to boycott English cigarettes:

> About the 15th February 1927 a Hylam Chinese teacher of the Bukit Pasoh Night School named LIM addressed the audience of the theatre at North Bridge Road Chinese Theatre after the performance was over and advised them not to smoke English cigarettes. This man was previously noticed giving lectures in People's Park on the political situation in North China.
>
> (item 63, Journal 1927)

The Special Branch coverage was extensive as the Hylam schoolteacher was first traced at People's Park before being noticed at the North Bridge Road Chinese Theatre. It was likely that he had been under surveillance by detectives. In fact, Lim, the school teacher, was a well-known political activist on whom the Branch had a file. The Special Branch linked Lim to the Trolley Bus boycott of March 1927 that resulted in severe public disturbances (item 81, Journal 1927). The boycott of English cigarettes was, therefore, to the Branch part of an orchestrated attempt to defy and subvert British rule.

The political security dimension determined every aspect of the Branch's work. For the most part the Branch did not concern itself with crime or policing. It was only indirectly that the Branch took an interest in criminal activities, that is when criminals were used for subversion. As long as the activities of the triads did not trespass into the political arena, the Branch was happy to leave them alone. However, when their actions deliberately or otherwise trespassed into the out-of-bounds areas the Branch would react strongly. The references made to triads or criminals in the SSPJ were always in the context of their likely challenge to the stability of British rule. The link-up between criminal elements and revolutionary elements was indeed an area of special concern to the Branch. As experience showed, the chances of riots and violence breaking out at political demonstrations increased substantially when that happened. The repeated attempts to co-opt the triads into the political programmes of various political parties worried the Branch. Sun Yat Sen himself had gained the support of the triads in his revolutionary struggle. The Straits government reported to Churchill in 1922 that attempts were made to recruit working-class Chinese, such as the predominantly Eng Hua rickshaw pullers and the Hokien

and Teochew coolies, as enforcers in a strike[2]. The tendency towards a
united front that would bring together the armed strength of the secret
societies and the convictions of political activism was strong.

Equally worrying was the rapid emergence of a militant trade union
movement that believed in direct action to force employers and the
government into giving in to its terms. As early as 1921 representations
were being made to the government of the Federated Malay States
that the Kuomintang, increasingly under the influence of left-wing
thinking, was a threat to security. The Department of Chinese Affairs
asked for the Kuomintang to be banned and its branches closed down.
Sir Lawrence Guillemard, the High Commissioner, wrote in a secret
telegraphic message to London that he had:

> information (that) shows conclusively that Kuo Min Tang is now working
> as a secretly reorganized anti-European Bolshevik body directly under
> Lenin and Soviet. Sun has admitted that there is in Singapore a large
> Anti-British Society working with increasing ramifications.
> (C.O. 717/27, Telegraphic Letter, Guillemard to Duke of Devonshire,
> 2 February 1923)

This militancy found ready expression in the hatred of the imperialist
expansionism of England. The sentiments elided easily into a hatred of
the English. British arrogance born of misplaced pride in the superiority
of their race and its culture often provoked a blind rage against the
white man. This characteristic is in fact common to a number of anti-
colonial movements: from the Boxers in China to Ghadr in India and
later the Japanese as well.

The Branch kept a sharp lookout for evidence of such anti-British
militancy infecting the Chinese in the Malay peninsula. In September
1928 (a critical year as far as the Special Branch was concerned and
which will be treated in fuller detail below), H K Lee was arrested for
subversive activities when he tried to organize the triad members in the
Kuala Pilah district, Negri Sembilan, as part of a secret nationalistic
group led by the communists. A document in his possession provided
evidence of attempts of the communist party to infiltrate and control
the secret societies for their own purposes. However, the specific interest
of the Branch was raised by the anti-British rhetoric of the proposed
group. Despite the inflated prose the intent was clear. The Wui Khwan
was intended to be a national united front that would organize the
Chinese into direct militant action against the British oppressors. The
signs were worrying enough for the Special Branch to append a specific
comment:

Further indication of the attempt by the Communist Party to utilize the Triad Secret Societies has appeared in the Kuala Pilah district. A Cantonese named H K Lee was arrested on 22 September and in his possession was found a book from which the following extracts are taken:

Preface on Wui Khwan

The Wui Khwan is a national organization. The establishment of the Wui Khwan is the formation of the mother-country organization on which everyone depends for protection and which civilization is based. Therefore, if my brethren do not unite, although the nation and civilization exist, they will not be able to stand in this world …. Foreigners will look at us with contempt. Our comrades should join together to deal with them and not allow ourselves to be despised.

Two three five tai fuk Wu San Kwei. Communism in territories. May the Hung family live for myriads of years. Great massacre of capitalists. The meeting at the Headquarters at Johore, Nanyang, decided to carry out a great massacre on the 15th day of the 8th month of next year, also a great massacre of the (people of the) National Government. After killing the British kill the Nationalists.

May the Communistic Hung rise high, and live for myriads of years. Let all join together (lit. be like hands and feet) to affect the (abolition of) Treaties.

There are many members in the five sections. Mobilize soldiers to take revenge for brethren and colleagues massacred in great numbers. Kill the English princes. Then the land will have great peace.

Tonight the Hung family rises. To restore (and enjoy) territories for myriads of years.
Tonight the brethren's army arrives. To kill Europeans
and bring peace.
To annihilate the English soldiers and mount the dragon throne.
Then peace to the Hung brothers.

(item 193, Journal 1928)

The document is a classic expression of the millenarian/populist movement with its evocation of instinct, pride and xenophobia relayed through the rhetoric of home, ethnic pride and nation. The conjunction of the discourses of triads, nationalism and radical politics is indeed a heady and dangerous brew. The flowery and ornate language of the translation, obviously a literal rendition, must not put us off from the significance of the document originally in Chinese. The network of allusions, which loses a lot of its effectiveness in English, appeals to the emotional pull of country and people. Similarly, the symbolic language of the Taiping Tienkuo (Heavenly Kingdom) uprising led by Hung Hsiu Chuan would have been familiar to the readers as the uprising was still fresh in the minds of patriots and underground workers alike. The language is woven cunningly into a series of populist appeals to national pride calculated to stir up ethnic sentiments. What would really have concerned the Branch would have been the call, even if somewhat crudely put, to settle the debt by slaughtering the British. The strongly anti-foreign rhetoric would have reminded them of similar pamphlets circulated by Ghadr or, worse, the sepoys at Cawnpore. The careful intertwining of triadic language with that of an anti-colonialist rhetoric further complicated the political discourse of the overseas Chinese.

It was not just the communists who cultivated and used the triads for anti-British actions. The Branch was aware that the Kuomintang had been doing the same thing for some time. In June 1928, the Special Branch intercepted a document which referred to the formation of a new society, the Gi Hua Bin. This time, though, the directive for a popular uprising came from the Kuomintang. Except for the party line, the strategy was the same as that put forward for the communistic Wui Khwan. The Kuomintang named their proposed society, Gi Hua Bin. A seized document advised its readers that the Gi Hua Bin:

> is to be formed by the union of Hokien and Teo Chiu Secret Societies.
> (item 120, Journal 1928)

So secretive was the Kuomintang that the Branch did not manage to arrest any of the ringleaders although the outline of the society was known through informers. While the Branch did not manage to arrest anyone this time around, it was nonetheless clear what the Gi Hua Bin was meant to be:

> It is uncertain from what source this pamphlet originates; it is undoubtedly of a Nationalist character, and is interesting in view of the fact that, in 1922, strong rumours of the Kuo Min Tang attempting to enlist the assistance of the Triad societies were rife throughout Malaya.
> (item 120, Journal 1928)

 That both the Kuomintang and the communists were seeking the support of the triads must have been particularly worrying to the British.

These efforts to forge a common platform with the triads showed that the political factions were preparing to escalate their struggles. The direct actions they were now seeking to use against the colonial powers needed the manpower and extensive underground network of the triads. The Branch knew that it was not just competition for the same objective that made both the Kuomintang and the communists form these groups. They were tapping into the strong feelings of resentment and injustice among the population. The cry for reform and freedom in China could just as easily be seen as an anti-colonial struggle.

More seriously these revolutionaries were not prepared to take the law into their own hands and resort to direct action to undermine society. Throughout this time, both the Kuomintang and the communists were much influenced by the anarcho-syndicalists. Contrary to popular misunderstanding, anarchism is a political platform as much as socialism and communism are. This is not the place to go into a history of anarchism but the emphasis on the rights of the individual, the reform of society and the distrust of government found fertile soil in Malaya and Singapore at this time. One of the strongest points of appeal in anarchism is its call for direct militant action. Basically anarchists reject the slow, gradual process of political manoeuvrings favoured by political parties. They argue that this compromises the integrity of the revolution. Moreover, it is only through the shock and confrontation of immediate direct action that would force a ruling power into making concessions. A case in point would be the anti-Japanese boycotts. Direct action was needed to send a clear signal of disapproval. They also saw a vital need in such methods to accelerate the political awakening of the revolutionary consciousness of participants and their class members.

The increasingly revolutionary rhetoric sometimes took a violent turn. Bombs were a recognized weapon in the anarchists' armoury. Goh Tun-ban, the founder of Malayan anarcho-communism, did not disapprove of the tactic if it were used properly, like in enforcing the trade boycott against Japanese goods. Goh was one of the prime movers behind the boycott which was called to protest against the injustice suffered by China at the Versailles Conference. Goh supported the actions of the Peking students against the pro-Japanese officials in China who had ignominiously handed over Tsingtao to Japan. In an open letter published in the *Yik Khuan Poh* on 26 May 1919, Goh called for a boycott of Japanese goods as the only way to force the Japanese into returning Tsingtao. Goh was arrested in Kuala Lumpur with five others on 29 July 1919 and banished on 15 November. The trial was considered so sensitive and likely to create trouble that it was held in Pudu Jail following which Goh was deported immediately. Coincidentally between September 1919 to February 1920 bombs were thrown at a number of shops in Singapore that were suspected of breaking the anti-Japanese boycott. Although the Branch did not discover any tangible links the timing and the modus operandi pointed to the anarchists. Although not so serious as the shoemakers' strike, these bombings were the first instances of urban terrorism in the island.

Even more outrageous and provocative was the attempt on the life of Daniel Richards, the Protector of Chinese for the state of Selangor. Around 10.45 a.m. on 23 January 1925, Wong San, described as a modern Chinese woman with bobbed hair, walked into Richards' office which he shared with W L Blythe. Pressing the catch of an attache case she had placed on Richards' desk, a bomb was set off. Luckily none of the three persons in the room were killed. In the subsequent trial, Wong San a.k.a. Wong Sau Ying revealed she was an anarchist with links to the movement in both Shanghai and Peking. While personal dissatisfaction with the British who had deported her lover, Mak Peng-cho, to China where he was subsequently shot may have been a factor, the evidence suggested that the anarchists had instigated the action. Indeed, the Special Branch believed that the Hsin-she, the anarchist headquarters in Canton, had issued the orders. Wong San was sentenced to ten years imprisonment for the attempted assassination. Following the attack, the Special Branch dealt a crippling blow to the anarchists by carrying out a wave of arrests, deporting a number of suspects to China.

It is possible to summarize the key concerns of the Special Branch. These areas will also provide indications of the deployment of its personnel in these years. By the mid 1920s, the last few items had become progressively more important. The Branch was looking at:

- Indian nationalist movements especially those with Ghadr or Hindustani affiliations.
- Islamic and, in particular, pan-Islamic activities.
- Seizure and movement of weapons.
- Japanese economic activities and immigration.
- Events in China particularly those involving Sun Yat Sen, the Kuomintang, the anarchists and the China Communist Party.
- Communist networks of sympathizers and agitprop with links to Europe, North America and especially the NEI.
- Trade union activities, boycotts and strikes that had a political dimension. The militant organization of workers was regarded as particularly worthy of attention.

- 'Front' organizations such as night schools, associations and triad groupings.
- Communist and anarcho-communist activities.

The men of the Special Branch were handpicked from the Police Force, usually after they had had a spell with the Detective Bureau. As far as we know morale was good and requests for transfers out of the Branch were rare.

The Special Branch needed at this time to be level-headed about the increasing disturbance from the Chinese population. It was crucial before any objective assessment could be made to get away from the stereotyped ideas and images of the race. Many colonial officials continued to imagine the Chinese as feudalistic clans of contending triads and *tong*. Only a few had the language skills or cultural sensibility to perceive the Chinese as they were. The need was as always to keep in mind the wider perspective as there were many different currents competing for the attention of the Chinese mind in its encounter with modernity. Political dissent could be sparked off by any of these motivations: triad affiliations, anti-Qing sentiments, anarchist impulses, patriotic protests against the unequal treaties imposed by foreigners, nationalist wishes, Kuomintang politics, communist radicalism, and progressive liberalism. The Special Branch had to determine which of these represented threats, some immediate, others, long-term. Clear and precise thinking on these issues was absolutely necessary if evaluations were to have any value. It was becoming apparent that communist radicalism would be at the centre of things to come. There were reasons for this. Communism was attractively meaningful to the labouring class who resented colonial arrogance. The ideology made historical sense of China's humiliation and promised a better future. Cadres from both the Comintern and the Chinese Communist Party sustained its momentum. The Malayan Communist Party would emerge as the most dangerous opponent of the Branch in the following decade.

The years after the war until the 1930s marked the first phase of Special Branch work in Singapore. It was much like a series of ferocious cuts and parries as the Branch's resolve and organization were tested and probed by nationalists, anarchists and communists bent on seizing the initiative. Events that repeatedly tested the authorities showed that the usual public security organs such as the police could not provide the answer. Even as the memory of the 1915 mutiny remained fresh in the minds, boycotts, bombings and attempted assassinations occurred. The first serious politically-inspired riot in Singapore took place in 1927. The police had to take severe repressive actions which left six people dead. Further riots, boycotts and even bombings followed this agitation. The early years of the Special Branch was filled with one crisis after another as political agitation spread throughout the peninsula. The Branch acquitted itself well despite the severe tests of its resources and skills.

Amidst the upheavals, the Branch continued to extend its organizational and operational capabilities. Indexing was introduced and over the years the Branch built up one of the finest collections of data in its registry. This information, second to none in the region, was matched by an easy to use retrieval and cross-indexing system that enabled the reader to acquire perspective and depth very quickly. In the approaching decade the Branch would reap rewards from all the painstaking work.

In its early years the work of the Branch was often reactive. By the time notice was taken of a problem, the damage had usually been done. In the 1930s though the operations of the Branch exhibited less of the parrying of threats than an operational willingness to anticipate and neutralize a threat before it could develop. As an example we can see that the Branch used not just informers but double agents. These were recruited or turned by the Branch at an early stage. Having infiltrated into the enemy organization they often provided high-grade intelligence because of their positions. These were the moles that had been planted deep within the enemy's camp. One such spy who infiltrated and continued to be active in the Malayan Communist Party for 15 years was Loi Teck. This agent provided a whole array of information on organization, arms and membership. It is useful to remember that a spy is only as good as his organization. Without the structure and framework of support that the Branch had put in place he would not have been as successful as he was. In the early years the Branch often had more than enough on its plate.

The deteriorating security and escalation of violence came to a head in 1927 which saw the start of two years of militant violence. What became known as the Kreta Ayer Incident or Shooting turned into a prolonged boycott of the trolley buses accompanied by riots and damage to property. The significance of this agitation was not lost on the British. An editorial in *The Straits Times* drew attention to the events, noting that:

> This was the first occasion that any disturbance has occurred in Singapore or any part of Malaya arising out of the political conditions in China.
> (*The Straits Times*, 14 March 1927, p. 8)

The Straits Times is not quite right, as the 4 May incident had also brought the protestors out on the street. Still, it was certainly the first time riots stemming from politics had reached such dangerous levels and caused so much damage to property. The paper might have added that it was also the first time that the colonial police showed signs of panic, responding with excessive severity to the attack by the mob. The indiscriminate shooting by the police produced unnecessary casualties. The riot demonstrated how ill-prepared the police were in handling civil unrest.

The origins of the riot appeared innocuous enough. 27 March 1927 was the second anniversary of Sun Yat Sen's death. Various applications were made to the authorities for an observance ceremony. The Secretary of Chinese Affairs rejected this as reports that the communists were going to use the occasion to create trouble and to challenge the government had been received. Circulars had been seen in town calling on the people to use the occasion to spread and advance the revolution. One such pamphlet put out by the communist-inspired "Main" school movement argued that with Sun Yat Sen's death and the evil machinations of the imperialists:

> it is insufficient for us merely to commemorate this date with the same pomposity as that of the anniversary of a great Saint or the festivities of Christmas. We should take this opportunity to instil (our principles) into the mind of the populace, to enlarge the organization of this school; and to recruit new forces.
>
> (C.O. 273/535, Peel to Amery, 18 May 1927)

The Branch also knew that the "Main" school and the Hailam night schools were gathering support from organizations for the proposed mass meeting. Some 15 organizations including *hoey kuan*, clans, schools and workmen's guilds had given their support. An invitation to a meeting at the Lam Oan Hoey Kuan to discuss the proposed commemoration went out from them on 4 March. This meeting was attended by some 30 organizations from which a preparatory committee was formed. Already events were snowballing rapidly out of control. Seizing the initiative another meeting was held the next day at the Man Yu Continuation School where it was decided that the organizations would put in an application to the Chinese Affairs for the ceremony. It was also recommended that prominent members of the community be approached to help with this application.

In due course another, by now the third, application for the ceremony was made. This time the Chinese Affairs could not dismiss so easily the application backed by 30 organizations with endorsements by reputable community leaders. Reluctantly, the Secretary of Chinese Affairs gave permission for the gathering. The Chief Police Officer added the proviso that there should be no speeches, parading or the shouting of slogans. While the community leaders agreed to these conditions they knew that the Hailams would object strenuously and might even use this as an excuse to stir up trouble. When Hugh Clifford wrote to Amery with his report on the disturbances, he was careful to point out that the Chinese leaders had attempted to avoid trouble:

> Leaders of the community, the Teochew and the Hokien were, in fact, aware that the Hailam intended to have a more demonstrative celebration on 12 March. They had made a pledge to the authorities that they would abide by certain conditions but knowing that the Hailam would object strongly they endeavoured to keep secret from the leaders of the Hailam that they had accepted the conditions. They held a meeting on 11 March after which they sought to render themselves inaccessible to the Hailam leaders during the remainder of that day and during the night that followed. They also made arrangements to have the contingents representing their several communities assemble at Happy Valley at an earlier hour than the Hailam.
>
> (C.O. 273/537, Clifford to Amery, 31 August 1927)

The leaders realized that they were in a fix but they were not prepared to face the wrath of the Hailam. They had to think of a way out of the situation.

On the morning of 12 March, the meeting to mark the anniversary of Sun Yat Sen's death was held at Happy Valley. The authorities appeared to have been lulled into a false sense of security by the assurances that nothing untoward would happen. Even the Hailam who were expected to make capital out of such an event declared that "they would rather cut their throats than have any trouble" (*The Straits Times*, 18 March 1927, p. 9). The observance ceremony went well at first. The Chinese streamed in to pay their respects by car, lorry and on foot. By noon, at which time the ceremony began, there were about 20,000 participants. People paid their respects to a portrait of Sun Yat Sen that had been set up on an altar. The police kept a low profile, not willing to run the risk of provoking any incidents. In fact, there were only a handful of police directing traffic at the roads to the periphery of Happy Valley. Given the subsequent development, strong police presence might have been preferred. As events would show, the police were not prepared for riot duties or handling civilian unrest. Unfortunately, it was these unsuspecting policemen busy with their traffic duties who were involved in the initial clash with the rioters. These policemen could hardly be expected to contain the mob that surged out of the park, catching them by surprise.

Trouble began soon after 1.30 in the afternoon when the Hailam appeared as a group. There were about 1,000 of them, one third of which were school children. The Hailam effectively took over the proceedings. They began to make speeches, shout slogans and distribute inflammatory pamphlets that attacked colonialism. Slogans attacking the Kuomintang and British imperialism were shouted. The masses were instigated to rise up in revolt. When some of the prominent Chinese among them, several Justices of Peace, intervened by pointing out that assurances had been given that there would be no speeches the scene turned ugly. Those who counselled calm and peace were set upon and assaulted including Ng Seng Pang, Teo Lye Hee and Wong Siew Yuen. The latter two were severely beaten and injured (Inquest by Solicitor-General, *The Straits Times*, 18 March 1927, p. 10).

Following the melee the Hailam streamed out of Happy Valley forming themselves into a procession. They had apparently come prepared for banners were soon unfolded. Accompanied by bands and with a good deal of shouting the procession moved to Kreta Ayer and Maxwell Road. Here they ran into the policemen who were on traffic duty. When these policemen tried to stop the marching column they were in turn set upon. The Inquest was subsequently told that knives were used to attack two constables, PC 226 and PC 670, severely injuring one of them. Driven into greater agitation by the clash with the police some of the Hailam led the march out onto the main road declaring, "We are going to have our procession; we do not care about any police regulations" (*The Straits Times*, 18 March 1927, p. 10). Was this an intelligence failure? Did not the Special Branch know of the Hailams' plans, notwithstanding the 'agreement' reached with the organizer that there would be no trouble?

After the procession had marched onto South Bridge Road events got a little uncertain. We may say that the second part of the event, which later became known as the trolley bus riots, began at this point. The Solicitor-General, Mr G G Seth informed the Inquest that at this stage, "one had to get together the threads of evidence as to what took place at Kreta Ayer" (*The Straits Times*, 18 March 1927, p. 10). Upon reaching Kreta Ayer, the crowd apparently blocked a trolley bus and "proceeded to thrash the bus conductor" (*The Straits Times*, 18 March 1927, p. 10) when he attempted to drive on. They then turned upon Inspector Hale[3] who was attempting to disperse the crowd, severely assaulting him and two police constables who had gone to help him.

Hale retreated to the nearby Kreta Ayer Police Station leaving behind one of his constables. By now the constables at the station had been alerted and were trying to prevent the crowd from getting nearer. Noticing that one of their numbers was missing the police charged with drawn batons to retrieve the constable. Not surprisingly, the crowd saw this as provocation and charged at the station. It was at this point that shots were fired, killing six rioters.

Much of the evidence for all this came from Oliver Thomson, Traffic Superintendent of the Singapore Tramways, who was on the trolley bus that had been stopped by the crowd. Thomson was taking the bus out for a test run from Tanjong Pagar to Kreta Ayer when the procession met him head-on. Thomson's testimony was later criticized as being prejudiced and one-sided, particularly since it was his trolley bus that was at the centre of the ensuing trouble. What Thomson left out in his evidence was that the driver, apparently acting on Thomson's instructions, had attempted to move his bus after the crowd (including young boys) had started to hit its side with sticks and other weapons. Roland Braddell and S B Tan who appeared for the Consul-General of China at the Inquest produced a witness, Low Hian Yin, a clerk in Cheong Joo Rubber Works who managed to take some photographs of the incident. Low testified that the trolley bus had attempted to move on despite the crowd. In the process it had knocked down a number of people, infuriating the crowd further:

> Witness saw a trolley bus in Tanjong Pagar which was stopped. A European got on the bus which started to move slowly forward and knocked one or two of the small boys who were in the procession.
> (*The Straits Times*, Inquest, 30 March 1927, p. 10)

The boys did not appear to have been injured but the crowd took this as sufficient provocation and surged onto the trolley bus, knocking down the driver. Fighting broke out soon after.

Six Chinese were killed and 11 injured. The Inquest could only ascertain that firing had taken place; who had ordered the firing remained inconclusive. Even Alec Dixon, who was on duty at the scene, could not provide a satisfactory account of the incident except to admit that shots were indeed deliberately fired into the crowd:

> The "some one" in the station ordered the constables to fire a volley over the heads of the crowd. This had little or no effect, and only when the constables fired into the Chinese ranks did the crowd retire. Hale emphatically denied giving any fire-orders during the riot, although he would have been quite justified in doing so. Certainly the firing went on

for several minutes and a large quantity of ball-cartridge was used. But to this day only the constables who were present at Kreta Ayer that afternoon knew how many rounds were fired into the crowd.

(Dixon, 1935, p. 133)

When news of this came out there was general unhappiness as it was taken as proof that the police were covering up for their own. The senior officer on the scene was, of course, Inspector Hale although it was a sergeant who led the men in taking up firing positions.

The police did not come out of this well. Inspector Hale admitted at the Inquest that he "did not anticipate trouble" (*The Straits Times*, 8 April 1927, p. 9). It was not just Hale that was unprepared, the Kreta Ayer Station which was manned by six NCOs and 18 men did not appear to expect any trouble or, worse, know what to do with a mob. On the second day of the Inquest, Thomson gave evidence of how when he first went into the Station he could not find anyone:

Whilst he was there, the men upstairs came running down the stairs. They were not in uniform. They took hold of rifles and batons.

There was no European there at the time and he could not say who was in charge. They felt that trouble was coming, and he had the same feeling.

He saw ammunition on the table and the men helping themselves. He did not actually see any rifles loaded ...

(*The Straits Times*, 19 March 1927, p. 9)

One cannot escape the impression that amidst all the confusion and fear someone had panicked. At least from the evidence the chain of authority had been lost, as the officers on the scene did not seem able to recall who had actually given the order to fire. As Turnbull sums up:

The ill-managed Kreta Ayer incident caused great bitterness among the Chinese.

(Turnbull, 1997, p. 131)

This bitterness turned into the long-drawn-out boycott of the trolley buses of the company Thomson worked for. His evidence in court and the unsympathetic manner he had treated the knocking down of the boys by his bus became the fuse for further rioting.

The whole situation was, indeed, badly managed. The police had reacted unthinkingly when the crowd rushed at the police station. Shots meant to kill were fired. The policemen could have lost their nerves when the riot started. The police were clearly not trained for anti-riot duties. They had not even contemplated the possibility of something going wrong in an emotionally-charged event like the Happy Valley gathering. They were also easily fooled by the assurances of the organizers. The Chief Constable himself accepted the assurances that the commemoration meeting would be peaceful and that it would not involve political issues. While there were detectives circulating among the crowd, the uniformed police were kept busy directing traffic. Hale himself testified that he had walked into the crowd armed with a "walking stick" (*The Straits Times*, 8 April 1927, p. 9). He told the Inquest that this was standard gear for policemen when faced with a rioting crowd. While this was all very heroic and entirely in keeping with the best of colonial propaganda it was clearly also very foolish. Practices observed later in anti-riot duties, such as the identification of the leader and, if necessary, arresting him as a warning to the rest, were not in place. Once again, as with the Indian mutiny, communication was lacking. Thomson could not find an "incidents room" to report the rioting; in any case he even had difficulty just trying to alert the rest of the police for reinforcements.

Significantly the Special Branch played a key role in dispersing the rioters. Onraet, himself, took the stand, giving evidence as Director of the CID. His title was a cover for his actual duties as Director of the Special Branch. The Branch clearly expected trouble. On the morning of 12 March Onraet had met A S P Dickinson, head of the Detective Bureau. Picking up two Chinese detectives they had gone down to Happy Valley to mingle with the crowd. Upon receiving information that trouble had broken out at Kreta Ayer, Onraet together with a team of eight or nine Europeans, proceeded there. As Onraet testified, when he reached the area he realized that:

> The temper of the crowd was such that witness saw that he would have to act at once.
>
> (*The Straits Times*, 7 April 1927, p. 10)

Leading the charge himself, Onraet dispersed the crowd in Spring Street before proceeding on to South Bridge Road. Cross-examined by the Solicitor-General, Onraet gave his views:

> His duty was very plain.
> If he saw people being assaulted by a crowd and he thought his men sufficient to disperse them without firing he would do so.
> If the men were not sufficient he considered that it was his duty to fire.
>
> (*The Straits Times*, 7 April 1927, p. 10)

Similarly, he would not hesitate to fire if there was a threat to his officers and the station they were protecting. Compare to the vacillations of the other officers, Onraet came across as firmly decisive. He was without doubt bloody-minded as well but at least he convinced the worried British residents who had been listening to the account of police incompetence that decisive action was possible. The speed with which he acted to disperse the crowd at Spring Street and the rapid deployment of picket lines ensured that the trouble would be contained for the moment.

From previous experience, Onraet knew that he had to send out a strong signal to the troublemakers and agitators behind the riots. He also knew that the Kreta Ayer shooting was not the end of the matter. The political agitators would not pass by such a golden chance to create further unrest. Indeed, playing upon the justifiable resentment of the Chinese as news of the shooting spread through the city, the underground agitprop swung into action. On the day after the shooting, the Hailam agitators were distributing hastily-printed handbills all over Chinatown. Some of these gave dramatic accounts of the shooting, others called upon the workers to rise up against the imperialists and avenge the martyrs of Kreta Ayer. Still others depicted a huge trolley bus mowing down innocent school children. The stage was set for the extension of the Kreta Ayer shooting.

A boycott (or *hartal*) of trolley buses was declared on 24 March. The Hailams threatened to manhandle and rough up any passengers who dared to disobey the order. Their immediate purpose was to hit the profitability of the Singapore Tramways, which by now had been turned into a convenient fall guy for anti-government action. Eight out of every 10 passengers carried by the trolley buses were Chinese. The boycott would deprive the Tramway of revenue, causing its stocks to drop sharply. An unstated but equally important aim would be to unite the different Chinese clans in a common cause against the colonial masters.

The *hartal* met with initial success. Two days after it was called, the trolley buses were almost empty. Passengers had been dissuaded by the threat of violence. Even the Straits-born Chinese whom the government felt had little to fear from the Hailam threats were staying away despite appeals in the press for them to carry on taking the trolley buses. Soon even bus routes to the suburban area of Katong were affected. Right from the start the political significance of the boycott was clear to the authorities:

It is stated that the boycott is a sequel to the shooting affair at Kreta Ayer police station on 12 March and the evidence given at the inquest. Another suggestion of the fact that the Traction Company has its headquarters in Shanghai has some bearing on the position. At all events the effort at boycott appeared to be successful by this morning. Trolley buses coming from Katong, which usually are crowded between the hours of eight and nine, contained few passengers, and Chinese were conspicuously absent.

(*The Straits Times*, 26 March 1927, p. 8)

By linking the boycott to the fighting then taking place in Shanghai between the various contending Chinese forces and its spillover into attacks on the Straits Settlement, *The Straits Times* alerted readers to the wider political context of the action. The boycott was called not just to express resentment of British injustice in the Kreta Ayer incident. It was part of a series of disruptions that underlined the revolutionary movements. It was also part of a strong anti-foreign campaign that was sweeping through southern China at this time. To give an illustration, on 28 March a mass meeting at Chapei, Shanghai, under the auspices of the General Labour Union, a communist-controlled front, passed a resolution asking for the intensification of the anti-British boycott in China.

In Singapore the boycott turned violent rapidly. On the evening of 27 March unruly crowds gathered first at People's Park and then at New Bridge Road threatening and, then, attacking the buses. The Fire Brigade had to be called out, using their fire hoses to disperse the crowd. Predictably, rioting broke out as the crowd turned upon the firemen, pelting them with crockery from the nearby food stalls, bricks and other available missiles.

Hooligans of all clans harassed the street patrols and received every baton charge with a hail of stones and brickbats. This stone-throwing caused so many casualties in the police ranks that on the second night of the riots every man in the Force was issued with a steel helmet.

(Dixon, 1935, p. 136)

Eventually the police had to mount a baton charge to clear the streets. In just one night of violence $750.00 worth of damage was done to 11 trolley buses that were attacked. Even three days after the event People's Park was "like a war scene" (*The Straits Times*, 30 March 1927, p. 9) with heavy police presence.

Given all the harm to life and property it was not surprising that *The Straits Times* expressed outrage at the lack of law and order and the seeming disability of the authorities to stop the agitation. By this time the actions had produced an atmosphere of "nervous tension and a readiness to panic" as described by the Special Branch then. In the light of what was by now regarded as deliberate subversion, many British residents agreed with the editorial of *The Straits Times* which called on the CID (Special Branch) to be given greater support:

> If the Criminal Investigation Department needs strengthening in personnel, there should be no difficulty in this being done. We cannot afford to neglect the subversive movement, which we assert, exists. If we do we are going to pay the penalty. The time has come for Singapore to show her mettle. We believe we are sufficiently strong and that there is sufficient self confidence to enable us to destroy the treachery around us and destroy it quickly.
>
> (*The Straits Times*, 11 April 1927, p. 8)

It is interesting to note that *The Straits Times* was not allowed to make any reference to the Special Branch. Onraet was referred to as the Director of the CID or Criminal Investigation Department.

The boycott of the trolley buses worsened steadily as the days passed and recriminations flew thick and fast about the Kreta Ayer shooting. Despite the strong police presence the crowds rampaged through People's Park, New Bridge Road as well as Havelock Road. Efforts by a deputation from the Chinese Chamber of Commerce to defuse the situation only met with more vandalism. The Branch received information that the action against the trolley buses was not merely in response to the Kreta Ayer shootings but part of a larger plan to undermine British influence. The same shadowy perpetrators behind the boycott of British cigarettes that the school teacher, S J Lim, had called for on 15 February 1927 in the North Bridge Road Chinese Theatre were also behind the present unrest. The revolutionaries were taking every opportunity to create turmoil, manipulating public opinion from behind the scenes with the aim of fanning anti-British sentiments.

In fact, documents seized on the day of the Kreta Ayer shooting already provided evidence of hidden hands. During the Inquest a number of handbills and pamphlets of a subversive nature had been tendered as evidence. When it was his turn to testify, A S P Dickinson of the Detective Bureau drew attention to one found in the pockets of a dead rioter. It urged:

Overseas revolutionaries, rise up!
Support the Northern Expedition.
Hasten the building of the national conference.
The whole population of the country should acclaim the abolition of
unequal treaties.
Support the Kuomintang and the Nationalist Government.
All the overseas revolutionaries shall back up the Nationalist Government
in its diplomacy.
Overthrow imperialism and militarism together with all its tools.
Everlasting success to the Nationalist revolutionaries.
The Immortal spirit of Dr Sun.

(*The Straits Times*, 7 April 1927, p. 10)

The memorial to Sun Yat Sen provided an opportunity to recruit new
followers to the Kuomintang cause as well as educate the people to the
key achievements of revolutionary China like the Northern Expedition
against the warlords.

The Special Branch and the police conducted raids almost every day
during the boycott. Intensive monitoring soon produced results. On
29 April, the Branch raided the Nanyang General Labour Union,
reportedly a branch of the Canton Overseas Red Labour Union, at
251 Orchard Road. Wong Kum Nam, the occupant, was detained.
Following this, the police raided 18 Duxton Road, which housed the
Union of the Overseas Chinese for Backing up Representations
Concerning the Disastrous Incident of 12 March. It was this organization
formed on 18 March that instigated and led the boycott of the trolley
buses. The Special Branch was especially concerned about this union as
it was successful in bringing together the different Chinese clans and
dialect groups to oppose the government. It used the term "curious and
dangerous" to describe this worrying development:

> This last named organization was undoubtedly the centre of the Trolley
> Bus boycott and is curious and dangerous for up to now all available
> information has pointed to the Hailam section alone being responsible
> for the revolutionary and subversive propaganda in Malaya. It is now
> definitely known that the Hailam have met with some success in their
> efforts to unite the Cantonese, Hokkien and Teochew in an organized
> boycott of the Trolley buses.
>
> (item 106, Journal 1927)

From a security point of view the Union of the Overseas Chinese at
18 Duxton Road was of especial interest since it showed features that
were quite different from the usual run-of-the-mill organizations the

Branch raided. Firstly, the Union was not concerned with just the Kreta Ayer shooting. It had larger, more sinister aims in seeking to bring together all overseas Chinese and their associations. Seized documents confirmed that the aims of the Union were:

1. to take vengeance for the 12 March incident,
2. to affiliate and rouse all local associations,
3. to unite the overseas Chinese to struggle for freedom and human rights.

The Union thus had a political programme that went beyond taking revenge for the Kreta Ayer martyrs. As the Branch dug more deeply they realized that the Union was not only ambitious in its aims but also well-organized. It had five departments: General Affairs (for secretariat work), Propaganda Department, Finance Department, Investigation Department and Picket Department. The sophistication of its structure would suggest a highly complex political presence.

The Branch was right to be worried. The Union was the first effective united front organization in Malaya pointing the way ahead to the communists. Secondly, this development showed that the Chinese were prepared to put aside their differences when they felt that the issues were serious enough. The consequence of this would be a political and security nightmare: a united force with links to hostile external agencies. As the Chinese were an essential component of the colonial economy unrest and disaffection among them would seriously damage British interests.

The Nanyang General Labour Union was an equal threat since it attempted to bring together not just the "Chinese tribes ... but (also) Malays, Javanese, Tamils" (item 196, Journal 1927). The Nanyang Union provided a network of politically aware activists that covered the key areas of British control and influence. Branches had been established in the Straits Settlements, the Federated Malay States (Port Swettenham, Seremban and Kuala Lumpur) and the Unfederated Malay States (Ipoh, Sepang Road, Kuala Pilah, Klang, Rawang, Rantau and Rasa), Sarawak (Miri) and Siam (Chooipon). After the split between the Kuomintang and the Communist Party many of these branches and their supporters went under the influence of the revolutionary left.

The events in Singapore confirmed suspicions which the Branch already had since the beginning of the year. A chance raid at the Phang Man School at Kuala Lumpur yielded a rich find. Seized documents revealed the existence of the 'Main' School:

a Chinese Extremist Organization which appears to be about a hundred and fifty strong. Its activities extend, according to documents found, throughout Malaya, the NEI and Siam. These hundred and fifty members would appear to be members of a committee who have used for subversive purposes the Night Schools and Labour Guilds throughout Malaya and sub-branches of the 'Left' KMT to spread subversive propaganda throughout the Malayan Archipelago and to aim at a large increase in the number of 'fellow students'.

(item 196, Journal 1927)

The papers showed that the 'Main' School was keen to forge links with the Javanese communists. The members of its executive committee had studied the failure of the Javanese communist revolt against the Dutch in 1926 and drawn lessons from it. The discovery of the documents was important, as the 'Main' School did not have a fixed headquarters. In order to evade the attention of the authorities, the 'Main' School moved from town to town, usually operating through the night schools of those places where their leaders congregated. These leaders and the headquarters would move again once it was felt that the authorities were getting too close for comfort.

We have here already an indication of the overlapping organizations, agencies and fronts that would later characterize the communist movement in Malaya. Not satisfied with one agency, the communists would often parallel their work by creating other organizations and fronts. The attention paid to secrecy meant that it was even harder for the Branch to stumble upon their headquarters and plans. In fact, the 'Main' School was so successful in carrying out its activities in spite of the vigilance of the Special Branch that from 1926 to 1927 they managed to help the affiliated Nanyang General Labour Union increase its membership from:

1,000 members with 5 branches in May 1926 to 6,000 with 42 branches in April 1927, a foundation which stood them in good stead throughout the rest of the 1920s.

(Yong, 1997, p. 74)

While the 'Main' School was an indication of the debates underlying the direction of the left which racked the movement at this time, its methods were a precursor of the tactics used with some success later on by the Malayan Communist Party. The secrecy made the movement difficult for the police to detect from without and suggest that it would be more profitable to infiltrate the organization, to plant a spy within their ranks. In fact, operationally this was the only way to cover the organization.

In the meantime, all these developments made it quite apparent that by 1927 a sustained campaign was underway to forge an anti-British revolutionary front. Despite Special Branch pressure, the activists decided to intensify their campaign the following year. So even before the memories of Kreta Ayer and the trolley bus boycott had receded the shoemakers' strike started on 12 February 1928. Normally a strike would not have attracted much attention except that Special Branch monitoring soon showed that it was "prompted by political rather than economic reasons" (item 18, Journal 1928). Starting from the Hakka workmen, the strike soon spread to the Cantonese and then the Hailam. Once again a unified political front in pursuit of a political objective was rapidly coming into being.

As with the trolley bus incident, the strikers showed a willingness to resort to force when their demands were not met. On 24 February explosive devices were set off. For the first time a sustained bombing and terror campaign to back specific economic/political objectives hit the colony. Despite an almost immediate raid resulting in the arrest of five men on 1 March at 100 Java Road, the bombings continued. A bomb was thrown at a shoemaker's shop at 35 Middle Road on 2 March and another two were found on 4 March at Merchant Road although these failed to go off. However, on the evening of 6 March bombs exploded at 777 North Bridge Road and 49 Middle Road. Both were targeted at shoemakers' shops, the intention being to terrorize both the owners and the general population. That same evening a bomb exploded in a hotel room at 101 Short Street, apparently while the terrorist was preparing it. Little of all this was reported in the press which provided only a summary of events when it was finally allowed to report on the incidents (*The Straits Times*, 7 March 1928, p. 10). A more detailed write-up subsequently, when the back of the bombing campaign had been broken, admitted:

> It is generally believed that at least ten shops have been bombed since the beginning of the strike, although only a few of the shop proprietors have reported the occurrences to the police. The bombings have undoubtedly had a very alarming effect, and additional police are now stationed in Queen Street and other districts.
>
> (*The Straits Times*, 12 March 1928, p. 10)

Instead of daily and up-to-date coverage of the bombing campaign the paper, presumably on Special Branch advice, only provided a summary of the situation. This method prevented panic from spreading as well as denied the terrorists any propaganda value from their bombings.

The Special Branch allowed some of its activities to be highlighted in the press, possibly with a view to assuring the public that the authorities were on top of the situation. Perhaps it was all a part of an intricate propaganda war for the hearts and minds of the population. In any case, on 2 March, *The Straits Times* reported the trial of Wong Wee Kam, a Hylam house servant in the employ of Mr Sammy of 10-C Chancery Lane. He had in his possession documents such as "How to Carry out a Revolutionary Movement in the South Seas" and "South Seas Provisional Commission of the Communist Party". It was revealed that the Communist Party would be placed under the direct control of China and that Cheong Yeok Kai would take charge of it upon his arrival from China. The court was then told that Cheong was actually an assassin, tasked with the shooting of Dr Lim Boon Keng. The documents also mentioned efforts to form a propaganda committee as well as a military committee. Wong Wee Kam insisted that the documents belonged to the previous occupant of his room. He was indicted for sedition after the DPP argued that all the documents suggested "an incitement to workers to overthrow British imperialism" (*The Straits Times*, 2 March 1928, p. 10). The shoemakers who were already striking took an extraordinary interest in the trial. They sent their men to make notes at the court hearings. The Special Branch watched their movements with great interest. One of them who made copious notes of the proceedings was arrested and charged.

The Straits Times reported the startling news of a raid on 8 March on a compound house in 59-B Balestier Road near the junction of Kim Keat Road. Two Chinese, one of them Wong Te Choi (a.k.a. Cheung Wan Seng), the head of the South Seas Revolutionary Party, was arrested. The paper reported that:

> A large assortment of seditious literature and Bolshevik publications was found ...
>
> (*The Straits Times*, 9 March 1928, p. 9)

The raid yielded a number of "completed bombs and material for their manufacture" (*The Straits Times*, 9 March 1928, p. 9). These were similar to those that had been thrown in the shoemakers' strike. What the paper did not report was that 59-B Balestier Road was in fact the military headquarters of the local communist organization (item 68, Journal 1928). Similarly the paper did not report a raid at 53 Owen Road which turned up documents showing that the Nanyang General

Labour Union was deeply involved in the shoemakers' strike and the trolley bus boycott. Over this period, from 30 January to 14 March, some 17 people were detained and eight on banishment warrant. One of these, C M Cheung, a Hokien, was suspected of being behind a bomb-throwing incident at Kuala Lumpur as well as the trolley bus riots. Goh Choon Peng and Liew Law Yin were detained for making bombs. The expansion of the Nanyang General Labour Union stopped after similar raids in Penang, Perak, Selangor and Pahang. Coincidentally the bombing campaign in support of the shoemakers' strike stopped and the strike ended soon after.

The Special Branch did not rest on its laurels. It was still after some key perpetrators. Its investigations met with success on 26 June when they arrested L Y Bok, a Hailam bookkeeper. It turned out that Bok:

> had first come to the notice in 1926 as a Committee member of the Lok Khuan Hylam Night School which was closed down on account of subversive propaganda.
>
> (item 124, Journal 1928)

Bok was said to have been present at the Kreta Ayer shooting on 12 March 1927. He also attempted to organize some sort of demonstration at its anniversary in 1928. He owned an unregistered company, Peng Peng Kongsi, which was used to finance the operations of the Koon Seng Hylam shoe shop in Middle Road:

> This place was for a long time the rendezvous and the Post Office for local Hylam Communists, and its staff took an active part in the directing of the recent Shoemakers strike.
>
> (item 124, Journal 1928)

With the arrest of Bok, the Branch ended the first episode of militantly violent industrial unrest in Singapore which had bombings used as a part of its tactics. The raids certainly revealed that the Branch had a fair amount of knowledge of their targets.

***

In the mid-1920s Singapore was a boom town. After a relatively mild recession at the start of the decade, prosperity returned. These were the years that saw enormous fortunes being made almost overnight. The entrepreneurs who became household names in wealth such as Tan Kah Kee, Lee Kong Chian, Tay Koh Yat, Tan Lark Sye and

Aw Boon Haw made their money at this time. The quality of life improved markedly with the affluence and the increased spending on public health and transport as government revenues soared. The Outram General Hospital and the Trafalgar Home for lepers were opened in 1926, the Woodbridge Mental Hospital in 1927 and the Kandang Kerbau Maternity Hospital in 1928. The first municipal power station was opened at St James in 1927 and the Pulai Reservoir in Johore began to supply water to Singapore in 1929. Many imposing buildings reflecting the majesty of imperial wealth also went up such as the Fullerton Building which included the General Post Office in 1928 and the new Municipal Building (later to be known as City Hall) in 1929. On the whole the colony experienced prosperity and growth.

The shops were flushed with expensive goods and the latest arrivals from London and the Continent. Its residents, particularly the British, traded, wined, dined, danced, and slept every night, confident in the paramountcy of imperial rule and the security of their homes and wealth. Robinsons was advertising its full-dress suit that was "lined finest quality silk throughout" and its "exclusive range of palm beach suitings". A discerning gentleman of wealth might also contemplate the latest Norton motorcycle from John Little and Co., a Falcon Knight Light Six-Sleeve Valve car from The Associated Auto Company, the more upmarket Studebaker's Erskine Six four-door sedan from Imperial Motors, or follow his Imperial Majesty in purchasing a Daimler from Guthrie and Co. This same gentleman and his wife could dine off fresh pork from Cold Storage's own farm at Bukit Timah or relax with a splash of Johnnie Walker, the dependable Black and White or Gilbey's Spey-Royal. In the evenings after dinner, an enjoyable time was available at the cabarets, theatres and cinemas. In February 1928 the cinemas offered 'The Gay Retreat' at the Alhambra, 'Out All Night' at the Pavilion, 'Son of Zorro' at the New Casino Cinema and 'The Waltz Dream' at the Straits Open Air Cinema. At the Raffles Hotel, Sea View Hotel and the Adelphi Hotel you could watch acrobatics, character and modern dancing, the Recherche Cabaret Dinner Dance, Cherpino's Broadway Follies or dance away the night to the music of Chas L Fischer's Orchestra. The British resident would have found many things to be pleased about in the colonies. Even if he was managing a plantation the journey to the cosmopolitan city of Singapore was now very easy. With the rail system and the good roads travelling was no longer demanding or hazardous. There were many things to recommend life in the Malayan colonies.

Once away from the bright lights of the commercial and entertainment areas we are presented with a very different picture. The 1920s were not just one long unending summer of prosperity. There were unhappiness and poverty. There were also those ready to capitalize on these contradictions. In dimly-lit rooms, dummy offices and safe houses plans were being laid to end imperialist rule. Behind the apparent peacefulness there was unfolding an increasingly brutal and relentless struggle for supremacy as the British presence was challenged by the rising tide of revolutionary fervour and nationalism in their Asian colonies. The prize was not just the political and financial future of the Malayan archipelago. It was also the right to determine the direction of events in Asia for the next century. These were years that tested the fledgling Special Branch even as it sought to put together a team that would prove capable of meeting the myriad of challenges.

The Branch weathered the storms well, beating back not just efforts at espionage and political agitation but also a number of attempts to foment revolts and instil fear. A number of major security threats confronted the Straits Settlements as a result of these. Not only was there the first political riot that ended in police shooting but it was followed by a boycott that united the most economically important group, the Chinese, in a common effort. This period also saw the outbreak of the first sustained terrorist bombing campaign in British Malaya. The 1920s also marked the rise of China and the Comintern as inspirers and supporters of the anti-colonial movement. The Comintern was a well-oiled machine with many arms. It operated as comfortably from Amsterdam as it did from Bangkok or Shanghai. A different level of professionalism as well as mindset was needed to counter its many efforts at subversion. It was just as well that the Special Branch had evolved into a highly competent force. An indication of its competence was the assurance with which it handled the bombings in 1928. Within a few weeks the Branch had seized the explosive materials, cutting off essential supplies to the terrorists.

The nature of the threats also underwent some far-reaching changes even as the broad theme remained the same. Germany and India were no longer important. Instead the USSR and the Comintern proved the more dangerous foes in the long run. Germany had challenged the imperial structure but, unlike Russia, it did not want to destroy the colonialism that went with it. It was the aim of the Comintern not just to eradicate colonialism but through revolutionary upheavals to alter the economic relationship and power of the old imperial world. The Comintern wanted a change both in the substance as well as nature of power and control. It set about this methodically, bringing the years of its experience working on the fringes of society to the task. In addition, as the imperial powers reacted with increasing hostility to the new regime, the USSR not only felt that revolution was an appropriate response but that its very survival depended upon underground activities. To these it added organization and method, key characteristics that allowed its control of hidden cells and agents. The rise of the Third Comintern with its call to spread revolution to the colonies would dominate the Special Branch's attention for the next decade.

One common thread that did remain and was, in fact, enhanced was the ideological battleground. In every case, subversion and sedition in the colonies had been appeals to the moving power of ideas. The new thinking would free the oppressed, allow them to reclaim their dignity and freedom and alter the relationships in power and resources between ruler and subject. The Ghadr movement, Turkey's declaration of *jihad* and Germany's efforts to incorporate these as part of an uprising against British imperialism had played upon the appeal of the liberating power of ideas to stir up the people. Increasingly, to use a cliche it was the "minds and hearts" of the colonized that were fought over. In the 1930s political subversion came to the forefront as the Special Branch felt it more and more necessary to counter its danger. Communism functioned above all as a complete system of ideas that was very appealing to the colonized. When knowledge is fused with sophisticated organization a powerful force will be formed. The Branch had forged its tactics and weapons none too soon.

Notes

1. The incident is attributed to reliable sources in Harper and Miller's book on the Singapore mutiny in 1915 (Harper and Miller, 1984, p. 237).

2. C.O. 273/516, Baddeley to Churchill, 29 July 1922.

3. *The Straits Times* refers to him consistently as Inspector Dale when his name should be Hale. A curious discrepancy indeed. Was this to protect his identity from revenge seekers? Certainly the mood was such that Sikh policemen were posted as guards around the houses of the European police officers as a safety precaution.

The Special Branch in the 1930s

The Special Branch was often a privileged but silent witness to the making of history. By the very nature of its work the Branch was aware of the hidden currents and motivations that swirl beneath the placid surface of daily life, the crucial yet absent details that are essential to our understanding of events and the often hidden but powerful impulses that influenced actions.

By the 1930s, communism had emerged as the primary threat to the security of British Malaya although the extent of Japanese espionage was also an increasing phenomena of security concerns. Communism affected not only the stability of the colonies through militant labour actions but also subverted the Chinese, an important component of the colonial political economy. Uprisings in China, French Indo-China and the Netherlands East Indies had shown that, if given the opportunity, the communists would resort to armed insurrection to seize power. Much of the Special Branch's efforts were to neutralize the infiltration of cadres, propaganda and weapons used for such ends.

A number of events heightened the apprehension of the Branch. The founding of Soviet Russia in 1917 made communism an attractive political inspiration for the anti-colonialist movements seeking alternatives to imperialist ideology. Despite significant vacillations on the "Eastern" question and the appropriate response towards colonialism, the Third Comintern saw advantages in helping the various national liberation movements especially those in Asia. By the time the Fifth Comintern Congress met in the summer of 1924 the colonial world was seen as the place where communism could expand. The Comintern's failure to bring about revolution in Europe as well as increased unrest in the colonial world convinced Moscow that the new strategy should be followed. At the meeting Manuilsky, a close confidant of Stalin criticized the European parties for their inability to address the issue of colonialism. There were, of course, severe contradictions on the issue which would damage the communist cause in time. However, whether it be the Manuilsky/Stalin line that collaboration with the national bourgeoisie remained central to the struggle against colonialism or the rejection of this in favour of the more vigorous class struggle espoused by M N Roy the die was now cast. The Comintern would support national liberation revolutions in particular those that would damage the European imperialists who were ranged against Soviet Russia. In fact, despite the reservations expressed by several Asian delegates including Roy, Nguyen Giap, Sen Katayama and Semaun the Comintern would step up its control of the nascent communist parties.

Inevitably its fingerprint would be much more obvious, adding to the suspicions of the colonial intelligence agencies.

The influence of the Chinese Communist Party became steadily important, owing as much to the sentiments it attractèd among the large Chinese population as from its financial and other contributions. As the Comintern was by now well established in China this made it easy for Moscow to use ports like Shanghai and Hong Kong to infiltrate Southeast Asia. Even when a second courier route came into use running from Malaya to Siam and on to French Indo-China its origin was still from southern China. By the 1920s China had emerged as the key arena for the Comintern, a test bed for the revolutionary doctrines of Soviet Russia. As the Comintern became more entrenched in China it directed a steady stream of battle-hardened cadres, propagandists and militants into the Malayan peninsula.

It is significant that organized communist activities in China and British Malaya took place at about the same time. In 1920, two Comintern agents, Grigori Voitinsky and Yang Mingzhai, helped form the first provisional central committee of the Chinese Communist Party. However, communist ideas were already circulating and well known to Chinese intellectuals who introduced them in turn to Malaya. In 1921 Mak Chau arrived in Kuala Lumpur where he founded and taught at the Nan Ming Hok Kwan. Together with a few others, Mak founded the Nanyang Critique Society, a radical organization that promoted the dissemination of socialist ideas. This organization may be regarded as the first communist society in British Malaya. The Special Branch named Mak and seven other Chinese active communists. Thus within a year communist activities were well in place in the two areas.

In the early 1920s cooperation between the Kuomintang and the Chinese Communist Party provided the opportunity for left-wing ideas to circulate freely. The Kuomintang itself had a left-wing section that was so active in Malaya that the British raided its front organizations several times. On the evening of 28 February 1926 the Special Branch raided the Chi Min Night School at 25 Blair Road where the fourth delegates' meeting of the Nanyang Public Bodies Union was being held. Forty-one participants including four delegates from China were arrested. From the amount of communist pamphlets seized the Branch thought mistakenly that they were dealing with the Malayan Communist Party (MCP).

Actually communism in Malaya tended to be spread through militant trade unions and guilds reflecting its anarcho-syndicalist roots. The syndicalists took their inspiration from Fernand Pelloutir who spread the message of revolution through the syndicated groups of craftsmen in France. Certainly the earliest communists or left-wing agitators were anarchists, hence the reference to them as anarcho-communists. In Malaya the 'Main' School founded in Singapore in October 1926 exhibited these characteristics: it drew support from a whole variety of left-wing groups including the Nanyang General Labour Union, the Hainanese night schools, the Nanyang Communist Youth League of China and Kuomintang branches. In April 1927 the 'Main' School was renamed the Nanyang Local Committee. However, this committee was in turn dissolved and superseded by the Nanyang Provisional Committee of the Chinese Communist Party (CCP) founded in January 1928. Whether it was the Comintern or the CCP that was responsible for the founding of this organization is not as important as the fact that the local party had been subsumed and brought under the control of external forces. From this time on the communists in Malaya would be directed by external agencies: at times this would be the Comintern, at others it would be the CCP. The consequence on the whole was disaster for the movement.

The Nanyang Provisional Committee crippled by incessant Special Branch raids was itself replaced on the direct orders of the Shanghai Far Eastern Bureau of the Comintern in 1930. The founding of the Malayan Communist Party in April 1930 was attended by delegates from the Nanyang Provisional Committee, the Nanyang General Labour Union and the Nanyang General Seamen's Union. Nguyen Ai Quoc (Ho Chih Minh) was present as the Comintern representative and chief minder. Almost immediately the new Malayan Communist Party suffered a blow when eight of their top leaders were arrested at 24 Nassim Road on the evening of 29 April 1930. In giving his evidence in court Onraet who had organized the raid produced a number of incriminating items as evidence. Among the papers the police discovered a notification on communist activities for the May Day rally, the translation of a Russian lecture on international communism, a call to communist youths to take concerted action against imperialism and accounts of the New Bridge Road branch of the party. The eight detainees were subsequently convicted and given two-year imprisonment for illegal activities.

Although the Special Branch was often successful in its interdiction of communist activities it could not afford to rest on its laurels. The Comintern was determined to penetrate the roots of communist ideology deep in the soil of Malaya. It sent one wave after another of emissaries to the region. These were added to by the activists who were among the refugees fleeing the unrest in China at this time. From these the Malayan Communist Party found replacements for those leaders and cadres that had been arrested or deported. Despite constant vigilance the threats that emerged in the 1920s intensified rather than receded in the years leading up to the Second World War. The rise of Japan and protests from the overseas Chinese against its encroachments in China further complicated the picture by arousing the political consciousness of the Chinese. Many of them joined communist-controlled organizations or fronts to campaign against Japanese aggression. It was at this time that Asian nationalism experienced a resurgence of resistance movements from Indo-China to India. Many of these were militant, advocating armed resistance or direct action against the colonial authorities. The revolutionary ideology of communism often attracted these nationalists as an appropriate alternative to imperialism. Moreover, both the Comintern and China were willing to help form underground movements as well as train the necessary cadres. Onraet's warning that outside influences often affected the security of the Malayan colonies is exemplified by all these developments.

In the first part of the decade the major sources of subversion were from the Comintern and its progeny, the Chinese Communist Party. By the very nature of their historical experiences these had extensive skills in the use of underground and concealed networks of agents, couriers and front organizations to carry out their work. Years of being hunted by various governments had taught them highly sophisticated ways of survival. The Comintern introduced these skills in planning, organization and agitation to those Southeast Asian countries that were receptive to communism. Trained Comintern agents stiffened and extended the effectiveness of the local movements. The Branch had to develop complex and thorough means of monitoring and surveillance over the years to counter the increasing sophistication of the communist networks. Vigorous policing was no longer enough as it could not cut off the secured bases of the Comintern Far Eastern Bureau in Shanghai or Vladivostok. The Branch was faced with a hydra against which merely reactive action was only momentarily effective. The Branch needed new instruments involving deep penetration operations and infiltration of the communists to achieve its aims. These new circumstances led the Branch to invest more in covert operations that attempted to penetrate the secrecy of the communist cells. The Kreta Ayer shootings of 1927 was a salutary reminder of how rapidly things could get out of hand:

It was, however, only after firearms were used by the Kreta Ayer Police on 14 March 1927 that the true communist and China-directed character of the trade unions was discovered.

(Supplement to Journal No. 1 1931)

The communist attempt to create popular uprisings meant that repressive action had to be selective. Once the situation deteriorated into a riot the police would have already lost. Trouble had to be forestalled and nipped in the bud before passions got inflamed. Intelligence thus became even more important.

The sepoy mutiny of 1915 for all its ferocity did not involve substantial parts of the population. It was not a challenge by an internal component of the system since the sepoys were essentially mercenaries brought in for garrison duties. In comparison, the To' Janggutt incident in Kelantan was more dangerous since it had a strong populist element drawing support from a wide spectrum of the state's residents including religious teachers and ordinary villagers. The British decision to display the crucified body of the insurrection's leader was drastic and barbaric in the extreme, but its political message was clear. It was similar to many atrocities in colonies such as Congo and Java that were meant to drive home the message of the futility of resistance against superior imperial firepower. The aim was among other things to subdue the population so that the uprising would not spread. In the 1930s, the security threat took on precisely this dimension, as the substantial and influential Chinese population became an increasing target for subversive and revolutionary action.

The Special Branch knew that repression was no longer sufficient to the task given the very different scenario they were now operating in. The key to successful internal security was a light touch with selective suppression when the need arose. Troublesome issues had to be neutralized and troublemakers removed before they could stir up enough enthusiasm. Experience with riots had shown that these were difficult to control once they started. In other words, it was best that the problem be resolved before it became ungovernable. The key to the Special Branch duties was therefore sound and timely intelligence that allowed for anticipation and decisive intervention. Put another way, it would be strategic vision, sound organization and superior skills that mattered. In addition the advantage would also come from a keen awareness of international events and trends in both neighbouring and faraway countries like China, Japan, Germany and the USSR. In meeting its adversaries organizational strength would be crucial. Not surprisingly, the Branch was quick to make those structural changes that would give it a competitive advantage.

Many of the major breakthroughs of the Branch in the new decade came from the careful evaluation and analysis of documents and other sources. These provided the Branch with a comprehensive map that allowed for the enemy's motives and intentions to be read. On the other hand the communists were astonishingly lax with their documents. The Branch found out a lot about the MCP's organization as well as other leads through these. Sometimes these revealed the dissension and tensions between the local party and its controllers in China. On 28 July 1928 in the course of searching a suspect's, N T Lo's room they found documents that belonged to the Printing Department of the local communist organization. These records showed that an indigenous communist party was being formed. In the light of the iron control that communist organizations asserted over their other organs this was a significant development. The documents criticized the Chinese Communist Party's directives to the South Seas (i.e. Southeast Asia) as being:

> defective in that it was made from men of too high education and intelligence and has led to what is termed "the influence of opportunism".
>
> (item 140, Journal 1928)

The document argued that the movement's direction needed to be rectified with greater control placed in the hands of workers rather than the intelligentsia. This split shows that there was resistance to the Comintern line which the locals felt was too abstract and removed from social reality:

> Reorganization in the South Seas is to take the place from the lowest upwards, for this alone will build up a genuine party of labourers and peasants led by men of their own kind.
>
> (item 140, Journal 1928)

This dispute is also an excellent illustration of how familiar the MCP was about events in China. The MCP was aware of the line that Mao Zedong had put forward in his report published in a CCP journal in 1927 on the Hunan peasant uprising. Mao had eulogized the peasants as the vanguard of the communist movement in China. The CCP, he recommended, should learn from these peasants who alone were able to carry out the destruction of the feudal class structure. He also argued that the CCP was too theoretical and removed from the actual situation. Views like these that did not fall in with the CCP's idea of what a revolutionary vanguard should be were frowned upon. In November 1927 Mao Zedong was censured and dismissed from his positions in the Central Committee and the Hunan provincial committee. Looking back from our vantage position, the document provides ample proof that those left in Nanyang were at this moment very alert to and influenced by the ideological debates in China.

Unfortunately, this independence was removed when first the Comintern and later (paradoxically) the Maoist CCP insisted on exerting control over the ideological direction of the MCP. Despite these early efforts at a more open debate, the Nanyang communist party remained essentially an elitist outfit that was controlled and even subservient to outside forces. This continued obedience to "Central", initially the Comintern and then the CCP, meant that the Malayan party was never able to fully address those issues that were really central to the people of British Malaya. Just one example of this restricted, tunnel vision will suffice: throughout its history the MCP remained a Chinese party that did little to forge a truly Malayan political platform that embraced the multiracial and multilingual realities of the peninsula. The MCP's faithful adherence to the directions of "Central" also meant that it accepted unquestioningly Loi Teck, the supposed emissary and Comintern liaison chief from Hong Kong, allowing him to penetrate into the inner sanctums of the communist movement without much difficulty. In this sense, the MCP's defence—its internal secrecy and its cadres' total obedience—was its Achilles' heel: a mistake that often proved fatal to many of its members.

In the meantime, the 1928 raid had exposed the entire structure of the communist movement in Nanyang. Two charts detailing the plans of the just-concluded Nanyang Delegates Meeting fell into the hands of the Special Branch. These revealed the projected reorganization of the Provisional and Standing Committees as well as the various branches and cells that made up the party.

The documents provided the Branch with its first precise idea of the Nanyang Provisional Committee and the hierarchical nature of its organization. Directly under the Standing Committee were six committees—Propaganda, Committee on Racial Movements, Secretariat, Women's Section, Organization Meeting, and Committee on Labour Movement. Of these the Labour Movement, the front of which was the Nanyang General Labour Union, was regarded by the Special Branch as "the section from which we had most trouble" (item 140, Journal 1928). The documents further confirmed the links of the Nanyang General Labour Union with the series of strikes and riots that had been taking place. Together with documents seized at the Phang Min School during a raid in 1927 there was now ample proof of the rumours and reports they had been picking up since 1926 when a raid on the Chi Min School in Singapore gave reason to suspect the existence of a controlling organization. The existence of a "Malayan Central" that controlled many of the night schools, fomented strikes and instigated riots allowed the Special Branch to focus its attention even more on these areas.

Armed with this tantalizing insight the Branch was able to dig out substantially more information about the underground organization until by the start of the decade they had a fairly comprehensive idea of its capabilities as well as weaknesses. Knowing the weaknesses of the party was particularly useful since the Branch could exploit them. Like the Comintern the Nanyang branch controlled its cells and active units through a more or less rigid line of command that taught never to question instructions from the Standing Committee. When taken with the isolation imposed upon the cells by constant police action and Special Branch surveillance this meant that the active units were often slow to respond to developing situations. In addition, orders from Central could not be easily clarified or questioned, leading to a culture of blind obedience to the party. This is one reason why charts setting out the organizational structure of the local communist movement have always been restricted materials. Not only did these alert intelligence agencies to the likely intentions of their enemies but, when used properly, were means through which the communists could be penetrated with ease. For instance, the documents seized from the 28 July raid listed a Secretariat with six sections—Printing, Communication, Finance, Propaganda, Military, and Organization. The existence of a Military Section was a disturbing development confirming that the communists were now clearly prepared to use violence to attain their ends as the trolley bus boycott and the shoemakers' strike had indicated. It also signalled the long-term plan of the MCP to create an armed resistance movement. This would take some time to realize; not until the Japanese invasion, when the Malayan People's Anti Japanese Army was formed, did a nucleus of trained fighters come into being.

The secrecy that kept the Standing Committee or "Central" apart from the other components of the movement was a central feature of the Malayan Communist Party as well. The lowest units—the cells—were separated from the Committee by six levels of leadership. At the divisional level this structure was duplicated, making the insulation even more marked. While this no doubt helped security it also isolated the Central Committee from the ordinary members, making it slow to react to new developments. Once adopted by "Central", a decision could not be challenged but must be carried out unflinchingly otherwise the loyalty of the member would be suspect. Ordinary members were often kept in the dark about the nature and quality of their leaders. Not surprisingly once an agent such as Loi Teck had been inserted into the central committee as the secretary-general not too many questions would be asked about him. In addition since Loi Teck was the secretary-general his word was final and his leadership regarded as paramount. The astonishing failure by the communists to detect this drastic breach of security is more understandable once we understand the way the Branch was using the organizational structure and internal operating culture of the communists against them. The failure was more than inept leadership; it showed up the fundamental weakness of the Leninist system of the Comintern. The sophistication and level of British counter-espionage activities would certainly have surprised the communists.

Still, it was already evident that communism could not be lightly regarded under any circumstance. The steady stream of information that became available from 1928 emphasized that the Comintern was intent on forming a party to carry out its plans for destruction of the colonial system in Southeast Asia, replacing it with a system friendly to Moscow. The events also showed that communism had a longer history and deeper roots than was thought. The Malayan Communist Party that was formed in 1930 had evolved through nearly a decade of revolutionary experience. The Party had its origins in left-wing trade unions such as the South Seas General Labour Union, which existed as early as 1920, as well as the left-wing faction of the Kuomintang (KMT). As the development of communism in China accelerated and, in particular, following the decisive split between the KMT and its radical members in Shanghai in 1927 these bodies became more militant than ever. The Chinese Communist Party also threw out its previous policy of collaboration with the Kuomintang which was determined to form its own branch.

Adding to this drift towards greater radicalism were efforts by the Bolsheviks, especially under Lenin and later Stalin to develop or take control of revolutionary movements. In an effort to break out of the encirclement of unfriendly countries and to encourage socialist revolution, Lenin had established the Third Communist International (the Comintern) in 1919. After its first congress in March 1919, the Comintern's policy was to make contact with overseas revolutionary, anti-colonialist and anti-bourgeois groups. In 1920 the second congress of the Third Communist International had met at Petrograd. The fourth and fifth paragraphs of the Supplementary Thesis presented to the congress outlined the response to the colonial question:

> The breaking up of the colonial empire, together with the proletarian revolution in the home country, will overthrow the capitalist system in Europe. Consequently the Communist International must widen the sphere of its activity. It must establish relations with those revolutionary

forces that are working for the overthrow of imperialism in the countries subjected politically and economically. These two forces must be co-ordinated if the final success of the world revolution is to be guaranteed.

The Communist International is the concentrated will of the world revolutionary proletariat. Its mission is to organize the working class of the whole world for the overthrow of the capitalistic order and the establishment of communism. The Third International is a fighting body which must assume the task of combining the revolutionary forces of all the countries of the world.

(Gruber, 1974, p. 285)

The rhetoric sounds worse than it actually was in practice since the Comintern was never able to stir up worldwide revolution. But the Comintern was willing and eager to spread the gospel of communism. It also sent emissaries, trained agitators, political as well as labour organizers, spies and weapons trainers to a number of Asian countries to kickstart and extend the revolution.

The formation of the Chinese Communist Party in July 1921 following the first plenary meeting in Shanghai also gave impulse to developments in the East. Lenin was particularly convinced that the feudal nature of China and the colonial status of other Eastern countries rendered them fit for revolution. Even before the second Comintern congress in July 1920 Lenin had despatched two agents, Grigori Voitinsky and Yang Mingzhai to China. It was also a Comintern agent, codenamed "Maring", who led the discussions at the first plenary of the CCP. Even though the CCP was too preoccupied with events in China to pay much attention to Southeast Asia, nonetheless, it played significant roles in their revolutionary struggles. Firstly the rapid expansion of the CCP provided a ready-made pool of cadres and agitators to replace those caught by the Special Branch. Secondly, conflicts between the CCP and the Kuomintang led to frequent social unrest that sent refugees fleeing to Southeast Asia. Finally, the CCP-liberated zones provided safe areas for the training and rearming of revolutionaries.

***

These larger international events framed the context of developments in Southeast Asia, or Nanyang as the region was called. By 1927, in keeping with the steady drift towards centralized autocratic control these various left-wing trade unions had come under the influence of an organization known as the 'Main' School, the existence of which was discovered after a raid on the Peng Min School in Kuala Lumpur. The

Special Branch initially thought that the name of the organization was the "Phang Man School". However, thorough investigations revealed the power behind the 'Main' School. In their "Review of communism in Malaya from 1925 to 1936" which was published as a supplement to the *Political Intelligence Journal No. 3* of 1937, the Branch noted that:

> By the end of 1927 the extremist elements of the KMT in China and Malaya reorganized on communist as opposed to nationalist lines. The 'Main' School became the South Seas (Nan Yang) Communist Party (NYCP) and the 'Middle School'—a nom de guerre also met with in documents—became the South Seas Communist Youth (NYCY). The entire organization was under the control of the China Communist Party Central Committee which in turn was governed by the Far Eastern Bureau, a Comintern organization in Shanghai.
>
> (Supplement to Journal No. 3, 1937)

The Branch had by now received information that the Far Eastern Bureau was directed by the Third International (the Comintern). It was the Comintern that directed the meeting of the Third Representative Conference of the South Seas Communist Party held in April 1930 that led to the founding of the Malayan Communist Party (MCP). Important things were clearly expected of this reorganized body as for a while the communist parties of both Siam and the NEI were attached to the MCP. Not only was the MCP to provide training and organization to these fellow parties but it was also tasked with the working out of an indigenous doctrine suitable for Southeast Asia:

> The main reason for this reorganization was to free the South Seas movement from the direct control of the China Communist Party which was making of it a Chinese movement.
>
> (Supplement to Journal No. 3, 1937)

The Comintern line presented at the meeting by its representative, Nguyen Ai Quoc, was that the colonial problem could only be resolved if the existing socio-political realities of the country were taken into consideration. Yet even Nguyen could not escape the irreconcilable difficulties of a party that was by now entirely under the control of Chinese elements. Although the meeting was advised to pay more attention to the Malays, with Nguyen telling the delegates:

> to study the Malay language and enlist Malay recruits as Communists not as Nationalists.
>
> (Yong, 1997, p. 130)

in the same speech, he gave his blessings to the Chinese leadership of the MCP.

Implicit within Nguyen's advice was the recognition that communism would not succeed unless it took account of local sentiments. The Malays were never brought in fully and the MCP remained a Chinese-based party. It is surely paradoxical and telling demonstration of communist hegemony that, having argued for the need to address local issues, the Comintern would, within a few years, reverse this position and insist that its line be followed totally. The blind obedience to Stalinist hierarchy destroyed the opportunity for the local communist parties to develop their own doctrines of revolution that would address the contradictions of their societies. In turn, once the CCP came to power, it would also demand the same rigid obedience to its doctrines. What would have happened if the MCP had achieved this goal of an indigenous communist ideology geared to the Southeast Asian landscape instead of the increasingly Chinese-based movement it became? Would the victories of the Vietminh have been repeated?

These are not just tantalizing questions for they showed that as early as 1930 some voices within the Comintern had the foresight to realize that an ethnically-based communist movement would not work. The success of the CCP could not be duplicated outside the specific historical conditions of the mainland. The true path of revolution needed to address historical specificity because the different pace of economic development determined the unique political situation of each country. Having recognized this it was then all the more a pity that the subsequent turn towards Stalinism led to insistence by Moscow that its doctrines be followed rigidly. When the CCP emerged triumphant in China they, in turn, ignored the unique historical experiences of the Southeast Asian countries and made repeated attempts to impose its Maoist vision upon these lands. It is interesting to conjecture whether the British had a hand in this foolishly blind adherence to an overriding doctrine. Since the British had planted Loi Teck as the secretary-general of the MCP, he would doubtless have influenced strategic and ideological directions. Did he push the MCP into a structure that was so openly Chinese chauvinist that it alienated significant portions of the population? Did he weaken their command and control structures by making them so unresponsive to events? Was the shift to an increasingly Chinese-based rhetoric and outlook on his advice? These are questions that the larger events which we have listed in a small way here are bound to raise.

The Special Branch was particularly keen to neutralize any attempts of communism evolving into an indigenous strand suitable to the conditions of the Malayan archipelago. Much of this was fought out in the complex arena of labour relations. It had been one of the key tenets of the Comintern that the subtext of any society, the force that determined its direction, was historical materialism. Labour was the ideal expression of this materialist historicity, the conditions of the working class brought into being that accounted for social realities. Both the Comintern and, for a while in its early years, the Chinese Communist Party subscribed to the view that the many different races and ethnic mix in Malaya could be unified through the theme of labour. In their view, once this is achieved an irresistible revolutionary energy would come into being that would compel the destruction of colonialism and its comprador politics. To the Branch labour agitation was thus a useful marker that could be used to identify pro-communist movements:

> The Malayan CY (Communist Youth) is identical with the China CY. It is perhaps more a purely labour movement than that in countries where the indiginous (sic) youth have formed labour or other associations, for labour *alone can be the nationalism, i.e. the uniting bond of the various nationalities of Malaya.*
>
> (Supplement No. 1, 1931: my emphasis)

The Comintern sought to convert all aspirations including nationalism into its own radical ideology. By disregarding nationalist or ethnic impulses the MCP weakened the base of its support. The Branch, however, knew that the matter had to be handled carefully as mass labour action involving the different races could easily turn into widespread discontent and revolt.

It was the view of the Special Branch that the MCP would only succeed if it could successfully evolve an indigenous political ideology that brought in all the other races. Bolshevism, Leninism, Stalinism (and later on, Maoist thinking) had to be modified and reinterpreted to meet the different historical and national circumstances. In Malaya the communists felt the disadvantages of the narrow appeal of their movement to the Chinese. Several attempts were made over the years to rewrite and revise the communist ideology. One such instance was through what became known as the "racial movement":

> Ever since 1928 the Malayan Communist Party has been trying through the medium of Chinese cultivators to graft the foreign plant of Communism upon the native soil of Malaya and has so far failed. Communism in Malaya still remains an almost entirely exotic growth, sponsored by aliens and subsidized by foreign money flourishing chiefly amongst Hailam Chinese, and whose comparatively feeble roots can be plucked out at any time by a drastic application of the banishment order.

> Moscow knows that if Communism is ever to take permanent root in Malaya and not remain merely a shallow growth among some sections of the immigrant population, fresh seed must take the place of the old barren methods of cultivation and to this end propaganda in simple and comprehensible Malay and with an appeal to the local Malay peasantry must be made available in large quantities before the Malayan field can ever bear the red harvest of Moscow. This is the meaning of the "racial movement in Malaya" upon which emphasis has been laid by the Party during the past three or four years.
>
> (Supplement No. 2 to PIJ, 1934)

The rhetorical flourish aside, this analysis identifies the central contradiction facing the MCP. The Comintern—and later China "Central"—continued to insist on sufficient control over ideological matters while paying lip service to the view that the local party must evolve its own theory. It is interesting to note that in this "race" figured prominently as a possible way out of the contradictions. In many ways this showed that communist discourse remained heir to the 19th century imperialist and scientific thinking. All these doctrines of which communism is no exception shared a common interest in forms of social Darwinism, "racial science" and eugenics.

The Comintern sent out mixed signals on this matter. It was loath to surrender control over the regional parties, yet it directed the MCP to resolve such a contradiction. In a significant document entitled "Letter from the Comintern Apparatus in Shanghai to the central committee of the Malayan Communist Party" dated 1 June 1934, the MCP was first criticized for its lack of progress on this issue and then counselled to adopt a:

> differentiated approach to the various national and industrial sectors of the masses.
>
> (Supplement No. 2, PIJ, 1935)

The need to adopt a "differentiated approach", that is to be aware of the multicultural textuality of Malayan life is further underlined at several places such as this direct reminder about:

> taking into account the peculiar national and social composition of the Malayan population in each region, centre, and enterprise ...
>
> (Supplement No. 2, PIJ, 1935)

However, the heavy-handed, bureaucratic approach of the Comintern repeatedly undermined such well-meaning advice. So despite the calls to accelerate the "training and promotion of Malay and Indian communists" (Supplement No. 2, PIJ, 1935) the local movement was never allowed to forget that the party line must be followed unquestioningly and that the "Leninist policy on the national question" (Supplement No. 2, PIJ, 1935) cannot be deviated from. This gives a hollow ring to all the exhortations to develop an indigenous point of view. There is a strong possibility that the Special Branch, given the chance, was doing all it can behind the scenes to ensure that these contradictions were not resolved and would remain a millstone around the necks of the communists.

The Special Branch was able to exploit these weaknesses because it often possessed precise and up to date knowledge of the intentions of the MCP. By the mid 1930s the Branch had not only an effective network of listening posts, informers and agents in place but had also penetrated the secrecy of the MCP. They would be expected to have used this to influence events, even to add on to the obvious mistakes of the MPC by encouraging them to adopt disastrous, short-sighted methods. They had inserted agents within the party. One of these, Loi Teck, rose to the highest post. As secretary-general of the MCP in 1939 he effectively guided the destiny and direction of the party. However, as nobody rises to such a high position overnight it would be reasonable to assume that Loi Teck had steadily worked his way up the senior ranks of the party. As a senior executive member he would have access to valuable and confidential information. Whether through Loi Teck or other similar agents in place, the Special Branch was throughout much of the decade in possession of a steady stream of high-grade and sensitive information belonging to the MCP.

However, with a highly successful penetration of the Malayan Communist Party, the Branch would have to grapple with a different dilemma. Apart from the perennial question of how much of the information should be used to cripple the MCP—to mount raids, arrests and disruptions—without jeopardizing the agent or agents, there was now the issue of 'control' over the MCP itself. By virtue of the success of the agent in gaining control of the leadership of the MCP, the other question arose as to how much should be allowed or tolerated by way of the MCP's underground growth in order to shore up the agent's credentials as a 'capable' leader without inadvertently creating a monster organization that the Branch could not neutralize in time. And yet, premature action or 'harvesting' of the intelligence access and control of the MCP through an agent like Loi Teck may simply cripple the organization temporarily, setting it back but not eradicating it. Was it not better then to keep the agent in place and manipulate the underground organization?

The British could not have succeeded in these plans without the support of a sophisticated and competent system of political evaluators and administrators. By the 1930s the war of espionage and counter-espionage was increasingly pitting systems and teamwork against one another. Here the Comintern was aided by its front organizations as well as specialized units such as the Glavsnoei Radzdivateinoie Oupravienie (GRU) established by Trotsky or the *hongse tewu* (Special Red Units) in China. Against them but sometimes working at cross purposes were the Special Branch in Malaya, the Public Security Bureau of the KMT, the *Services de Renseignments Politiques* in Indo-China and other agencies such as MI6 or the Dutch colonial police (or Research Organizations) in the Netherlands East Indies. The agency with the most efficient system won the day as it was now the system that enabled the effective deployment of agents or the running of covert operations.

The Special Branch was fortunate in the capable leaders that it had. These were able to identify the operational needs of the Branch as well as to create within a short time an appropriate system to address the key threats. The foundation laid by the exceptional David Petrie who went on to head MI5 was developed as we have seen first by G V Savi and then Rene Onraet. When Onraet became Inspector General of Police, A H Dickinson replaced him. All this while the Branch was known as the Criminal Intelligence Department which, despite its title did no essential criminal police work. In September 1933, the Special Branch officially replaced the Criminal Intelligence Department while the Criminal Investigation Department was from then tasked with looking after criminal matters. A H Dickinson became the first head of this Special Branch. A year later in November 1934, W L Wynne took over as Head of the Special Branch. He was succeeded by J P Pennefather-Evans who was in turn replaced by L F Knight just before the Second World War. With the exigencies of military operations, the Branch was then absorbed into the Malaya Security Service.

The structure of the Branch emphasized the specific areas of security threats to British Malaya. By studying its various sections we are provided with a fascinating window into the political thinking behind the realities of empire in the early days of the 20th century. By 1934, the basic establishment structure of the Branch was in place with key areas under the control of respective section heads. However, the Branch preferred to see its organization as a means to an end rather than an end in itself. It was always prepared to dismantle and reshape its sections. In 1935 the Branch underwent a significant change in these sections. As a result there were five main sections backed up by an Internal Administration unit which looked after such areas as the Central Registry, translation and secretarial work. The five sections were the Anti-Communist Section, the Japanese Section, the Security Section, the Aliens Section and the Political Section (in reality, the counter subversion). There were several other areas placed usually under one of the five main sections. For instance, Assistant Superintendent A H Sym's Anti-Communist Section supervised the Chinese section as part of its duties.

An important new development was the creation of the Security Section on 1 October 1935. A E G Blades was transferred from the Detective Bureau to head the new section. On paper the Security Section appeared very much like an inter-agency liaison unit:

> The Security Section, which works in close liaison with the newly appointed Services Defence Security Officer and the Intelligence Officers of the Three Fighting Services, undertakes enquiries and investigations in connection with the Local Defence Security measures.
>
> (Special Branch Report for the Year 1935)

In practice the new section was in charge of counter-espionage. In 1937, just two years later, it was already reported that:

> The two main functions of the Security Sub-Branch are:
> 1. Counter-espionage
> 2. Enquiries on behalf of the Fighting Services, undertaken in cooperation with the Surveillance Sub-Branch.
>
> (Special Branch report for the Year 1937)

We must not be misled into thinking that this section was merely a local defence unit concerned with guard duties and the security of the military installations. The title and description serve to conceal its counter-espionage duties that included the handling of covert agents.

The new Security Section confirms that by now the Branch was not a mere police unit dealing with political matters but a proper intelligence agency. This was also underlined in the change of name in 1933 when the Criminal Intelligence Department was renamed the Special Branch to differentiate it further from the Criminal Investigation Department. The new Security Section also pointed to the increasingly complex orientation of the Branch. Instead of arrests and seizures the Branch now dealt with long-term undercover operations that yielded high-grade intelligence rather than a series of arrests of suspects. The Branch's most spectacular success was its thorough knowledge and 'management' of the communist movement which they gained from active intelligence operations. In contrast its signal and obvious failing was the inability to read Japanese penetration in Malaya during this period. Although the Branch was fully aware of unhealthy Japanese intentions, lack of manpower and the demand of the communist threat meant that it could not give this area its full attention. It is, of course, one of the big 'ifs' of history as to what would have happened in 1941 had the British penetrated the Japanese in Malaya as thoroughly as they did the Malayan Communist Party.

The Branch itself was aware of this deficiency although:

> It has endeavoured with the limited means at its disposal, to keep itself informed of the Japanese aims and activities in the political and economic spheres generally throughout the world and particularly in the Far East, and at the same time it has attempted to obtain a better appreciation of the distribution and activities of Japanese residents in Malaya.
>
> (Special Branch Report for the Year 1935)

The resources needed for this intensive intelligence were simply not available. In addition, the Japanese threats were not regarded as the special purview of the Branch as there was a plethora of competing organizations including those from the military and navy. There were also MI5 and MI6, regarded as the senior services in matters of political espionage. For a while, until the arrival of Major Morgan, the Japanese section was under the charge of Chief Inspector Prithvi Chand who also looked after the Political Section when its head, Sardar Bahadur Balwant Singh, retired. The Political Section had by this time diminished substantially in importance as much of its most sensitive work was taken over by the Anti-Communist and the newly-formed Security sections. Similarly, the Aliens section, which monitored the presence of visitors and arrivals in the port, was involved in the more routine aspects of security work.

The posture of the Special Branch clearly indicated that during this period it was focused on anti-Communist and counter-espionage activities. In fact these two areas were intricately linked since most of the communist activities in British Malaya were controlled by outside agencies, either through the Chinese Communist Party or the Comintern. The task of containing these threats had to assume an international, overseas dimension. In addition it had become obvious that the most suitable response was not merely through the arrest of suspects and seizure of documents but through high-grade intelligence that allowed the selective removal of key personnel from the movement. The knowledge of intentions, motives and plans had taken on critical importance in this fight. The Special Branch had thus to reorientate its approach and its manpower deployment.

The establishment strength of the Branch remained modest despite the new areas of its responsibilities. In 1935 the approved establishment of the Branch was:

Superintendent	1
Assistant Superintendent	2
Supernumerary	1
Inspectors	2
Asiatic Inspectors	6
Detectives	13

The detectives attached to the Special Branch were different from those with the Detective Bureau or the Criminal Investigation Department. It was, however, not easy to recruit people of the right temperament and quality for the Special Branch. If Onraet and Wynne were anything to go by, the candidates had to be men of methodical patience, true scholars and possess a deep intellectual curiosity of the world they were to police. Onraet's *Police Story* is a well-written account of his work while Wynne's standard book on the triads is a masterly piece of scholarship.

By 1937, the growing importance of the Branch was reflected in the allocation of more manpower as well as the enhanced status of its officers. In 1937, the establishment strength had grown to 54 officers although the actual strength was only 49 officers. The Director of the Branch was upgraded to the rank of Commissioner and the four deputies were pegged at the rank of Assistant Commissioners under him. Stringent selection continued to ensure performance with high morale and almost no resignations.

The 1930s was one of the high points of the Branch. Benefiting from its successful penetration of the Malayan Communist Party, the Branch came into a steady stream of highly valuable information about the structure and directions of the Malayan Communist Party. Through this the Branch was able to selectively weed out the really dangerous elements even as it became aware of the origins and development of the Party. The success came largely because the Branch had become convinced by the closing years of the 1920s that in the face of deliberate, sustained subversion more superior organization would win the day. The Branch understood that the Comintern was bringing to the area not just ideology but methods of agitation and mass mobilization which would have to be countered. As an indication of this a dangerous nexus had developed between the schools and the trade unions. The schools provided not just revolutionary propaganda but also tactics of agitation against the government. The trade unions provided the means for mass mobilization and agitation. The Branch could no longer just react but had to seize the initiative at each turn before damage could be done.

The emerging security scenario was not simply about military control but a struggle for the hearts and minds of the people. This meant the allegiance the people were prepared to give or be co-opted into, the thinking they were willing to have their lives shaped by as well as the kinds of behaviour and livelihood they were prepared to be governed by. Success, the Branch recognized, would lie not just in politics or economics but the intellectual and cultural impulses that stimulated existence. Both the communists and the British were competing to seize the centre stage upon which the ideological narrative would be acted out. The one who gained control of the ideas, the beliefs and the intellectual outlook of the Malayan people would triumph. To achieve this required strategic vision and intelligent organization:

> Subversive agitation connected with the Hailam night schools has become continuous since 1925. In 1926 the Hailam night schools were definitely recognized as a part of the labour trade union organization, which was then known as the Nanyang General Union, a communist body. The effect of this teaching was very noticeable at demonstrations organized by the Labour Unions whether they used the cloak of KMT and anti-Japanese boycott, or came into the open as communists on May Day and other similar anniversaries. The young demonstrators were by far the best disciplined, most militant and most honestly convinced of the righteousness of their cause. In 1928/29 the history of individuals arrested for subversive acts showed that those who had been CY members were the most capable, enthusiastic and unrelenting. *Their training had given them method and the faculty for organization.*
>
> (Supplement to Journal, 1931: my *emphasis*)

This objective account of the disciplined belief and dedication of the communist youth wing showed that the Branch was prepared to give credit where it was due. The MCP was rapidly developing the knowledge and strategies that allowed it to train cadres in the manipulation of mass movements. Threats came not from individuals but from well-planned and well-thought-out actions of organized bodies dedicated to subversive ideals. Violence was not just a blunt instrument of random impulse but a means to a political end as the shoemakers' strike had demonstrated so cogently.

Increasingly, Special Branch work required the strategic depth and vision of a well-played chess game. Foresight and the careful ability to think ahead were now the key ingredients of its work. Increasingly the Branch itself used these terms to describe the communists. In an incident at Tangkak, Johore, on 29 January 1931, rioting broke out soon after the police had halted a demonstration. In its report, the Branch stressed the method and organization that the communists displayed:

> This demonstration shows method and organization; the Police Station wire to Johore was cut, and is known to have been part of a scheme of demonstrations for the Johore district ... Such demonstrations may be expected in townlets where authority is only represented by a few native policemen.
>
> (item 13, Journal 1931)

Faced with such an orchestrated challenge the Branch could no longer react simply to each provocation. To carry on doing this would be to lose the strategic initiative and allow the enemy to undercut the Government's authority and seize control of the ground by default. Moreover, the communists showed, as the Kreta Ayer riots and the trolley bus boycott, that they were ever ready to aggravate any provocation. The Branch had to retain the initiative at every step, ensuring control of the overall situation. This was only possible if up-to-the-minute and detailed intelligence of intentions and motives were on hand. It was useless arresting perpetrators after an event had occurred as the political and propaganda points had already been made. Moreover, as long as the guiding hand was located overseas it was almost impossible to eradicate the source. The Branch was confronted with a situational hydra of sorts. There were always new recruits ready to take advantage of the unrest. The game had to be played differently under the circumstances. Fire-fighting was good but it was far better to snuff out the sparks of resistance before they could take hold and spread. The strategic dimension of the threats, rather than their local, tactical, irritation mattered. It was preferable strategically to penetrate the enemy deeply and gain sustained access than to close down an underground cell or cluster of cells as and when discovered. The overall play of the game and its final end-game became the object rather than the episodes and segments of the play.

This strategy saw perhaps one greatest intelligence coup of the British in Malaya when the Branch recruited and inserted Loi Teck into the Malayan Communist Party. The British agent managed to gain access to the very nerve centre of the Party becoming its secretary-general in 1939. In that position he was not only a steady and reliable source of sensitive information to the British but also did much damage to the communist movement by decimating its key cadres. In addition, Loi Teck was not the only agent the British had in place. Documents available from the 1930s suggested that the Special Branch was routinely reading confidential communist documents and most aware of its courses of action.

Special Branch action against the communists became precise and focused during this period. The Branch knew with unerring accuracy who it should detain and the places it should raid. In February 1932 effective intelligence led the Branch to the arrest of:

> 105 leading communists in Singapore (who) were detained, identified, and after prolonged enquiries, banished.
>
> (Supplement No. 9, PIJ, 1933)

While the Branch had the quiet satisfaction of reporting its crippling of the various organs of the communist party the success came from hard work behind the scenes:

> This action entirely disorganized the Communist Party, Communist Youth and Red Labour Union; Its effects are still being felt.
>
> (Supplement No. 9, PIJ, 1933)

With one fell swoop a number of key cadres and activists were arrested and served with banishment orders. It was not just the number that was arrested that mattered. In the 1930s, six secretary-generals of the MCP (an astonishingly high number that could not have done any good to the Party's ability to organize any revolt) were arrested and five banished. So the culling, if we may so describe it, of the party was carried out with such ruthless efficiency that the Special Branch knew almost who exactly to go for! In fact, figures revealed that mass arrests of suspects had by this time become the exception rather than the rule. Significantly, arrests declined steadily while the percentage of convictions (the yield of the raids) remained constant, suggesting the greater efficiency of the Branch. The following table provides figures for raids and the number of persons arrested by the Special Branch from 1931 to 1935:

	1935		1934		1933		1932		1931	
	Total Raids	Number Arrested	Total Raids	Number Arrested	Total Raids	Number Arrested	Total Raids	Number Arrested	Total Raids	Number Arrested
Singapore	12	7	33	13	95	78	118	84	174	44
Penang	26	2	33	4	34	8	70	12	14	11
Malacca	4	1	5	2	8	2	60	–	–	–
Total	42	10	71	19	137	88	248	96	218	55

While the number of raids fell, and particularly so in 1934 and 1935, the number of arrests as a percentage remained the same and actually went up for Singapore where the Special Branch efforts were most concentrated. Rather than indiscriminate raids the Branch focused its efforts on key meetings where it could be certain of netting the most cadres.

A similar pattern is revealed when we look at the actual number of convictions for those charged in court. The numbers show that those produced in court were invariably convicted, given the weight of evidence against them.

	Total detained	Released after inquiry	Charged in court	Convicted in court
Singapore				
1935	35	17	17	13
1934	164	118	31	26
1933	661	411	48	48
1932	462	216	213	189
Penang				
1935	13	–	13	4
1934	17	7	7	5
1933	36	13	21	2
1932	54	20	34	24
Malacca				
1935	12	4	7	6
1934	17	5	2	2
1933	132	62	55	51
1932	101	61	28	14

Even as the number of arrests went up, the percentage of convictions also improved. These two sets of figures provide convincing evidence of the efficiency of the Special Branch in these crucial years. This efficiency extends throughout the later half of the 1930s. In 1937 the Branch reported that "the number of raids carried out continues to decrease year by year, but the number of raids yielding results has remained fairly constant since 1934" (Special Branch Report for the Year 1934).

More significant is the number of postal censorships to China. Censorship of mail, which began in 1928 (when events in China had taken a turn for the worse), increased steadily until 1931 when it began to drop. Once again the pattern is repeated. From mass censorship the Branch refined its system to checking only the mail of certain categories of people.

Postal Censorship

Year	1935	1934	1933	1932	1931	1930	1929	1928
Number of articles inspected	350	459	522	1,260	1,465	896	345	*

(*Censorship began. No records kept.)

It should be emphasized that while raids, court charges and censorship all go to show that the Branch had by 1933 a clear picture of who and where the threats were, the level of communist activity and attempted subversion continued to remain high. It was that the Special Branch had become more discriminating.

There are other signs that the British had penetrated the MCP. In a measured, understated, comment in "Supplement No. 1" to the *Political Intelligence Journal* of March 1935, the Special Branch took its readers through the intricacies of "A Statement of the Malayan Communist Party Accounts". The Branch had been aware for some time that since 1933 the Comintern in Shanghai had agreed to pay a regular subsidy of $300.00 in gold a month to the MCP. All in all $4,000.00 had been received to date. However, with the arrests of the Comintern members in Shanghai and related developments in Malaya the subsidy was no longer available by the beginning of 1935. The Branch was aware that frantic efforts had been made to re-establish contact with the Central in Shanghai so that the subsidy as well as instructions from Moscow could be restored. However, the Branch did not expect this to take place till at least May that year. In the meantime the Branch had obtained the financial accounts of the MCP for the period of November 1933 to September 1934. This was a major triumph for the Branch as the accounts detailed not just the monies received but to whom these were being paid.

The identities of executive members, paid agents, sympathizers and front companies were now revealed to the interested eyes of the Branch. The list also included companies (printing presses, unions such as the Malayan General Labour Union and aid associations) as well as individuals (party members, executive committee members, runners and sympathizers). This was a major coup for the Branch as at one blow the activities of the MCP were now fully known. There were names, and confirmation of names. The accounts provided a comprehensive map of the clandestine activities of the MCP between November 1933 and September 1934. Even beyond this period the clues thrown up by this document allowed the Branch to continue its operations to unearth the communists underground.

***

There is evidence that the MCP had no knowledge that their secrets had been revealed. The Branch had referred to its access to the accounts as being in "temporary possession". This probably meant that the document had been lifted without knowledge of the MCP:

> In December 1934, the Special Branch was fortunate to obtain temporary possession of the original accounts of the Malayan Communist Party, covering the payment of this subsidy and its disbursement between November 1933 and September 1934.
>
> (Supplement No. 1, PIJ, 1935)

After being photographed the accounts were returned. The MCP thus remained in the dark, unable even to take any defensive measures.

Another piece of information the Special Branch came into and which they commented on made it quite clear that they had an agent in place who was feeding them with high-grade intelligence. On 5 October (although the information was not released till April 1935) the Branch obtained confidential Comintern documents that implicated Moscow in the revolutionary activities in Southeast Asia:

> A typewritten document in English together with a draft manuscript translation thereof in Chinese came into the temporary possession of the Special Branch on 5 October 1934. Both documents have been photographed.

The original in English is believed from a reliable source to have been brought to Singapore by To Mong at the time of his return from Shanghai in August 1934, with funds for the Malayan Communist Party.

The document is of importance as it affords proof of Moscow's intention in this part of the world and is unique in that it is in English and is clearly the work of a European (or rather from its style, an American) communist directive brain, applied exclusively to an analysis from the Communist standpoint.

(Supplement No. 2, PIJ, 1935)

Once again the language confirmed that the document had been lifted, photographed and then returned. The remarks also suggested it was likely that an agent was in place who could reliably confirm the circumstances surrounding the letter. Those running the Branch were no longer interested in the momentary triumph of simple grab and arrest operations, but were more concerned with deep covert operations that emphasized information over routine arrests. The timing of these two highly confidential documents the Branch came into at this time indicated strongly that it had a source (or a number of sources) within the MCP which was providing it with information.

More was to come. Supplement No. 5 to the *Political Intelligence Journal* in 1935 provided "An Analysis of the Numerical Strength of the Malayan Communist Party and Subsidiary Organizations for the Years 1931–1934". This was strong proof indeed of how closely the Branch had its fingers on the pulse of the communists. The Branch was skeptical of the figures, especially those of the subsidiary organizations. It felt that many of the so-called members had been duped into joining a front organization of the MCP. Still, it was reassuring to see that the MCP was relatively small: a total of 12,716 members. In 1933, the Party proper had only 709 Chinese members, 9 Malay members and 4 Indian members. The racial predominance of the Chinese was even more pronounced in the Malayan Communist Youth which reported a membership of 209 Chinese, 1 Malay and no Indians. The "racial movement" upon which the Comintern and the MCP had pinned their hopes to bring about an indigenous version of the ideology was not getting anywhere if these figures were anything to go by. The Special Branch had little to fear of a pan-Malayan communist movement emerging, at least not for the time being.

So complete was the Branch's knowledge and penetration of the MCP at this time that the security forces were almost like reading over the shoulders of their opponents. Just days after the MCP launched its "Purification Campaign" on 16 May 1935 the Branch had obtained a copy of the form that the Party members were required to fill out with all their personal details. We know though that in 1939 the Special Branch "came into possession" of a report as well as details of the biography of all the members of the Working Committee of the Perak Communist Party. The MCP had also insisted that each member provide a signed account of his anti-government activities. The admission of seditious activities was in each instance enhanced by the fact that it was handwritten:

> The Special Branch has recently come into possession of a 45-page report submitted by the Perak Communist Party Central. This report dealt with various political and economic questions affecting the Perak Government, and gave a full and comprehensive account of the personnel and future plans of the Perak Communist Party. Each member of the Working Committee had submitted in his own handwriting details of his own history and activities in connection with communism.
>
> (item 9, PIJ, 1939)

It is tempting to imagine an agent provocateur instigating such a campaign of signed confessions. In fact it is almost certain that Loi Teck, by now secretary-general of the MCP, would have known and given his approval for such action.

The success of the Special Branch was not the result of arbitrary good fortune but the consequence of careful and methodical work. The arrests of key agitators, interceptions of documents and the penetration of the MCP seen from a historical perspective were part of a carefully-orchestrated strategy. The instruments ensuring the success can be traced back to the 1920s when Petrie, Savi and Onraet laid the foundation of the Branch and its work. The more immediate impulse of these events came from arrests made in 1931. Nothing shows more clearly the long-drawn-out and patient work of the Special Branch than the closely-linked but too easily overlooked series of events that stretched through these years. The Branch worked very much like an artist with his palette. Imaginative genius allowed the artist to identify patterns and forms. Pure scientific reasoning with its blind insistence on mechanistic routines was inadequate, more often a deterrent than an aid, to the acquisition of such vision. The pieces of knowledge a Special Branch officer came into were often substantial but meaningless in themselves unless he discovered the pattern they were part of. From then on careful checking and gathering of evidence would confirm or deny his perspective. This was the case with events that happened in 1931.

On 27 April 1931 Serge Lefranc, a French businessman arrived in Singapore from Hong Kong on the *S.S. President Adams*. He had good credentials, claimed to represent Establissments Cidlo, a firm manufacturing steel products, and soon set up business at No. 32 Winchester House in a respectable business quarter. Lefranc did legitimate business, selling his steel products to various interested parties. But it was all a cover-up for his real activities: organizing and stimulating the Malayan Communist Party. In due course when Lefranc was arrested the French Police could not trace the firm. Lefranc was actually an agent of the Comintern reporting to Shanghai. He had been sent to Southeast Asia on the order of the Far Eastern Bureau to promote the cause of the new Malayan Communist Party. He was an agent carrying out the orders of the Moscow Politburo to advance its plans for revolution in Southeast Asia.

Despite Lefranc's elaborate efforts to conceal his movements, enough evidence had been gathered over a month's surveillance to convince the Branch of his:

> connection not only with the local communist movement, but what was of international importance, his direct connection with the Pan-Pacific Trade Union Secretariat in Shanghai.
>
> (Supplement No. 4, PIJ, 1932)

The PPTUS was already known as a centre controlling Comintern activities in the East. It was based in Shanghai and was the directive agency of the Profintern, the name given to the International of the Red Trade Unions. More to the point, the Profintern was directly under the Comintern and was tasked with the organization and preparation of labour and wage earners for the coming revolution. The Branch felt that at this stage the Comintern was not only a *subversive* but also an *espionage* agency as it was a front for Moscow:

> The Komintern (sic) is the council of the Third International, which in turn is directed by a committee known as the IKKI. This committee numbers among its members several members of the Polit Bureau, the organization of 9 or 10 men who jointly form the head of the Government of Russia.
>
> (Supplement No. 4, PIJ, 1932)

The PPTUS with this clear link to planned and directed operations. In fact, one of Lefranc's specific tasks was to get in touch with Abdul Rahman Wadoed (also known as Bassa), a Javanese intellectual who was trying to form an All-Malay communist party that would complement the existing Chinese-dominated Malayan Communist Party. There is evidence to suggest that the Branch even managed to manoeuvre Inspector Prithvi Chand, one of its officers operating undercover to work for Lefranc!

The presence of Lefranc and Foo Thai Kheng, who was arrested in Lefranc's company, indicated outside forces at work. At the founding of the MCP it was Foo Thai Kheng who translated Nguyen Ai Quoc's English speech into Chinese. Subsequent events would show that the trail not only led to Lefranc but to his controller in Shanghai as well as to the Southern Bureau of the Chinese Communist Party operating out of Hong Kong, and to Nguyen Ai Quoc (Ho Chih Minh) of the Vietnamese Communist Party. As the Branch noted:

> The power of the PPTUS was therefore enormous; it had at its disposal almost unlimited funds. The presence in the Straits Settlements of an agent of the PPTUS entrusted with the organization of communism in Malaya, Siam, Burma and the Netherlands East Indies constituted a danger of the first magnitude.
>
> (Supplement No. 4, PIJ 1932)

The strong phrasing itself was quite unusual, reflecting the alarm and concern felt by the Branch at this unwelcome development.

On 1 June 1931 the Branch arrested Lefranc (sometimes written Lefranca) while he was having a meeting with Foo Thai Kheng and Wong Muk Han at his office in Winchester House. Foo Thai Kheng and Wong Muk Han were both standing members of the Malayan Communist Party. In addition Wong, a member of the PPTUS was in Singapore illegally, having been banished in 1929 for subversion. It turned out that Lefranc's real name was Joseph Ducroux (a.k.a. Dupont). Ducroux was born in 1904 at Bellville-sur-Saone, Department of the Rhone, the son of Joseph Ducroux and Claudine Sautier. For a while he studied at Bristol and then London. Since 1923 he had been a militant communist and a member of the *Federation de la Seine des jeunesse Communistes*. He was thought to be one of those who introduced the cell system to the French Communist Party.

As is usual, Ducroux's Comintern controllers moved him around constantly to evade attention. His revolutionary career reads like an adventure story. In 1925 after a short journey to England he surfaced as an interpreter of the Thomas Cook Agency in Marseilles. While there he also used the name Dupont to establish and to teach at a Leninist school as well as write a regular column for the Young Communist

International. By this time Dupont was already deeply involved in anti-imperialist and colonial agitation. He was suspected to be involved in the murder of Sir Lee Stack by the revolutionary movement in Egypt and was known to have helped M N Roy with the smuggling of subversive literature into India. Moving further eastwards, Ducroux next turned up in Shanghai where he worked for the firm Chapeau Freres. He was also believed to have acted as secretary to J H Dolsen, the radical American journalist who was also a member of the Pan-Pacific Trade Union Secretariat.

Given new instructions to motivate and reform the communist movement in Southeast Asia, Ducroux took a characteristically tortuous and roundabout route, hoping this would throw the authorities off guard. In 1930 he returned to France where he applied for a new passport. However, his application for a British visa to Colombo was rejected. This should have alerted Ducroux to the fact that the Special Branch was already on to him. However, notwithstanding this, Ducroux obtained another passport under the name Serge Lefranc and the necessary visa for Southeast Asia. Once again taking a circuitous route, Ducroux (or by now Lefranc) reached Shanghai in 1930 by the Trans-Siberian railway. No doubt the journey through Berlin and Moscow would also have given his controllers time to brief the new representative to the Far Eastern colonies of the Third International.

The ring was already closing around the spy. In Shanghai Ducroux's residence at the Palace Hotel and his PO Box (1518) which he used for correspondence was already under surveillance. It was in Shanghai that he received instructions from the PPTUS and, in particular his controller, Hilaire Noulens, about his mission in Southeast Asia. Ducroux spent much of March travelling to Saigon, Hanoi and Campha. Nguyen Ai Quoc who was himself being watched by the French Surete wrote to the communist Central in Indo-China about Ducroux's visit. Unknown to Ducroux, his travels in French Indo-China were already closely monitored by the British and French intelligence services.

The arrest of Ducroux and his two Chinese compatriots on 1 June was therefore not accidental. Since the middle of May Ducroux had been under intensive surveillance. The Special Branch had even managed to plant one of its own officers, Prithvi Chand, as a clerk in Ducroux's office! The Branch's expectations that the Comintern representative would lead them to other hitherto undiscovered plots were well founded. The arrest of one of Ducroux's associates, Foo Thai Kheng, led to the seizure of the MCP's printing presses as well as a number of documents. In follow-up raids, the Branch netted a number of other prominent local communist agitators. All in all 14 others were picked up.

Next to Ducroux, Foo Thai Kheng (a.k.a. Fu Ta Ching) was the most important person to be detained. Foo was a member of the Chinese Communist Party who had been sent to organize the Nanyang Communist Party in the 1920s. Together with Nguyen Ai Quoc he was thought to have been behind the founding of the Siam Communist Party. Foo was also thought to have worked with Tan Malaka in the fomenting of Indonesian unrest. Foo was certainly one of the key inspirations behind the founding of the MCP. In comparison Wong Muk Han was relatively junior, having "merely" been banished by Onraet for running a bomb-making factory in Balestier Road. However, his evading a banishment order got him the most severe punishment!

In his memoirs, Onraet sums up the key tasks that Ducroux was expected to carry out in Singapore:

> His purely local activities included a thorough survey of the Malayan position and the establishment of direct communication with the PPTUS in Shanghai, the reorganization of Red Labour Unions, the payment of subsidies to the Malayan Communist Party, to the Malayan Trade Unions and the Malayan Communist Youth, and finally, the proper use of 50,000 dollars (gold) set aside by the PPTUS for work in Malaya and Burma to enrol the native element.
>
> (Onraet, n.d., p. 113)

Despite the amount of information that the Branch had on him, Ducroux could only be charged under the Societies Ordinance Act. The charges against him were for:

1. being in possession of seditious literature,
2. assisting in the management of an unlawful society, to wit, the Malayan Communist Party, and
3. using as genuine a false passport.

Sentenced to 18 months' imprisonment, Ducroux was last heard of in French Indo-China where he once again got into trouble with the authorities. He was jailed for using false documents before disappearing into the mists of history.

The Special Branch was rightly furious that the legal authorities did not treat such attempts at subversion with sufficient seriousness. Unfortunately this is often all too true. The law did not impose sufficient punishment for subversion. The authorities were often quicker and more willing to react to crimes and public disturbances. Thus, murders, gunfights, robberies and riots elicited a readier and more immediate reaction than espionage. The Special Branch was also hampered by the very nature of its work where success was often measured in terms of prevention rather than arrests. For instance, it was better for Ducroux to be arrested **before** he committed any offence than to nab him **after** he had done damage. Of course after the damage had been done the perpetrator becomes that much more obvious and few would deny the need to punish him severely! However, security services exist precisely to deter such actions, which if allowed, often have consequences far in excess of their immediate harm.

Comparing Ducroux's rather light punishment with the severe justice meted out to his compatriot, Hilaire Noulens in China, Onraet wrote with some obvious bitterness:

> Serge Lefranc and his Malayan confederates were more fortunate as they profited by the stubborn and almost childish unwillingness of some men to take these subversive activities seriously. At the time of his trial it would have been impossible to disclose most of what has been written in these pages; but as there was ample proof of his connection with an unregistered and therefore an unlawful society he, the two Chinese arrested with him and fourteen others mopped up in the police raids that followed were charged in open court as being members of an unlawful society.
>
> (Onraet, n.d. p. 114)

Onraet's view was that the existing laws were grossly inadequate for the prevention of subversion. Most of the existing statutes dealt with criminal procedures and were unsuitable to the prosecution of subversion and espionage cases. Often the hands of the Branch itself were tied since they could not disclose their sources without compromising their safety.

Ducroux's dubious claim to fame lies as much in his arrest as a blunder that led the security services to his controller in Shanghai. In the process the security services uncovered the operations of the Far Eastern Bureau of the Comintern. Ducroux had, in fact, been very careless. Confident in his disguise as a respectable businessman and certain that his encryption was safe, he had attempted to contact Shanghai through a letter. As postal censorship of letters to China had been implemented since 1928 it was not surprising that the Branch intercepted and read his letter.

Ducroux had used a code of five-digit number groups to encrypt his letter. In itself this was not a very wise thing to do as the numerical codings invariably suggested some sort of secret transmission going on. The Branch managed to decipher most of what he was trying to conceal. In his letter Ducroux informed Shanghai that the censorship of telegrams in Singapore had made communication almost impossible. He also complained about the shortage of adequate personnel that made the reformation of the MCP a harder task. Providing details of his progress, Ducroux wrote:

Dear Sir,

Comrade W*ong Muk Han* says that he has been sent here by 39016 48395 48727* to collect information and that, only for a limited period of time—two to three months at the most—he is to return to *Shanghai*. Please inform me whether this is correct or not. If it is a fact, it will be necessary to send some one to replace him. In any case, it is clear that I cannot let him go before his relief arrives, because it is impossible for us to accomplish all that has to be done without some one to devote himself particularly to the *Trade Union Movement (Profintern)* in all these countries. Will you discuss this question with Mr Jack[1] and give me an early reply?

Can you give me some information *about the censorship of telegrams in China* and what must be done in these circumstances? We are in progress of organizing the *Singapore Bureau* which will be composed of three, *one foreign representative of Profintern* and two *Chinese members of the Chinese Communist Party*. In all the measures which we have already undertaken and which I have communicated to you we try to establish *good connections* with *Java* which is indeed difficult on account of the lack of qualified personnel and the almost total absence of information about the situation of XX 26575* activities.

Yours sincerely

(item 50, Journal, 1931)

(*Not deciphered. The words in italics have been deciphered from five-digit number groups.)

In the same way as it intercepted letters the Special Branch successfully interdicted the couriers and broke the links between the local MCP and their foreign controllers. Agents were forced to resort to the postal system because the steady pressure of the Branch had broken off the usual links. However, the carelessness evinced by Ducroux and a number of agents showed how the Special Branch had succeeded in concealing the methods it was using against the communists. These subversives and spies were often unaware of the efficiency or competition of the Branch until they were caught.

Having broken the code and read its contents, the Branch alerted the Shanghai Municipal Police to mount the necessary surveillance on its destination, a PO Box 206[2]. Their patience was rewarded when Ducroux's controller, Hilaire Noulens, collected the letter in due course. The Shanghai Special Branch followed Noulens to his home at 235 Szechuan Road and subsequently to his office at 30C Central Arcade (49 Nanking Road). On 15 June 1931 the Shanghai Municipal Police arrested Hilaire (Hillyer) Noulens on charges of espionage and subversion.

Hilaire Noulens operating under his cover as a Professor of the French and German languages was actually the controller for the Comintern's Far Eastern Bureau in Shanghai. He was also directing the operations of the PPTUS for Moscow Central that was used to channel labour agitators to Southeast Asian countries. Noulens had arrived in China on 19 March 1930 and assumed his front soon after as a teacher of languages. At his office at the Central Arcade the police search turned up three steel boxes that contained the archives of the PPTUS and the Far Eastern Bureau of the Comintern. The information was so sensitive that it crippled the Far Eastern Bureau for the next few years. The police also detained Mrs Noulens and other associates in a series of follow-up raids.

Noulens (and, to a certain extent, Ducroux) underlined the international dimension of the communist conspiracy. The fronts they employed showed the extent the Comintern was willing to go in order that its top agents were allowed to operate in safety. Each agent was furnished with a cover story (a "legend", as some intelligence agencies describe such an operation) that explained their lives, occupations and interests. The British may have taken a leaf out of the Comintern's book, creating an elaborate 'legend' for their agent, Loi Teck. The low-level Annamite communist was reinvented and assumed all the glory of an international emissary of the Comintern.

Returning to events in Shanghai it was soon shown that Noulens was indeed a man of many faces and disguises. He and his wife were known variously as Ruegg, Vandercruyssen, Motte, Beuret or Beret and Herbet. For a while even the French police thought that he was actually Paul Ruegg (or Rugg) born in Zurich on 30 March 1898. Noulens had come to the notice of the police for the first time in Basel in 1922 when he surfaced as a Central Committee member of the Swiss Communist Party. As was usual with spies like him, Noulens disappeared for a while to reappear in Brussels in December

1929. He had acquired a Belgian passport under the name of Ruegg then.

From Brussels, Noulens went on a characteristically long and roundabout journey designed to throw his pursuers off his trail. He was known to have visited Berlin, Moscow and the Balkans before reaching China via Manchuria. Not surprisingly it turned out Noulens was actually:

> a Ukrainian NKVD agent named Luft who had served as a Balkan trade unions specialist in the Soviet Embassy in Vienna between 1925 and 1929.
> (Wakeman Jr, 1995, p. 149)

While in Vienna he met his wife who was at that time serving as a secretary to the Soviet Embassy in Rome.

Noulens protested his innocence vigorously, challenging the right of the Chinese courts to charge him with espionage. Brought before the Chinese court in the International Settlement on 19 June 1931 he claimed first Belgian and then Swiss citizenship, arguing that the Chinese had no jurisdiction over either a Belgian or Swiss citizen. However, the Belgian Consul General and the Swiss Consul General rejected his claims and refused to extend their help. Throughout this, the Soviet Embassy kept a studied silence, preferring to operate through a law firm, that frequently acted for Soviet interests.

In the meantime the Comintern sought to exert international pressure on the Chinese. Noulens' trial soon assumed something of the status of a *cause celebre* through the orchestration of various sympathizers. In Europe a Noulens Defense Committee which included Henri Barbusse, Victor Margueritte and Jacques Sadoul took the lead in trying to secure his freedom. Demonstrations were held in places as far as Sydney and America. In China itself the campaign attracted the support of Edgar Snow, Agnes Smedley, Harold Isaacs, Theo Thackeray and even Soong Ching Ling, Sun Yat Sen's widow. Despite these voices pleading on their behalf, the Noulens were committed to trial at the Jiangsu High Court in Nanjing. They were sentenced to capital punishment in July although Chiang Kai Shek later commuted their capital punishment to life imprisonment. The Noulens were freed when the Japanese occupied Nanjing. After a short presence in Shanghai they disappeared. Some reports conjectured that they were sent to the Gulag since Moscow Central did not take kindly to failures.

The arrests of Noulens and his fellow conspirators provided the security services a rich harvest of incriminating documents. These were circulated and shared among the interested agencies: the British, the

Chinese and the French, with severe consequences for the communists. In particular, the efforts of the PPTUS and the Comintern to use Shanghai to penetrate and direct operations in Nanyang (the South Seas or Southeast Asia) were crippled. Surveillance on Ducroux that blew the cover of Noulens and the Far Eastern Bureau in Shanghai paid off handsomely, buying at least half a decade's time for the Special Branch. More importantly, it alerted the Special Branch to the long-term intentions of the Comintern. For the Branch, it was the documents and the insights they yielded that were of greater value than mere arrests. The information were the real treasures of the case, exposing the secret intentions of the Comintern giving the Branch a competitive edge in their counter-espionage work.

In July that year, the Branch received a report from the Shanghai Municipal Police underlining the significance of this case:

> The listing and analysing of the archives of the Pan-Pacific Trade Union Secretariat and other papers and articles found in the various addresses used by Mr and Mrs Noulens alias Vandercruyssen, alias Motte, alias Beuret, was completed during the month. There were altogether two hundred and eleven documents and one thousand and eighty-one other books and papers. Of the documents, which were in English, French, German, Russian, Japanese and Chinese, seventy-three deal principally with 'red' revolutionary activities in China, eighteen with similar work in Japan, four with Korea, one with Formosa, fourteen with the Philippine Islands, fourteen with Indo-China, ten with the Straits Settlements and India and one with Indonesia. Some of the documents contain details of the amount spent monthly by the organization and the manner in which it was disbursed. The investigation of the case shows that Mr and Mrs Vandercruyssen had seven different aliases, five different Post Boxes, four different telegraphic addresses and besides having $50,000 deposited in seven different Chinese banks, were in possession of large sums of cash in foreign currencies. The case against them which is being tried at the Shanghai Special District Court, was on remand at the end of the month.
>
> (item 61, PIJ, 1931)

The Ducroux-Noulens network was neither an amateurish set-up nor a small-scale operation. The Shanghai police alone seized 25,000 copies of 'red' books, pamphlets and handbills as a result of the case. Together with other leaflets the haul amounted to 83,984 articles in Shanghai alone. The large amount of cash, number of secret addresses and comprehensive details of various efforts at infiltration show skilful planning, careful method as well as huge resources at work.

Following leads found in Noulens' documents, the Hong Kong Special Branch arrested Nguyen Ai Quoc on 6 July 1931. The Malayan Special Branch had been after Nguyen since 1939 when they learnt that he was at the founding of the Malayan Communist Party in Johore, Investigations revealed that Nguyen was a senior Comintern member as well as the Chairman of the Indo-Chinese Communist Party. But he was, on the relatively lax attitude of the law, sentenced to only two years' imprisonment.

All these developments confirmed that a large spy ring was at work in Shanghai with its activities covering East and Southeast Asia. The documents also revealed the presence of a Dutch East Indies Bureau that oversaw the re-establishing of the PKI (East Indian Communist Party), maintained the necessary connections with the PPTUS as well as worked together with the Malayan Communist Party. The Comintern was deploying its pieces, treating Southeast Asia as a single chessboard as far as its strategy was concerned:

> From the documents seized the following information was obtained relative to the projected movements and activities of Javanese communists:
>
> TAN MALAKA   was to go from Amoy to Rangoon to work in Burma.
>
> ALIMIN @ DIRDJA   was to follow Tan Malaka.
>
> MOESO   was to act as liaison officer between the above two and the Far Eastern Bureau in Shanghai.
>
> BASSA   who had not been noted previously was described as a Javanese intellectual aged 27, a member of the Communist Party who took a leading part in the 1926 rebellion in Java, and went to China in 1927. He was believed to have been in Malaya about the time engaged in the election and despatch of Malay students to Haborvosk.
>
> (Supplement No. 5, PIJ, 1938)

Throughout this period the Comintern was very active in starting national resistance movements that would challenge the colonial ideology.

***

The Comintern was clearly determined to destabilize and foment revolutions that would help it install its own regime. It saw developments in the region as being interrelated; local parties were relevant to the extent that they played a part in this overall orchestration. The Branch was correct, monitoring and surveillance could no longer be treated as matters of local intelligence but had to bear in mind the depth of communist strategic thinking that cut across borders. It was of little use to pinch out disturbances when they occurred. The deterioration of the world situation saw the rise of extremist ideology such as fascism, communism, militarism and the revival of sectarianism.

The Branch adopted a dual strategy. While emphasizing covert action, it stepped up its policing of the dissidents. Raids continued to weaken the MCP apparatus and manpower. Often the Branch used the banishment order that had been introduced to contain trial activities:

> The strength of the Party was kept in check by a steady weeding out and deportation of headmen and organizers, and by ceaseless raids on their various secretariats, printing presses and, on two occasions, bomb-making centres.
>
> (Onraet, n.d., pp. 112–113)

There is by now sufficient evidence to show that the Special Branch acted neither randomly nor indiscriminately. Most of its actions had become by the mid-1930s almost surgical in the precision with which it detected and removed subversives. Since the arrests of Ducroux and Noulens, the Special Branch had gained an important initiative, possessing a comprehensive picture of communist intentions. Successful raids in both the Straits Settlements and Shanghai had disrupted connections between the local parties and their bases in China. The MCP was forced to operate very much in the dark at this time, often unaware of Comintern directives or ideological developments. This ignorance coupled with their continued reverence for the authority of Central benefited the Special Branch, allowing it to insert agents or collaborators, especially those with external antecedents that was difficult to verify. It hatched a plan to introduce a double agent into the ranks of the Malayan Communist Party. Through Loi Teck, the Special Branch 'offered' the MCP an apparent saviour in the form of a hard core militant communist, a messenger of the Comintern, who arrived at a time of a party crisis and who entrenched himself as leader after purging the party of its 'problematic' elements categorized as the opposition function of the MCP Central Committee.

The Branch knew that the MCP was trying desperately to re-establish contact with Central China. The Branch's agent, it was decided, would be very knowledgeable on these issues, a trusted member of the

Comintern hierarchy who was held in the highest confidence by its leadership! The Branch knew, for instance, that next to the mainland Chinese, the Annamite, with the example of Nguyen Ai Quoc in mind, were held in high regard for their revolutionary zeal. In making their undercover agent an Annamite, there would be key advantages: he would share in the aura of Vietnamese revolutionary consciousness, be less likely to be recognized by the Chinese and would also be in a position to play off the Comintern against the Chinese Communist Party. The Branch also knew that Nguyen Ai Quoc often dabbled in the affairs of the Southeast Asian communist parties. An Annamite Comintern emissary fitted the bill, satisfying everybody.

So an Annamite militant, with impeccable revolutionary backgrounds in Russia and China and well versed with every directive of the movement would be a godsend to the Malayan Communist Party which was in disarray and out of touch with Central. The Annamite would be helped by the selective arrests of those in power who were likely to question him. Other troublesome party members could be hunted down as likely traitors or terrorized into acquiescence. The iron discipline of the Party which demanded and enforced obedience to the Central (the Standing Committee) ensured that not too many questions would be asked about a person once he had reached a sufficient status. Moreover, the Party practised an administrative system that isolated units and departments from one another. Constant Special Branch raids meant that the MCP would be forced to depend on the cell structure for survival. The advantage to the Party was better security, the disadvantage was that it kept knowledge among party members to a minimum.

The Branch knew that it had to move before the advantages were lost and the communist regained the initiative. They had on their side a good sense of the strengths and weaknesses of the adversary, a comprehensive map of their intentions and effective penetration that allowed them to intercept and arrest key personnel. However, the Branch knew that the Comintern would not rest. It was the long-term penetration of communism into British Malaya that worried it. The threat was compounded by its international dimension which was deteriorating rapidly. This congruence of events posed the most severe challenge to the Special Branch.

Subversion and espionage are often explained as events brought about by a person or a group of like-minded people bound by common belief and conviction. Someone hurls a bomb. A group of terrorists takes over a government building. Another group distributes subversive pamphlets. Such actions are usually traced back to the causes or a series of interrelated causes. Just as there are events in history, so there must be causes that brought them about. Unfortunately life often refuses to be so neat. People do things for various reasons; in fact, they may not agree with each other although in the indeterminate zone of living they may decide to travel along the same path as long as it is convenient. Thus they may appear to share the same discourse and even pursue the same actions for a while. What happens after that is another thing altogether. History is often silent on what happens after an event. Do these people stay together? Do their convictions continue to sustain them? Or, do they go their separate ways of their own beliefs and behaviours?

Nothing illustrates this better than the upturn in the fortunes of the Malayan Communist Party in the late 1930s. To all intents the movement was well and truly beaten. The crucial links and subsidies from Shanghai had been cut, the Party itself was infiltrated and its secrets exposed, and continuing vigilance by the Special Branch made active reorganization difficult. However, a series of events gave the Party renewed life, allowing it to ride on the rising tide of Chinese nationalist fervour against the Japanese. From the apparent jaws of defeat, the Party once again posed a threat even as the Branch succeeded in its infiltration of MCP Central. As Japanese military aggression against China increased, many Chinese were drawn by nationalist and patriotic feelings into joining the various resistant bodies and Anti-Japanese societies that were formed. Many of these were communist-inspired if not controlled. Yet it would be simplistic to say that all those who agitated against the Japanese or who joined the societies were communists. Many of them did so out of a wish to express their outrage and anger. In other words, it was now harder to separate the communist from the non-communist. The shape of events became less distinct in an increasingly grey landscape. Significantly this was the landscape the British would send their agent, Loi Teck, to map. Once again events in faraway lands brought things to a head. Addressing his Reichstag on 30 January 1937, Hitler had promised, "The time of so-called surprises has been ended" (Shirer, 1968, p. 413). Stalin certainly did not believe his empty promises. He was aware that Soviet Russia crippled by years of mismanaging the armed forces was ill prepared to meet any German onslaught. In the face of the impending onslaught from the West, Stalin decided to use colonial wars to stir up the situation. As with Lenin who tried to use the Third International to break out of the encirclement of unfriendly capitalist countries, Stalin decided to use the communist movement to improve his country's strategic position.

The Seventh World Congress of the Comintern in 1935 revised its previous call for an all-out militant struggle against capitalism in favour of preparations to combat fascism. This meant a radical change of directions as the International worked with the national bourgeoisie in the fight against the common enemy of fascism. Advocating the popular or united front movement the Comintern argued that contradictions of capitalism could best be exploited to serve the advances of Marxism by the formation of political alliances and groups. The common enemy was to be the fascist movements that now threatened all workers. Of course the hidden agenda was that fascism was now threatening the borders of Russia and whatever could be done to impede its advance was welcomed.

It still remained the stated aim of communism to end capitalist modes of production but now it was not wrong for the contending groups to forge an alliance against the evils of fascism. In China, for instance, the CCP abandoned its avowed fight against the Kuomintang to enter into a united front against the Japanese. The Xi'an incident where Zhang Xue Liang kidnapped Chiang Kai Shek to demand a national front against Japan had struck a chord with many Chinese. The Japanese conquest of northern China had aroused patriotic fury across the political divide of Kuomintang and the communists. To the CCP this was an opportunity to widen and rebuild its bases. This was especially advantageous in Southeast Asia where there was an extensive supply of funds and fresh manpower to tap. The conditions were ripe internationally for the united front tactics espoused by the Seventh Comintern.

The MCP decided that the moment was right for it to restart the militant struggle against the British. It felt that this time the chances of success would be much better as it could reach out and harness the patriotic anger of the Chinese. A wave of strikes hit Malaya in the closing months of 1936. By the next year, it had reached an "unprecedented" intensity. The wave of strikes soon spread to the Straits Settlements:

In September 1936 there began a series of strikes involving unskilled as well as skilled workers which, by the end of March 1937, had attained unprecedented proportions. The first group of strikers was set off by Chinese cutting "coolies" at Singapore and Johore pineapple factories. These strikes involved perhaps 1,500 workers, lasted for about three weeks and spread to Chinese building workers, between 4,000 and 5,000 of whom stopped work for one or two weeks. The unrest communicated itself directly or indirectly to the multi-racial Singapore Traction Company employees and to Chinese night-soil "coolies" at the Singapore municipality, both of whom staged brief stoppages in September and then, their demands not being met, further stoppages in October and December respectively, the latter spreading to a total of 13,000 Indian and Chinese municipal and government employees.

(Stenson, 1970, p. 14)

Often the strikes turned violent as they did in Selangor. Workers at the Malayan Collieries at Batu Arang, the Sungei Besi Tin Mine, the Tong Sang Tin Mine and pineapple factories at Morib and Klang created much problems for the police. The first strike took place at Batu Arang in November 1936 but an even more serious one broke out on 24 March 1937. It rapidly fell under the control of the communists who declared a workers' soviet. The "soviet" was an internal council of workers that included an elaborate defence scheme as well as a court to deal with criminal offence and to settle civil disputes. It had all the makings of a dissident government. Although the "soviet" took pains to ensure order and that Europeans were not threatened, a fact that even the Inspector General of Police admitted:

The European management of the mine was defiled but not molested.

(Onraet, n.d., p. 117)

the political implications of this insurrection were obvious. The situation was regarded to be so unstable that the Inspector General of Police put an alarmist spin on the matter, emphasizing in rather purple prose that:

The Federated Malay States has passed through the most serious crisis of its history. It was within an ace of dissolving into temporary chaos as a result of communist intrigue. The evidence is now clear that Batu Arang was to be the trial of strength between the Communist Party and the Government. Had the organization there not been crushed and crushed quickly it is almost certain that there would not only have been a general strike but that this country with its European women and children living in scattered bungalows on estates would have been in very serious danger of being overrun by angry and desperate Chinese mobs. The time when looting of food shops would have started was perilously near.

(quoted in Onraet, n.d., pp. 116–117)

In fact, there never was any danger of a Cawnpore-like massacre of European women and children. Rather the alarmist report was deliberate disinformation reflecting fears that an alternative system of political and economic control was being established at the Bukit Arang mines.

The British would never tolerate such a challenge to their paramountcy since it effectively meant that the government would collapse. On the evening of 27 March, some 300 policemen with two companies of the Malay Regiment on standby raided the mine and, after some shooting, arrested 116 of the strikers. This broke the back of the strike. The colliery, Malaya's only coalmine, went back to production soon after. The strike was a frightening reminder of how easily a political challenge could emerge from the escalation of militant labour strikes. It is not surprising that the Branch took strong objections to the strike.

While the Batu Arang strike was a significant turning point in the history of labour relations in British Malaya, not all is to be attributed to the communists although most scholars accept this. Yeo Kim Wah, for instance, argues that the strike marked the:

> beginning of really deep Communist penetration among Chinese workers, a development sharply accelerated by the Communist involvement in the (China) National Salvation Movement after July 1937. Through this movement, the MCP succeeded in organizing a growing number of trade unions among Chinese workers, ostensibly for the collection of financial and other contributions for China's resistance against Japan.
>
> (Yeo, 1976, p. 57)

There was no doubt that the communists took full advantage of the patriotism of the Chinese to stir up and capture the trade unions. The agitation at the Bukit Arang mines fell in with their strategy to make use of the rising spirit of patriotic anger. This found expression in the challenging of British dominance.

A confluence of events and emotions added to the state of social and labour unrest. Agitation came from expressions of patriotic awareness, assertions of self-identity, calls to resist Japanese aggression as well as the desire to punish Japan. Communist agitation and manipulation added to these feelings but cannot be said to be the entire inspiration behind the upsurge of troubles. There were also similar attempts by the KMT and its front organizations to appeal to and work up the Chinese ground. Branch reports at this time tended to downplay the communist inspiration behind the unrest. Certainly the Branch did not subscribe to the Inspector General's fears for the safety of British women and children. It knew that the remarks were spun as propaganda against the communists. The Branch knew that real danger came from the "soviet", the alternative political system that was being experimented with at the Batu Arang colliery. It was this political experiment that made the strike quite different. The Branch resorted to a display of force and an overwhelming number of arrests. The speed with which the Branch reacted—a raid being mounted within four days of the strike—suggested that the Branch had information on the events. This would not be surprising as Loi Teck was thought to be active in the organization of the strike. The miners could not have chosen a worse leader or the British a better one under the circumstance.

The Branch's response to the events in the late 1930s was calculated but measured. By this time they had probably infiltrated the Standing Committee of the MCP and knew the areas of greatest danger. The communists were trying to take advantage of the strikes. In some cases they even instigated them. However, harsh repressive actions would merely evoke even greater sympathy for the communists. As Stenson pointed out:

> In reality, evidence of communist instigation, far less control of the strikes was most remarkable for its paucity. Illegal, communist-sponsored associations were undoubtedly behind the initial strikes of the pineapple factory and building workers and every attempt was made to extend the final strikes of rubber tappers and Batu Arang miners. Nevertheless, the most marked characteristic of the strikes as a whole was their spontaneity and absence of disciplined, coordinated direction. Almost every stoppage began on a limited scale, usually as the result of some incident at the work-place, and was then spread by word of mouth or by bicycle-riding "agitators".
>
> (Stenson, 1970, p. 15)

Special Branch records confirmed this view. The pineapple cutters' strike in Singapore appeared to have been "actuated by motives of revenge on one of the foremen of the factory who was unpopular with the coolies" (Special Branch Report for the Year 1936). It was more of an attempt at revenge than a politically motivated incident. However, just to be sure, the Branch continued with its by now familiar strategy of detaining key cadres of the MCP. The Branch was not panicked into indiscriminate action; rather it picked off the cadres and agitators with routine ease each time they surfaced to create disturbances. The Branch dealt with the increasing number of strikes in a calm and collected manner that did not display an excessively harsh reaction.

It would appear that the very successes of the Branch in the early years of the 1930s made it more difficult to anticipate the communists. The MCP had for the moment lost its hitherto tight organizational structure. They thus confronted the authorities by default with a series of guerrilla-like actions initiated by loose groupings and cells. The split in the MCP exacerbated this disarray even further. The disagreement within the Party over the correct ideological direction to take came to a head in 1935, when a number of cadres were killed. One result was the decentralization of the MCP as cells lost contact with Central. Unwittingly the MCP had stumbled on an effective response to the Special Branch. The question remained as to whether they knew how to use it to their advantage. Although the fluid, unplanned actions that were sparked off by local abuses and resentments could be fanned by police intervention, disruption of the picket lines and arrests of the leaders, the unorganized actions made it difficult to predict communist actions unlike in the past. The Branch admitted:

> It is no easy matter to obtain a clear view of present day communist organisations and activities in Malaya since the breakdown of the orthodox organisation which was previously operating in this country. The functions of the Committees are now very indefinite and vary according to the ideas of the leading members and circumstances. *The Central Committee has little hold over the local and town committees.*
>
> (Special Branch Report for the Year 1936)

The very disorganization of the MCP made it even more of a danger. The intelligence dimension was just not present!

While the MCP continued to suffer from the split in its party its situation was helped by the fury of the Chinese population towards Japanese aggression in Manchuria and Eastern China. This created a new threat: a growing sense of political awareness and spiritedness now animated the Chinese consciousness. There was at this time "a fairly sophisticated awareness among the mass of workers" (Stenson, 1970, p. 15) which together with an assertive determination over identity provided a focus for the Chinese workers. Their sentiments found ready focus in the events that were taking place in China. Throughout Malaya and Singapore a number of national salvation groups, self-help movements and backing-up groups were formed by Chinese of all political persuasions. The communists naturally sought to gain from this situation. Anti-Japanese feelings had always been strong and were likely to get out of hand. The Governor's, Sir Thomas Shenton's, visit to Penang was disrupted by a boycott of Japanese soybean. This situation soon turned into a searching and burning of shops owned by collaborators. For 48 hours Penang was, as Onraet himself noted, like a city being sacked. It was almost as if a sense of spiritual disruption and personal panic were in the air as war drifted ever nearer.

Although on paper the strength of sympathizers increased by leaps and bounds, membership proper of the MCP remained constant, showing that it did not make as much headway as was feared. As the Special Branch noted many were hoodwinked into joining the MCP front organizations that passed off as patriotic bodies supporting China. Cheah Boon Kheng agrees with this assessment:

> Probably because of its successful appeals to the Chinese, the MCP's strength increased during the anti-Japanese campaign. According to British records, its supporters more than quadrupled from 1934 to 1940 to an overall total, including Communist-affiliated organizations, of more than fifty thousand. Membership for the same period in the MCP proper, however, remained constantly around fifteen hundred to seventeen hundred ...
>
> (Cheah, 1992, p. 31.)

In fact, the use of the China situation to attract members simply meant that the party remained Chinese dominated. The plan backfired over the long term as the various races the MCP sought to sink its roots into polarized increasingly along ethnic lines:

> The gains in membership achieved by the Communists among the Chinese during the anti-Japanese campaign, therefore, appeared to have had an opposite effect among the Malays and Indians.
>
> (Cheah, 1992, p. 31)

The Comintern's instructions to develop a pan-racial indigenous communist movement, which the British feared above all, never took off. The MCP remained a Chinese-dominated and supported group that had little appeal to the other races. The failure to reach segments of the population would in the long term prove decisive in the defeat of the movement.

Even as these events were taking place the structure and scope of the Special Branch underwent further changes in the closing years of the decade. In 1937 the work of the Branch was centralized into three main areas:

1. Anti-communism,
2. Counter-espionage, and
3. Detection and prevention of other subversive activities.

By now the Branch was organized in terms of Sub-Branches rather than sections. There were five: the Anti-Communist Sub-Branch,

Security Sub-Branch, Japanese Sub-Branch, Aliens Sub-Branch, and the Surveillance Sub-Branch. The most important were the first two while the last which dealt with surveillance merely provided the manpower in response to the needs of the other Sub-Branches. While the Anti-Communist Sub-Branch remained the most important the Security Sub-Branch, responsible for Counter-espionage, was now of equal relevance as the international situation deteriorated and war drifted nearer. The Security Sub-Branch acting as liaison with other intelligence agencies of the British government also provided the ideal mechanism to run operations that were international in scope.

Other changes were also important in underlining the development of the Branch. The Political Section of the early 1930s had disappeared by this time, replaced by the Surveillance Sub-Branch. The Political Section that used to be a kind of catch-all unit was now reorganized in recognition of the specialized work contributed by the Anti-Communist and Security Sub-Branches. The detection of a security threat and its neutralization was in any case inseparable from its political context so a Political Section would be a tautology. In its report in 1937 the Branch acknowledged that:

> In the past the work of the Special Branch had been mainly anti-Communist. During the last two years, with the addition of the Security and Japanese Sub-Branches, increased attention has been paid to counter-espionage though this work is still hardly out of its initial state.
> (Special Branch Report for the Year 1937)

Another significant development from a security point of view was that the Branch took over the screening and vetting of its employees. In due course this duty was extended to the screening of all government employees.

One advantage of the new structure was that it afforded greater security to ongoing investigations and cases. Previously, detectives had been part of an ongoing case. They had full knowledge of the implications of an investigation, the reasons behind an inquiry or whether information for an arrest had come from an informer or just fortuitously. The reorganization delinked field agents from the evaluators or desk officers who handled an ongoing investigation. Thus a detective asked to follow the movements of Mr XYZ would have less chances of knowing the significance of the task or, indeed, who Mr XYZ actually was. The new structure emphasized the need to put in place procedures that isolated the Sub-Branches from one another. Moreover, surveillance and investigation were now separated from the collation and interpretation of data. With this the modern Special Branch was in place. In an interesting way, the secrecy emphasized that the Branch was engaged in deep penetration operations which required above all else the protection of its agents who had infiltrated the communist camps.

By 1937 the Branch had an establishment strength of 54 and an actual staff of 49. It remained highly selective in its recruitment, refusing to fill its establishment by simply accepting the first recruit to come along. It wanted candidates who had a special feel and knowledge of local conditions. It was the empathy and almost intuitive awareness of the Malayan situation rather than the qualifications. On 1 February 1937 L F Knight who had been posted to the Detective Bureau was transferred back to the Branch on 21 June 1937 as its Acting Director.

The Branch had by the end of the 1930s matured into a tight professional outfit. However, its orientation still emphasized threats that came from external agencies and forces. Communism was given a new lease of life by the events in China, bringing other patriotic groups. The Kuomintang was also revitalized by the troubles in the mainland. However, an even greater threat was the military ambition of Japan that increasingly demanded the Branch's attention. Japanese infiltration was altogether different from that of the communists. The Japanese advanced and carried out their underground work behind an array of apparently legitimate businesses and semi-official agencies. Although that part of history has been well told as the Colonial Office has released significant documents regarding infiltration methods the story is worthy of attention as Japanese espionage often became intertwined with communist efforts to organize Chinese resistance.

Notes

1. "Jack" is Jack A Hoeg whom Ducroux met in Shanghai in February 1931. Obviously a nom de guerre his identity has not been established.

2. Frederick W Deakin and G R Storry, *The Case of Richard Sorge*, London: Chatto and Windus, 1966 refers to a scrap of paper in Ducroux's possession referring to "Hilanoul, Box 208". The reference is picked up and repeated by Frederic Wakeman Jr, *Policing Shanghai 1927–1937*, Berkeley, University of California Press, 1995. It is almost certainly wrong in the light of Special Branch files on the matter.

Red Sun Rising

Japanese Espionage Activities

Japanese military ambitions towards the rich lands of Southeast Asia with their rubber, oil, minerals, rice and cheap labour are well documented. An irresistible chain of greed, arrogance and even misunderstanding culminated in the attack on the American Pacific fleet in Pearl Harbour on the morning of 7 December 1941 and the simultaneous invasion of Malaya. The Japanese conquest of Malaya and Singapore brought three years of suffering and hardship to their people. It would also change forever the nature of the relationship between Britain and its subject population. Despite the victorious return of the Allies, the hollowness of imperial power became apparent. Moreover, it was now clear to many including the more astute British residents that the interests of the colonies far away from London might not always have priority in the calculations of the politicians.

But prior to the declaration of war, the Special Branch had been aware for a substantial time that Japanese intentions towards the region were hostile. Although the war started with surprise attacks, there had been all the time signs of Japanese aims to seize control of the region. The Special Branch had been monitoring the extensive Japanese activities and presence for some time. On the eve of hostilities, there were indications that the Branch had intelligence that showed the disposition of all significant Japanese in the peninsula. They had also identified many of the likely agents. It is one of the sad stories that their findings were never given sufficient weight as the Colonial Government was felt that the Japanese were an external, military threat. Whatever improprieties they committed in Malaya that posed an internal security issue, they could only be contained through local action. Even then many attempts such as Rene Onraet's proposal to restrict Japanese presence in Singapore were rejected because they might offend and spark off Japanese retaliations in other areas such as China against British interests. Onraet certainly had no such fear. By the mid-1930s he felt that the threat was serious enough to set up a Japanese section recruiting Major K S Morgan from Indian intelligence as its first head. Major Morgan and the Japanese section of the Special Branch compiled an extensive Japanese file as well as issued a monthly Japanese Diary from 1938 onwards that tracked the many efforts to infiltrate and subvert the security of British possessions.

The Branch's attempts to contain the rising tide of Japanese espionage and subversion were hampered by London's unstated policy of appeasement. The British knew that their military strength did not allow them as yet to fight a war simultaneously in Europe and Asia. As the home front was clearly more important, that meant the Japanese should not be provoked. However, it was not just this attitude of appeasement that often stymied the efforts of the Branch. The contradictions within Britain's imperial ideology returned continually to haunt her policies. Here a comparison of British responses to the espionage threat of the Japanese with that posed by communist activities will throw up interesting insights. It will also highlight the strengths and weaknesses of the Special Branch as the Pacific War loomed nearer and nearer.

The major contradiction affecting British internal security policy was that it shared similar aims with its erstwhile enemy, the Japanese. Both countries expressed their imperial designs in terms of trading opportunities, capitalist investments and most favoured nation treatment in business. The British were hoist by their own petard as it were. Just as the East India Company did, the Japanese advanced behind a screen of trading companies, investment houses and research institutes that concealed their espionage. It was difficult for the Special Branch to move against these as long as the two countries were not at war. Any attempt to close down a company, deport traders or detain a researcher, risked a diplomatic row and a worsening of relations. These were risks that London was not prepared to take as long as they hoped that time could be bought by appeasing the Japanese. The colonial legislators were, hence, unwilling to take stern steps. Onraet's suggestion to the Governor of Singapore to introduce legislation that would limit the number of Japanese workers was turned down.

Moreover, significant as it was, the wealth of the Malayan colonies had to be weighed against other British investments that might be adversely affected if hostilities erupted. Certainly by the 1930s the considerable British interests in China would be easily threatened by Japan since it had already a marked military presence there. This created a major headache for internal security with regard to Japanese business and its personnel in Malaya. While the Special Branch officers were aware that there was active espionage, they were forced to curb their hands. Moreover, the military, which was also monitoring Japanese activities, was focused on the external dimension of the threat. The Japanese did not hesitate to take advantage of this situation, inserting many of their operatives under the cloak of commercial or diplomatic passports.

In fact all these three players on the stage at this time share an uncannily similar view of the region. The South Seas or British Malaya to the Special Branch, *Nanyang* to the communists and *Nanyo* (or, more precisely *Omote Nanyo*[1]) to the Japanese was regarded as a strategic economic prized possession that had to be won if their different causes were to be advanced. It was only their ideology that identified their characteristics and accounted for the difference the British saw between Japanese and communist subversion. So while all three were competitors for the region their approaches were different, shaped by the irresistible logic of their outlook. The British and the Japanese fought as fellow colonists essentially for the economic wealth of the region. Their conflict was a consequence of competition for profitability and the politico-economic dominance of the colony. In that sense, the British felt they understood the strategic aims and more importantly the actions of Japan. Both were after all replaying the scramble for colonial possessions that had marked much of the previous century.

The communists, of course, ultimately shared the same aim of economic dominance but for them the political control and victory was not the means to economic dominance but to a new political world order. As far as the British were concerned, that made them the more immediately dangerous opponent. 'Red' actions in the trade unions, plantations, ports and mines also threatened the wealth of Britain which was needed even more now that war with Germany seemed inevitable. The left wing activists could not be allowed to disrupt the central tenet of colonial policy which remained as it had from the beginning—the uninterrupted exploitation of wealth. For that the colonies needed to be stable with as little disorderliness as possible. Moreover, communism in Southeast Asia was, as British intelligence saw it, but one aspect of the worldwide struggle for power between capitalist and socialist ideology. If the communists won in one place no matter how remote, it would embolden the proletariat within UK to rise up. To stem communism was, therefore, not just a matter of retaining possession of colonial resources vital to Britain's wealth but also the defeat of likely class unrest back home. When the communists seized power in the August revolution in Vietnam, their rhetoric echoed precisely this view. They were celebrating not just a Vietnamese victory but the start of a worldwide advancement of their ideology:

> The August 1945 revolution was an extremely important event in world history—perhaps the most important event since the 1917 October Revolution in Russia. It was the first time in human history in which a revolutionary national movement under Communist leadership had succeeded in overthrowing the power of a colonial state and establishing and maintaining its own new, independent form of social and political system.
>
> (Hodgkin, 1981, p. 1)

To the British, the left wing threat to the stability of their colonies was a global battle for ideological dominance that would decide the outcome of events at home. There were, as Special Branch appeared to believe, no indigenous nationalist movements even late into the 1930s. There could by that same token be no labour or class movements or nationalist awareness in the region. In a way, this was a charade perpetuated by the British to justify their colonial regime. If there were any dangerous ideas, these were introduced from the outside—to use a metaphor, they were contaminants that infected and upset the otherwise balanced harmony of the body politic. So the British argued that organizations like the Comintern and the CCP sowed dissension and spread rebellion by manipulating the innocent locals. Security threats and subversions were introduced by outside elements. If these were weeded out or interdicted before they could put down roots, there would be no trouble. Better still, the Branch wanted to keep such dangerous people and ideas as far away from Malaya as possible so that their spores would not settle on the fertile ground. Colonial ideology found in the gardening (or agrarian) metaphor a perfect description of its intentions and aims.

The methods of the Special Branch are similarly also metaphors that reveal the ideological basis of their origins—quarantine, surveillance, censorship, banishment, preventive detentions and passport controls were all widely used instruments in the effort to combat subversion. These same methods were, of course, employed on the Japanese when that threat became apparent. However, there was a significant difference. The British recognized Japanese espionage to be imperialistic in nature. It came as it were from the same cut of cloth as theirs. This was a creature the British, past masters of the game, felt at home with and could understand. Perhaps it was because they felt that they could understand Japanese intentions that they did not devote the amount of time and effort they spent on the monitoring of the communists until quite late in the day. Since the Japanese were regarded as imperial competitors, defensive measures were, more often than not, military with inadequate resources devoted to the home front. So right until the last moment, the Special Branch did not think that segments of the population would receive with enthusiasm the ideology of pan-Asianism put forward by the Japanese.

This British view of Japanese espionage was somewhat naive, based upon a simplistic view of the world that came from the old habits of commercial colonialism. Despite their own experience, they ignored the newer, more frightening realities of commercial militarism. Ironically, the Japanese and the communists shared the same view of subversion and espionage. For them, there was little or almost no distinction between intelligence and other activities like trade or diplomacy. To engage in one was to be involved in the other. Espionage meant subversion and agitation as much as the gathering of such routine intelligence necessary to a business company. There is a revealing anecdote in Lieutenant-General Iwaichi Fujiwara's account of his *kosaku* (intelligence operations) in Malaya and Thailand that underlines this. In his book, *F Kikan*, Fujiwara provides an anecdote recounting the meeting of Colonel Tamara Hiroshi, Military Attache at the Japanese Embassy in Thailand and Lieutenant-Colonel Kadomatsu Shoichi, an agent of the Imperial Army huddled together in a steamy downtown Bangkok office to discuss the steps to be taken in the forthcoming invasion of Malaya. Tamara argued that there could only be three unequivocal means:

> The first possibility was the co-operation with the IIL (Indian Independence League) ... The second one was to co-operate with "*Harimau* of Malaya", a pseudonym for Tani Yutaka whose home was in Trengganu on the east coast of Malaya. *Harimau* means Tiger in the Malaya language. His family settled in Trengganu in the late Meiji period and ran a barber shop for their livelihood. In the early days of the Manchurian Incident when the local Chinese staged an anti-Japanese uprising, Yutaka's six-year-old sister was kidnapped and murdered in cold blood. Following this incident, his personality suddenly changed and he joined a group of Malay bandits ... The third possible alternative was to incite Chinese, particularly coolies in the port of Singapore ...
>
> (Fujiwara, 1983, p. 9)

Fujiwara may have felt that these recommendations were "devoid of a principle that would inspire the cooperation of alien nationals" (Fujiwara, 1983, p. 10) yet in substance this was what Fujiwara himself did when his Department F or the "F-Kikan" launched its subversive campaign in Malaya. Fujiwara made no distinction between espionage, subversion, anti-colonialism or political unhappiness, since it was not what these stood for but their appropriate use in the service of the aims of the Japanese Army that was important. Fujiwara's own actions also showed that subversion and intelligence gathering were complementary. To gather intelligence meant the subversion of those with information or secrets to sell. It was always a short step from the routine gathering of intelligence to the deliberate subversion of worthwhile targets. Japanese intelligence in this sense is comprehensive and not compartmentalized since every soldier or civilian was assumed to work single-mindedly for the interest of the nation. Unfortunately, for a long while the British authorities were unaware of the multi-dimensional nature of the threat facing them.

The disparity many observers have written about between the posturing of imperial naval might and the rapid collapse of British resistance once the Japanese landed has been blamed not so much on military incompetence as the unwillingness of London to match its words with adequate gestures. Almost right until the day the Japanese invaded, the popular view of Japanese militarism held by many politicians and Churchill, in particular, was that it was essentially China's problem. It was also felt that the problem would probably be resolved in northern rather than Southeast Asia. After all, that was where Japanese militarism was most obvious. Throwing China to the dogs would be painful but less so than losing the imperial colonies in the south. The truth of the matter is, as Ong Chit Chung's excellently researched study of Britain's war preparations against the Japanese between 1918 and 1941 points out, that Churchill was unwilling or unable to recognize the extent of the Japanese challenge. Ong places the blame squarely on Churchill:

> The battle for Malaya was lost, even before the first shot was fired, in the corridors of power at Whitehall. Malaya was starved of the necessary reinforcements and the commanders on the spot were expected to make brick without straw. The responsibility or blame must *rest squarely on the shoulders of Churchill*. It was Churchill who consistently underestimated the Japanese threat. And it was Churchill who sacked Brooke-Popham (Commander-in Chief, Far East) and changed horses in midstream.
>
> (Ong, 1997, p. 249)

Churchill richly deserved this censure but his blindness to the typhoon racing towards British Malaya was not just personal prejudice. He had compelling reasons to delay the war by any means he could since Britain was simply not prepared financially or militarily for a war. Churchill's policy had its roots in existing and long-held political views about the best ways to defend imperial interests given inadequate war funds. As late as November 1938 the First Sea Lord, Admiral Sir Roger Backhouse, admitted:

> The trouble is that we are now trying to take on more than we are really able to ... and we simply cannot produce more than we are doing.
>
> (cited in Calvocoressi, 1999, p. 830)

It had been increasingly clear for some time that the resources both in terms of money and equipment were not there to fight a two-front war in both Europe and Asia. Even if Britain set about rearming which it did with increasing urgency from 1931 after the Manchurian Incident, defence planners realized that the war was unwinnable unless the United States was brought in. Until that happened the best course of action was to delay a conflict even if appeasement was necessary. Non-provocation would be an important diplomatic means to help ensure that war would not break out or that if it did it was only with one opponent. When the Germans invaded Poland on 1 September 1939, it became necessary to defend England at all cost particularly after the German blitzkrieg in Western Europe beginning May 1940 had shown that England would have to fight on alone for some time. Given the limited resources, it was at best possible only to defend the Mediterranean and India. Southeast Asia would have to look after itself with what limited weapons and men that could be spared from the European front.

Fighting the war in the East on limited means was not helped by the extensively detailed Japanese preparations. From the beginning of the century, the Japanese had carried out extensive surveillance of conditions and defensive measures in British Malaya. They had gathered considerable detailed information on the peninsula using the networks of its citizens that had sprung up at every majoir city. Above all, the Japanese realized that reliable political and social information was essential if their invasion of this faraway land was going to be successful. The nerve centre of their operations was their Consul General in Singapore supplemented by various front organizations such as the Commercial Museum. These collated a steady stream of reports from all aspects of activity including business, culture, travel and study. In addition, diplomats were often expected to carry out espionage as part of their duties.

However, in contrast with Western methods of espionage, there was no master plan, which fitted all these elements together. Their infiltration and colonization often took place by a process of gradual accretion The effort was total but the planning often decentralized. Thus, varying elements came into play at different moments, their importance depending upon opportunity and what the situation demanded. As an example, a Japanese traveller might start a small trading outpost because there was the opportunity for business. In time, it would grow, drawing in other Japanese. In due course, these would form a tightly knit community with their own schools and clubs. Occasionally, a cultural association promoting Japanese values would be formed with strong links to one or the other of the organizations back home. So trading presence would evolve into cultural assertion followed by military occupation and colonization. Aggressive business and ideological tactics backed up by military power was the norm in a weak state like China. In British Malaya though, such obvious strong-arm methods would not have worked. The Japanese preferred to infiltrate, gather information and await the arrival of the troops. Japanese advance was in any case always preceded by an aggressive business presence. In China, this approach was supported by supplanted secret societies. These societies were the harbinger, the shock troops, of the Japanese advance. This will be elaborated on later.

Japanese expansionism inevitably led to conflict since the Western powers did not willingly allow their colonial dominance to be displaced. Japan was prepared to take this risk since her militants believe that only through colonialism could she sustain the kind of growth that would bring about her manifest destiny as a great power. By the end of the 19th century the first thrust of colonialism had already exhausted itself in Asia. The richest lands had been carved up and distributed essentially among the Europeans and Americans. Japan a late pretender to colonialism did not have much choice nor found it so easy to form colonies. She could only do so by challenging or displacing the existing powers or through deliberate military aggression against weaker neighbours. Throughout the 19th century, the Japanese advance followed these principles as she advanced steadily. The China incursions were naked aggression as Japan tried to muscle her way into the mainland. First she took over the German possessions in Shandong; this was followed by the seizure of the Chinese island of Formosa (now Taiwan) and the aggressions in Northeast China. Japan also increasingly coveted the wealthy resources of Southeast Asia which were divided among the French in Indo-China, the British in Malaya, the Dutch in the Netherlands East Indies and the Americans in the Philippines. If the Europeans could be challenged through gradual encroachment and gains of business colonies and settlements so much the better, but it was becoming clear by the 1930s that Japan would have to resort to force of arms. The Americans and the Europeans were not likely to surrender their colonies without a fight.

***

As alluded to earlier, much of the work of this expansionist drive was carried out by the secret societies that had become ubiquitous both in Asian and European politics. In Japan, their adherents took over and dictated much of the direction of the national and government policy. As early as 1881, Kotaro Hiraoka, Mitsuru Toyama and Ryohei Uchida had formed the *Genyosha* or Black Ocean Society to promote expansionist policies. Uchida, who went on to form the *Tenyo Kyodan*, or Society for the Spiritual Salvation of the Oppressed, to penetrate Korea was regarded as a dangerous extremist. This society was implicated in the murder of the Queen of Korea and starting the Sino-Japanese war of 1895. The *Genyosha* took its name from the straits called the *Genkai Nada* that separated northern Kyushu from the mainland of Korea. It was formed specifically to penetrate the Asian mainland preparing the way for a military takeover. As Richard Deacon rightly pointed out the *Genyosha* could therefore be regarded as

> the first real external branch of Japanese undercover espionage ...
> (Deacon, 1983, p. 36)

Obviously, Uchida took his work of promoting Japanese expansionism seriously and with not just the Asian mainland in mind. A branch of the *Genyosha* was active in the Philippines for a while in the 1890s. In 1900, Uchida came to Singapore but was deported soon after as the authorities viewed his presence on the island with deep suspicion (Robertson, 1979, p. 2).

Uchida's interest in and visit to Singapore marked the beginnings of sustained Japanese espionage interest in this part of the world. It also signalled the general framework by means of which such activities would be carried out. Military and commercial information were inseparable under this rubric as they contributed to a comprehensive picture of their areas of operations. In addition, the controllers of Japanese intelligence were also convinced that it was the patriotic duty of every citizen to contribute such information as may advance the greater good of *Dai Nippon Teikoku* or the Empire of Great Japan. Thus there was little of the compartmentalized distinction between the professional intelligence agent and the citizen who was asked to cooperate in an operation. This interlocked relationship was often instigated and supervised not just by the government but by societies such as the *Genyosha*. Spying was not just for the military but a sign of the citizen's manifestation of loyalty to the nation. It was as the militants saw it the duty of loyal subjects to ensure the manifest destiny of Japan as a powerful modern nation. Every citizen was expected to put national interests above self.

All had their place in this scheme of things. In the 19th century, the proliferation of societies, academic associations and organizations provided fertile ground on which a fraternity of fellow believers espousing such patriotism could grow. It was not just mere desire for power that brought them together. Such was the idealistic conviction and resolute belief in the historical rightness of their cause. These societies provided the ideal platforms through which the militants could carry out radical actions, instigated subversion or set up espionage cells without embarrassing the government. So as the 19th century progressed Japanese penetration and espionage were undertaken increasingly by groups of individuals, some of which banded together in organizations that often had revealing names like the *Genyosha* and the *Korkuryukai* or Black Dragon Society. This is, of course, not to suggest that there were no military or government units training spies. In addition to routine military intelligence, both the Army and Navy used *tokumu kikan* or Special Services Organization that carried out subversion and other duties. Among these were the *F-Kikan* that directed subversion in Malaya and the *Minami Kikan* that directed the Burmese Independence Army. The Foreign Ministry had its own political intelligence agency that ran the myriads of diplomats, businessmen, journalists and professionals who were spying overseas. In January 1938, the well-regarded Nakano School of Intelligence was set up in January 1938 to train junior intelligence officers from the Reserve Officer Training School. By the end of the war, it had graduated more than 3,000 officers and non-commissioned officers. In his *kosaku* mission in Malaya, Major Fujiwara of the *F-Kikan* was accompanied by six of these graduates who acquitted themselves well.

Nonetheless, it was the societies that made very significant contributions to external espionage and penetration. Some of these, such as the aptly named *Ketsumeidan* (League of Blood) and the *Aikoku Seiji Domei* (Patriotic Government League), were openly nationalist. Others chose to hide their real intentions behind names that apparently promoted learning, trade or culture. Thus, we have *Toa Keizai Chosa Kyoku* (East Asiatic Investigation Bureau), the *Dai Ajia Kyokai* (Great Asia Society), the *Zenkoku Keizai Chosa Kekan Rengokai* (Association of Japanese Economic Research Bureaux, or more immediately relevant to Singapore, the *Nanyo Kyokai* (South Seas Association). A number of the so-called academic societies preached a form of pan-Asian ideology, seeking to draw all those unhappy with colonial and white rule into making common cause with the Japanese. It was good propaganda for attracting a number of adherents who went on to form such anti-colonial movements as the Indian Independence League even if there was never any doubt that the Japanese would control things. Many of these secret societies often reflected the vision of a dominant personality. Thus the *Kokuhonsha* (Great Asia Society) formed in 1933 had Prince Konoye as its first President. The Prince was a well-known militant who among other things demanded a "fundamental solution to the Sino-Japanese relations" (Crowley, 1966, pp. 338–339) after the Luguoqiao (Marco Polo Bridge) incident of 1937.

There are interesting parallels between these secret societies and the united front organizations that the communists were trying to form. These provided a means, which drew together people of disparate views for a common cause, often manipulated by a hidden power. They multiplied easily like spawning hydra-headed units. As they operated under many guises, it was hard to determine their real agenda, let alone root them out. This method of garnering information has been described, perhaps over-dismissively and patronizingly, as the mass method system[2]. However, there are obvious advantages in collecting a spectrum of information. A significant advantage is, of course, that the opposing counter-intelligence found it difficult to determine what the real target was. On the other hand, the disadvantage was duplication and the need for a large and strong back-end collation outfit to sift through the information deluge. Also, it was an approach that was wasteful in terms of manpower resources. However, since many of these spies were not paid for by the Japanese government, expense was perhaps not so significant a factor. There is, though, at least one significant difference in aims from the united front the communists were trying to create in their efforts to penetrate and destabilize colonial regimes. This was in the overall game plan of the espionage effort. The Japanese regarded intelligence very much like a game of *wei-chi* (or *Go*) the ancient Chinese board game. In this, black or white stones are placed randomly on a grid, with the aim of creating a pattern of encircling chains. Thus, when enough of these are in place they form a pattern that signals victory when their interconnection is revealed. Japanese intelligence tactics follow this method. A shop here, a farm there or a trading company in another place. It was not their individual reports that were valued but the sum total of their findings that revealed the strength or hollowness of the enemy that was highly prized.

The advantage of this kind of operation lay in the fact that their initial penetrations were not likely to alert the authorities since these often appeared innocuous or disorganized, hardly a threat to the well-entrenched colonial military system. Moreover, data gathering appeared incidental to the military aspects of intelligence. Perhaps, a failure of Western counter-intelligence of the time was that its analysts continued to view the Japanese threat in terms of its own operational paradigms. Since Western intelligence was expressed through a rational and hierarchical organization, it assumed that the same was true with everybody else. Thus, if it could not detect a perceivable organization behind an act of espionage, for instance, it may very well have written it off as an isolated, local phenomenon. This causal relationship between event and origin was derived from the logical positivism of 19th century scientific thought. The failure to anticipate Japanese intentions is, thus, not just a matter of military incompetence but also a striking demonstration of the shortcomings of an outmoded way of thinking. Although this so-called scientific system of thought had successfully underpinned much of European colonial expansion, its drawbacks were soon to be apparent.

The Japanese attracted a number of recruits to their cause by playing up the arrogance of colonialism and its overt racism. Throughout Asia, organs such as the Institute for the Study of East Asiatic Races challenged the "white domination" that was oppressing the Asian races. That the Japanese turned out to be as equally racist and cruel is another matter but they managed to gain adherents to their cause through such propaganda. The appeal to nationalist sentiments often worked well, posing a grave subversive threat to the colonial rulers. As early as the Ghadr movement and uprisings such as the failed 1915 Christmas day revolt in Bengal, the Japanese had been cultivating nationalist movements seeking to create a pan-Asian anti-Western front. When Rash Behari Bose fled to Japan after the failure of the 1915 uprisings, he was given protection. Among his supporters who ensured his safety was the eminent Mitsuru Toyama who had formed the *Genyosha*. Toyama was also the inspiration behind the even more powerful *Korkuryukai* (Black Dragon Society) founded in 1901 which took its name from the Chinese characters for the Amur River, clearly spelling out its agenda. Toyama not only befriended Bose but, according to reports, also treated him like a family member, even helping to arrange his marriage to a member of the *Korkuryukai*. After Bose, the next prominent Indian allied to and groomed by the Japanese was Subhas Chandra Bose (no relation to Rash Behari Bose) who went on to form the Indian National Army that fought against the British on the side of the *Dai Toa Kyozonken* or the Great East Asia Co-Existence Sphere.

Western military sources often passed these off as isolated cases of aberrant behaviour. In fact, anti-colonialism and the promise of pan-Asianism proved to be a popular rallying cause recruiting quite a substantial number of disillusioned natives to the Japanese side, in particular the unwilling colonized people. The goodwill felt by these people, however, did not last long, squandered away by the ruthless brutality of the Japanese. What would have happened, one wonders, if the Japanese Emperor and the *Rikugunsho* (War Office) had heeded the warnings of far-sighted counsels like Nobuyoshi Muto, who was proconsul to the Manchurian government at Mukden in 1929 as well as special *taishi* to Manchukuo, the Japanese puppet state. A man of good conscience and vision, he unreservedly condemned the excesses of the *Kempeitai* (the Japanese security police). He felt that such indiscriminate cruelty would lose the Army the goodwill of the locals necessary to the future stability of Japanese rule:

> He endeavoured to use the Japanese Secret Service to report on *Kempeitai* excesses in an attempt to curb them and to have the worst perpetrators repatriated to Japan. He prepared a report for the *Rikugunsho* on the matter which was "lost" in the Japanese bureaucratic system. At length he made a personal report to Emperor Hirohito concerning the excesses, underlining his intent by committing *seppuku* (ritual suicide) on 27 July 1933.
>
> (Lamont-Brown, 1998, p. 73)

If the *Rikugunsho* had listened to officers like Nobuyoshi would things have turned out differently with Japan's quest for a co-existence sphere? What would have happened if the Japanese had succeeded in uniting the colonized people against the Western powers? Would there have been the massive onslaught against Western imperialism she had hoped for if the soldiers had not alienated so many of the local population with their brutality?

The Japanese doctrine of One Asia was seductively appealing especially to people who were oppressed by colonialism. It must not be forgotten that Western treatment of colonial subjects was often both routinely harsh and arrogantly racist. There are many instances of brutal punitive actions by colonial troops. In October 1930, when the French colonial administration realized that the Nghe-Tinh uprising in their territory of Cochin China was not a mere local outbreak, they punished the rebels with characteristic savagery:

> Punitive raids on villages were intensified, accompanied by burning, looting and summary executions. Many thousands of peasants were imprisoned in makeshift gaols attached to the military posts and subjected to a terrible range of tortures, inflicted by the French Foreign Legion. "Each post had its preferred method of torture, its local 'specialties'." In the Vinh provincial prison peasants were shut 150 to a room fifteen metres by six, chained night and day,
>
> (Hodgkin, 1981, p. 255)

To those who had been at the receiving end of such treatment, the rhetoric of anti-colonial politics was eagerly received, as was the Japanese slogan of "Asia for Asians". As Major Fujiwara, head of the Japanese black ops unit, the *F-Kikan*, stressed, the Japanese should win the friendship of the local population by promising to help them gain independence:

> Our activities must be consistent with our practice of helping the national independence movement of the Asian people who agree with our ideals and principles. We ought not to force our will upon them and interfere in their affairs.
>
> (Fujiwara, 1983, p. 35)

It is easy to dismiss all this as lies or propaganda, which it certainly was as much as the incessant talk of the superiority of British or American culture over everything else. In that age and time, pan-Asianism struck a certain resonance and did work upon the hopes of some of the subject people. Indeed, one legacy of the Japanese occupation of Malaya was that it signalled the death knell of British colonial power and its prestige throughout Asia, not just by the defeat of its armies but also by the alternatives it opened up. The Japanese occupation reminded locals that they had to fend for themselves and look after their own security. The nature of security had to change for it was clear that when the crunch came, the British cared more for themselves than their colonies. With this sea-change, the whole idea and expectation of internal as well as of external security had to be looked at now from local interests. Many Special Branch officers were highly suspicious of military intelligence after the war because they felt that it was they and not the army that truly understood and defended the security of the new Malaya that emerged after 1945.

The Japanese were, in this sense, more successful than the Germans had been in 1915 when they were trying to foment local uprisings against the British. Fujiwara's *F-Kikan* not only subverted the morale of many Indian troops but also successfully formed the Indian National Army (INA or *Azad Hind Fauj*). Even if the INA was never really an effective fighting force, the propaganda value was substantial. Fujiwara's cultivation of the anti-British Amar Singh and Pritam Singh, respectively the leader and the secretary-general of the Indian Independence League (IIL) in Bangkok paid off handsomely. On 28 December 1942, barely three weeks into the invasion, the IIL formed a military wing, the Indian National Army in Taiping, Perak. The INA which fought on the side of the Japanese for the rest of the war was led by Mohan Singh whom the Japanese promoted to general.

The formation of the INA was consistent with Japanese intentions to create as many resistance groups as they could to embarrass and harass the British. These included Raja Mahendra Pratap's Aryan Army, Burmese Independence Army, the *Hakurokai* (Society of the White Wolf), the pan-Turan Society of Budapest and the Grey Wolf Society in Turkey. The men who fought in these units were nationalistic or religious men who fought for what they thought as their freedom from the colonial yoke. That the Japanese often used them for their own purposes is another matter. Given the complexities, it was very difficult to condemn these fighters entirely as traitors as the Allies did after the war. Indeed, the Japanese cast their net wide to rope in all manner of anti-colonial forces. While substantial attention was focused on stirring up Indian sentiments since the advantages of such an alliance for the strategic situation is obvious, they also cast their nets as far as Central Europe and the Middle East:

> Their aims were three-fold: first of all to secure Asian and Middle East allies against Russia, to ensure a free flow of intelligence from Budapest, Istanbul, Ankara and to some extent places inside Moslem Russia and Mongolia, and, finally, to encourage Japanese-Muslim friendship.
> (Deacon, 1983, p. 137)

There is an object lesson here which also serves to underline a critical difference between Japanese and Western intelligence methods. Most intelligence operations need considerable investments of valuable time, energy and resources. Some demand extraordinary amounts of these. To most Western intelligence agencies, accountability for the expenditure incurred was fairly short-termed, predicated as it was upon the financial years that controlled the expenditure of even the biggest spy agencies. The pressure was, therefore, there to show results after a source had been cultivated over a fairly short length of time. The Japanese treated intelligence gathering differently and with greater patience. They were less pressured than Western agencies that needed proof of some obvious military or political value in a target since for them, economic, social and cultural information was accepted as equally valuable within the overall scheme of things. Japanese intelligence had, thus, not only a *different time frame* for its activities but, accompanying this, also a *different conception* of the value of a source.

This patience paid rich dividends when things came together for them. Peter Elphick and Michael Smith in their excellent book, *Odd Man Out*, have traced how Captain Patrick Heenan was turned into a traitor working for Japanese intelligence in the crucial months before the invasion of British Malaya in 1941. Heenan was that rare spy, a "walk-in". Like all walk-ins he was the best kind of catch—someone who volunteered his service and knowledge. Heenan was all the more dangerous since the normal coverage of anti-espionage would not have picked him out. It was hard for the British to imagine that one of their own, an officer no less, would sell out. However, the signs were always there had the British been more alert to the iniquities of their class system. In their book, the authors investigated Heenan's growing bitterness and disillusionment with a system that continuously reminded him of his inferiority. If the fault was ultimately Heenan's for betraying his country, *Odd Man Out* points out that it stemmed from the very nature of the British social arrogance and its proliferation of class divisions and racism.

Growing personal dissatisfaction led Heenan to his fateful move. Sometime between the end of 1938 and the first part of 1939, Patrick Heenan went on long leave to Japan where he took the opportunity to make contact with the Japanese Secret Service. Although at that time only a lowly subaltern on secondment to the Royal Indian Army Service Corps, he was made to feel that he had great value to the Japanese war effort. Above all else, this sense of being valued was what Heenan needed:

> In his lowly position with the Indian "Rice Corps", he must have been a very small cog in the Japanese intelligence machine, but at least they seemed to want him. The Japanese had won a friend for life. Their investment in him had cost them little, but within the space of a year, it was to pay dramatic dividends.
>
> (Elphick and Smith, 1994, p. 118)

At the end of October 1940, Heenan by now transferred to the 2/16th Punjab Regiment of the 6th Indian Brigade disembarked in Malaya which was the target of Japanese ambitions. By early 1941 the regiment had settled into its new camp at Arau in Perlis, close to the Thai border. The events that followed strained belief except that they were, unfortunately, true. They were apt testimony to the confusion exhibited by British military planners at this time.

Patrick Heenan was transferred out of the 2/16th Punjab on 18 March 1941 after a number of unauthorized trips across the Thai border had suggested to his commanding officer that he could be up to something fishy. However, in a terrible instance of sheer incompetence, Heenan was transferred to 300 Air Intelligence Liaison (AIL) at Alor Star as a GSO III (Int), that is a Grade Three Intelligence Staff Officer. To all accounts, the 300 AIL was engaged in extremely sensitive work crucial to the military security of Malaya. The outfit:

> helped plan the perimeter defences of the north-western airfields at Alor Star, Sungei Patani and Butterworth, and probably those in the north-east as well, since there was no equivalent section based in that area. They also took part in the preparation and implementation of the air defence scheme for Penang.
>
> (Elphick and Smith, 1994, p. 172)

Despite his CO's suspicions of him, Heenan now found himself in an ideal position to provide high-grade intelligence about the air defence of northern Malaya to his Japanese masters. Moreover, as part of the 300 AIL, Heenan would also have known in some detail the army's defensive plans through his role in the liaison and planning group of Malaya Command. In November 1941, three weeks before the Japanese invasion, Heenan was actually promoted to second in command of the Alor Star AIL after the unfortunate death of Captain Lindsay. As the number two man, he had access to even more military secrets. By the time Heenan was arrested on 10 December 1941, irreparable damage had been done. Whether it was entirely Heenan's doing or whether there were, in fact, other spies in place, the Royal Air Force in Malaya was exterminated within a week of the invasion. The vital northern airfields that could have threatened the Japanese beachheads in Kelantan were rendered unusable by Japanese light bombs that would allow them to eventually repair and put the runways back into use. Two of Britain's mightiest ships, the *Prince of Wales* and the *Repulse* were sunk off Kuantan, caught without the necessary air cover. As the Far East Combined Bureau (FECB) which collated British intelligence confessed belatedly in November 1941:

> Japanese espionage and intelligence activities are widespread, efficient and comprehensive .... It can be assumed that their reconnaissance of the country has been largely completed; there can be no doubt whatever that their information is much more complete than ours.
>
> (WO 208/1915, FECB Report No. 5401, November 1941, PRO, cited in Elphick and Smith, 1994, p. 136)

Heenan's activities added to the thorough and precise information that the Japanese had possessed by this time of all aspects of the country including its defences. If anything, this was a clear illustration that the Japanese did carry out systematic espionage in Malaya as a prelude to their invasion.

Even if Heenan had been arrested earlier, not much difference would have been made. So thorough was their coverage that the Japanese would have known of the details anyway. His case is an example of the success of the Japanese "humint" programme in Malaya. There was a certain quiet confidence among the British services that while the Japanese were able to recruit an Asian collaborator, they were not likely to be able to recruit a British officer. Heenan as it turned out may not be the only British spy run by Japanese intelligence. But the Heenan episode demonstrated the political confidence the Japanese had of running a British officer, and to do so even though as a 'walk-in' he was very possibly a provocator or a 'double'.

On 18 January 1939, raids under the Official Secrets Act were conducted on:

1. Ohara Tomoyoshi, Head of the Japanese Trade Bureau, at his office in Toyo Hotel.
2. Eifuku Tora, proprietor of the Taichong Kongsi, at 14 Queen Street.
3. Aoki Jiro, Assistant Manager, Pilot Pen Company, at Sakura Hotel and
4. Watanabe Genkichi, Kataoaka Kazunobu and Kuramochi Hiroshi of the South Maunchuria Railway.

The raid on Watanabe Genkichi yielded a confidential FMSR publication which Genkichi claimed under interrogation to have obtained from the Japanese Consulate-General, Singapore. When the police, in a follow-up operation, raided the Japanese Trade Bureau, they found 12 RAF official secret air photographs in the desk of one of its staff, Tate Assajiro, who was Head of the Japan Industrial Bureau. Tate claimed to have obtained these from Shirai Sadahiko who had been deported earlier in 1938 for security reasons. Documents found in the possession of Ohara Tomoyoshi also revealed evidence of organized spying as well as active propaganda in Malaya against China. The aim was to weaken Malayan Chinese support for the Nationalist Government of Chiang Kai Shek as well as to create an anti-Chiang party. The Japanese hoped through this to further the aims of Wang Ching-wei who was in charge of their puppet government in Central China. Wang had once been a trusted lieutenant of Sun Yat Sen and had also served as a second in command to Chiang Kai Shek. He had been bought over by the Japanese who used him to split up the sympathies and support of the overseas Chinese for the Nationalists. The documents seized in these raids revealed the presence of an inter-departmental intelligence committee of the Foreign Office, Colonial Office and Commerce and Industry Office directed by the Japanese Consul-General. These documents confirmed that the Consul-General's office functioned as the nerve centre of Japanese espionage in Malaya.

Heenan's ready co-option by the Japanese emphasized the other equally important aspect of Japanese espionage, which was the encouragement and manipulation of local discontent. Despite being an English officer, Heenan's loyalties were turned in this way as he sought redress for his shoddy treatment by an arrogant officer corps because of his suspected mixed parentage. Heenan wanted revenge against this racist contempt he felt from his fellow officers. Here, the Japanese had a potent and ready weapon in the appeal of their pan-Asia ideology. They passed themselves off as Asians fighting to free the oppressed races from the tyranny of Western and white domination and tried with varying degrees of success to convince the Chinese, Indians, Malays and other colonized people to join their cause. The Japanese made the Asian crusade into a propaganda weapon that they spread among their own troops. In the pamphlet, "Read This Alone and the War Can Be Won" distributed to all their troops on the invasion fleet, the anti-colonial message was clear:

> Three hundred and fifty million Indians are ruled by five hundred thousand British, fifty million South-east Asians by two hundred thousand Dutch, twenty-three million Indo-Chinese by twenty thousand French men, six million Malayans by a few ten thousand British and thirteen million Filipinos by a few ten thousand Americans. In short, four hundred and fifty million natives of the Far East live under the domination of less than eight hundred thousand whites. If we exclude India, one hundred million are oppressed by less than three hundred thousand.
>
> (Tsuji, 1960, p. 301)

This message to rise up and throw off the racial humiliation by the arrogant white races found much sympathy until the Japanese showed that they were just as cruel and often more brutal than the previous colonial masters. However, it was certainly part of the complacency of the British that they remained so convinced of the appeal of their own superiority until the walls came crashing down about their ears.

***

Rash Behari Bose had been befriended and protected by Toyama of the Black Dragon Society not without motive. From that time, the Japanese supported and sought to use the Indian revolutionary activities to undermine the morale of both the native civilians and troops. In 1940, the Special Branch noted with concern:

The existence of a gang of revolutionary minded Indians in Singapore, calling themselves the Hindustan Socialist Republican Army or the Hindustan Communist Revolutionary Army, came to notice early this year on the appearance on 25 January 1940 of cyclostyled handbills in Hindi preaching non-co-operation. Similar handbills in Hindu and Urdu appealing to the Indians to celebrate Indian Independence Day were posted in the town on 5 April 1940. These handbills purported to have emanated from the "Hindustan Socialist Republican Army" and were signed with the letters H.S.R.A.

(item 85, PIJ, 1940)

The claim to being socialist was as much propaganda as an effort to mislead the authorities. However, the real aim of the party was clearly to instigate Indian troops against the British. It was Ghadr nationalism all over again, only this time more serious as more than half of the troops defending the Malayan peninsula were not Europeans.

As the war approached, the anti-colonial seditionists stepped up their inflammatory attacks against the British. Most of these took the form of an appeal to Indian pride and nearly all were designed to inflame passions. With British troops heavily committed in Europe and the Mediterranean, Indian soldiers formed the bulk of imperial defence in British Malaya. It was natural for the Japanese to subvert them and Fujiwara's *F-Kikan* was one of those units formed to achieve this. The prize was certainly worth fighting over. In December 1941, the 23 battalions of Indian soldiers in Malaya accounted for 49 per cent of military strength. Of these 18 were regular Indian army units while five—the 1st Bahawalpurs, the 1st Hyderabads, the 1st Mysores, the Kapurthalas and the Jinds—were Indian State Forces raised by the Indian princes. These five ISF battalions, with their preponderance of Indian officers leading the platoons, became prime targets for the Indian revolutionaries and the Indian Independence League. A typical piece of subversive (*boryaku*) propaganda carried out by the Japanese was the anonymous letter circulated on 16 December 1940, which the British attributed to the HSRA. With time and less urgent concerns, we are less likely to be worried by its inflammatory content. Instead we can see its pretentious gestures, its empty pontifications, superficial appeals to ethnic pride and laughably hollow threats. However, we must not forget that in the context of the 1940s with the resentment towards British arrogance and the stirrings of nationalism especially in India and China, such efforts to incite were clearly dangerous and easily sparked off trouble. The handbill certainly made sense to quite a few of its Indian readers:

Dear Brother,

What you have done and are still doing, that is, helping the British Imperialists and appealing to your countrymen to do the same thing, are known to us. Until now, nothing was done to you for you are an Indian. Now we want to stop. If you refuse, then we may be forced to take a drastic step against you.

There are thousands of Indians in Malaya today suffering from unemployment, and you never do anything to relieve them. Moreover, Indian women are molested by the British troops in Bombay. They were forced to dance on the road and are even sometimes raped. Thousands of your countrymen were thrown into jails and murdered for preventing these things. You are to blame, because if it was not for you, the British dare not do anything. We would gladly accept such treatment, but we are much against, when innocent people suffer.

Therefore, we hope that you will alter you ways, and start to remedy the wrongs you have done.

Commander-in-Chief
of the ISRA

The Special Branch was soon aware that the ISRA was but another calling card of the Hindustan Socialist Revolutionary Army. A raid on their headquarters followed in July 1941 resulting in the arrest on banishment warrants of its two leaders, Krishna Dev Rai and Ram Adhar Rai.

Beginning 20 February 1941, the local propaganda war was strengthened by a series of radio broadcasts from Tokyo and Formosa that aimed to create uncertainty, panic and resentment especially among the Indian troops. The Special Branch monitored what it denounced as:

A series of hostile lying propaganda news items that have been broadcast from Tokyo and Taihoku (Formosa) in English, Dutch, Javanese, Chinese, Malay, Siamese and Hindi to the effect that unrest exists among the Indian troops who "show an increasing anti-war sentiment" and their British officers. In one case, it was alleged that over 300 casualties occurred; that desertion into Thailand by Indian troops had resulted, and that alarm had been caused to the civil population. There have also been similar lying broadcasts of insubordination among Australian troops recently arrived in Malaya. Although repeatedly officially denied by the Singapore and Penang Broadcasting Stations, these mischievous and mendacious broadcasts continue.

(item 18, PIJ, 1941)

Soon such tactics began to have their desired effect as first signs of discontent and a lessening of morale especially among the Indian troops could be detected.

It was, for the British, a nightmare replay of the 1915 Mutiny by the 5th Light Infantry that had led to the formation of the Special Branch. Now the old fears of native rebellion surfaced with perhaps even greater urgency as the Japanese, unlike the Germans, were already at the door and ready to take advantage of any signs of weakness. Soon those native troops, who were unhappy, became increasingly emboldened in their actions. In March 1941, the 1st Bahawalpurs complained against the unreasonable behaviour of their Commanding Officer (CO), Lieutenant-Colonel Roger Fletcher. Matters went from bad to worse and, despite the mediation of the military adviser to the ISF, Major-General F Gwatkin, a number of officers had to be sent home. The incompetent Fletcher, whose arrogance aggravated the situation, was himself replaced by Major H E Tyrrell. However, the new CO could not do very much as news spread among the dissident troops that they had scored an important point against their British masters. Not surprisingly, a number of men from the 1st Bahawalpurs went on to join the INA, among them Colonel G Qasim Gilni, Captains A D Jahangir, Mahmood Khan Durrani, Shaukar A Malik and Lieutenant Sanuallah. Another ISF unit, the 1st Hyderabad stationed at Kota Bahru, went to pieces and ceased functioning as an effective combat force soon after nightfall on 8 December upon believing a rumour that Japanese troops had reached their perimeter. According to reports, their morale was not helped by the reported panic of Australian aircrews. Within a short while, the defensive line collapsed at a critical stage of the battle and the troops fled. The Japanese soon established their foothold in Malaya.

However, it was not just ISF troops that were affected by subversion and low morale. Even regular Indian Army units experienced trouble. In an incident reminiscent of the mutiny of 1915, insubordination struck the 4th Battalion 19th Hyderabad Regiment at the Tyersall Park Camp in Singapore. At one stage, it was considered that the situation had deteriorated so badly that men from the all-white Argyll and Sutherland Highlanders, who shared the same barracks, were put on stand-by and ordered to mount guard over the weapons and ammunition of the Indians. In this case, first the Ahirs of 'A' Company and then the Jats of 'B' Company had refused to obey orders. The tension was only resolved when Lieutenant Zahir-ud-Din, who had been summarily transferred to India for his outspoken views on independence, was allowed to address the men. So the sedition was rampant also among the INA troops who could have been expected to be more resilient. After the British surrender a number of prominent officers of the Indian Regular Army joined the INA. One of these, Captain Mohan Singh of the 1st Battalion 14th Punjab Regiment became General of the INA.

The Japanese did not just focus their efforts on the Indians. Their doctrine of pan-Asianism attracted other nationalities. We find a number of references to these in the Special Branch notes. In December 1939, the Branch reported that:

> Mohammed Ghaus Mahjoeddin, an Indonesian doctor trained in Japan had arrived in Singapore on 3 November 1939. He was looking for work in the Johore area. Mahjoeddin was known to have been in touch with Rash Behari Bose and A.M. Sahaya. He was also known to be in touch with Mitsuru Toyama, inspiration behind the Black Dragon Society and General Inwane Matsui, leader of the Great Asia Society.
>
> (item 160, PIJ, 1939)

The connections were not just with those out to foment unrest. As a number of writers have pointed out, the Japanese were generally well regarded by the peasants and working class who admired their economic drive and technological development. Thus the current of subversion actually ran deeper as it fed upon popular sentiments:

> These Malays, mainly peasants and labourers associated Japan with a new hope of economic prosperity. This hope, which early in the occupation proved to be unfounded, was brought about in part by an avalanche of Japanese textiles, bicycles, toys and chinaware which poured into the local market during the 1930s ... Even Malays who never met any Japanese before 1942 viewed them favourably, saying that they were different from the allegedly egoistic British expatriates. These Malays looked forward to the arrival of the Japanese army ...[3]

The subversive network was both extensive and multi-faceted, making it difficult for the Special Branch to close down its main threats.

By operating behind a screen of cultural or academic societies, the Japanese often managed to evade specific charges of espionage. There was an uneasy feeling that many Japanese commercial organizations were engaged in some sort of spying although much of this appeared to be legitimate data gathering, map collecting or photography necessary to their business. Each apparent act of espionage found an easy explanation. Sometimes it was business information, at others a hobby, still others had something to do with business plans. The strategic concentration on plantations in an arc along the Johore highway was justified in terms of the need for synergy and ease of transportation. Mines along the East Coast followed the logic of geology and the need for ports to ship out the ore. Fishing vessels going along coastal waterways and into ports of every description were merely going about their legitimate business. Cultural societies that extol the virtues of the Japanese system and of its vision of pan-Asianism were there to introduce interested members of the public to a different way of life. Thus, it was argued that the Singapore Commercial Museum not only promoted Japanese goods but also needed to sponsor a significant number of inspection trips into the interior of Malaya. These collected information, maps and data, which were justified as meeting the needs of commercial companies. However, the Special Branch knew that the Commercial Museum was controlled and run by the *Nanyo Kyokai*, the South Seas Association. While on the surface a private organization the *Nanyo Kyokai* had extensive links with the Japanese Ministry of Commerce and, through it, controlled the Japanese Chamber of Commerce in Singapore. It was also an espionage organization that was controlled by their Foreign Ministry. So there were layers upon layers of bureaucracy and offices over it. If this duplication and proliferation of espionage fronts made no management sense nowadays, it served an important purpose in diverting British counter-espionage attention.

These business fronts and secret societies had been critical to the efforts of the militants to penetrate and take the army and then the government. Along the way, they instigated many incidents that facilitated the intervention of the Japanese Army in their territorial expansion. So it is difficult to see these organizations as entirely innocent pawns in the espionage game. They were deeply implicated in the plans of the military, for the gradual conquest of Asia. Through their proliferation, incestuous cross-engendering and sheer multiplicity coupled by a policy of tolerance, they managed to evade the attention of Western intelligence for a long time until their work had been done. It has sometimes been suggested that while they provided a legitimate front for espionage they were never really very effective. This is to misunderstand their real function within the baroque maze of cutouts and dummies that often makes it extremely difficult for outsiders to penetrate their real intentions.

There is no doubt that these companies complemented the work of military intelligence to a great extent. No less a person than Masanobu Tsuji, who master-minded the invasion of Malaya, admitted that his team of planners:

had learned a lot from commercial companies and private individuals, and in particular the Reverend Mr. Kozui Otani immediately after his southern tour.

(Tsuji, 1960, p. 6)

Japanese commercial attaches often had dual identities. In addition to their legitimate business duties many would belong to societies that were quasi government or hold other official titles. For instance, the Commercial Consul in Singapore in 1937 was also a member of the *Takumusho* (Colonial Office). What this says about his commercial interests is interesting since Singapore was declared a Japanese colony after the occupation. There are many examples of innocuous dentists, cooks and even barbers who turned up wearing military uniforms to welcome the invading army. Nakajima, the proprietor of a photo saloon outside the Singapore Naval Base well patronized by British servicemen, was an army colonel working in intelligence. There are too many of such cases for us to dismiss these as rumours or baseless speculations about the fifth column as invasion fever grew. Even individuals had their own stories to tell. Yap Hong Kuan recalls how a Mr Mitsui who used to rent his father's shop was an avid fisherman and photographer, who would spend all his weekends inspecting Lumut and Pangkor, coincidentally the most convenient spots for a landing from the sea. In fact, it was here that the British Force 136 smuggled in their operatives.

A comparison here with similar attempts by the Comintern to create such a smoke screen is useful. The communists had also tried to achieve a cover of apparent legitimacy for their infiltration through parallel organs, dummy organizations and united fronts. However, they never really succeeded. The biggest obstacle to such plans was that the Comintern was regarded as a hostile agency right from the start. In addition, the Comintern was declared an illegal organization right from the beginning and the full weight of the Special Branch was directed at it. Although it had politburo support, the Comintern was separate from the Soviet government and could not operate under the protection of diplomatic or commercial cover. Japanese espionage activities, on the other hand, worked behind the diplomatic and commercial protection of their consular offices. Moreover, they attracted little attention since they appeared to present little immediate threat. They were left alone as the British did not want to risk a diplomatic row. This was the dilemma the Japanese presented the Special Branch with. Unlike the Comintern that had identified itself as the enemy straightaway by declaring that its primary objective was to instigate and foment revolutionary changes to replace existing governments, the Japanese did no such thing. Indeed, they often established trade and diplomatic links with the colonial power and sought their protection. Thus, the Police intervened to protect Japanese property and trade at the height of the communist inspired AEBUS (Anti Enemy Back Up Society) campaign to boycott Japanese trade. It was indeed strange that the Special Branch knew that some of the Japanese companies protecting were up to no good against British interests and yet it was compelled by diplomacy and the law to help them.

In fact, the British often found themselves on the same side of the fence with the Japanese where communism was concerned. With their extensive and at times interlocking trading and imperial interests, both governments felt that communism was a threat to their social stability that had to be vigorously destroyed. Many Europeans sympathized with Japan:

> Westerners with foreign contacts, specially the businessmen resident in the Far East, had on the whole been well disposed to Japan. Japan professed to be the champion of foreign business interests. It claimed to be taking steps—in putting down bandits, in removing the Chinese officials who were the bane of traders—which the other countries had taken it upon themselves to do from time to time in the past and which they would have continued to do had they the resolution to stand up for their interests without regard for distractions elsewhere. Chinese xenophobia was the enemy of all who had to do with China. And, for a long while, Japanese action received a great deal of sympathy from certain sections of Westerners.
>
> (Calvocoressi et.al, 1999, p. 845)

It was, in a sense, unfortunate at this juncture of history that the underlying thrust of Japanese expansionism coincided somewhat with British views of events as far as trade went. This gave both nations powerful incentives to compete against each other and destroy those that worked against their common aims. Commercial competition was regarded as the main reason for Japan's aggressive behaviour. It was something that the British who increasingly equated imperial survival with competitive paramountcy could understand and negotiate with. Even if in some quarters there were those who believed that Japanese military expansion beyond Northeast Asia to Southeast Asia was a real threat, the prevailing view was that Japan could be brought to her knees through an economic war. While they feared Japan as a first-class military power, the advantages of economic might would sooner or later allow Britain to triumph once she had gained enough time to rearm. Meanwhile, it was best not to provoke Japan, not to take too strong a line in case she over-reacted irrationally. Thus, it was perhaps also best to afford some appeasement to her demands, unreasonable though these were:

> The British tended to favour the well-trodden pathway of Appeasement, a policy based upon "moderation" and conciliation which had served Britain's perfectly respectable selfish aims throughout the preceding century or more.
>
> (Calvocoressi, et. al., 1999, p. 824)

In any case, the British saw no harm in this. After all, such delicate balancing and trading of interests had worked for the Empire for the last hundred years or so. Paradoxically, the British did not at heart respect the Japanese whom they regarded as nothing more than Asian upstarts. They argued that once the British had rearmed, the Japanese would amount to nothing very much.

However, this did not mean that they were unaware of the dangers posed by Japanese militarism. Awareness and resolution are, unfortunately, two different things especially in diplomacy. The local authorities, in particular the Special Branch, had been aware of Japanese ill-intentions since the turn of the 20th century. Thus, the view that they were lax, blissfully ignorant of Japanese intentions or of their manifold espionage activities cannot be sustained. In **Operation Matador**, Ong even argues that the whole notion of the somnolent British administrator numbed into obliviousness by the Malayan heat and his gin was a myth:

> It is evident ... that from 1909 onwards there was a clear perception of the Japanese threat in London and Malaya. This was no fleeting suspicion or momentary ire. Through the calculations of national interests and considerations of power politics, the defence planners consistently assumed that Japan was the one and only likely and potential enemy in East Asia.
>
> (Ong, 1997, p. 6)

As Ong pointed out it was the British imperial defence planners back in London and not the soldiers on the spot that let British Malaya down.

***

Yet the truth of the matter is that Britain and Japan often found themselves in broad agreement on many matters since their strategic concerns were born of commercial rivalry and dominance. For instance, the British strategic planners found themselves agreeing with Japanese militarists where the danger of left-wing ideology was concerned. Revolution was something that both systems regarded with repulsive horror and went out of their way to combat. Similarly, the treatment of China was often determined and reconciled between the two parties by shared perceptions of trading and commercial advantages. This spirit of cooperation even extended to the treatment of the Chinese during the occupation. The English-educated Chinese were on the whole treated far better than those who spoke only Chinese since these were regarded as enemies. Patricia Lim asserts that:

> The MPAJA and the MCP were supported mainly by the Chinese-speaking Chinese but the English-speaking Chinese were less concerned with the war in China and did not harbour as deep an animosity against the Japanese. The Japanese were aware of this distinction.[4]

I do not happen to agree with this view as many English-speaking Chinese fought the Japanese as well. However, it is true that the Japanese had a special hatred of the communists whom they regarded as the one ideological enemy standing in the way of their colonial dominance in China. A number of fanatically militant societies had an irrational hatred of communism. The *Kokuhonsha* (Society of the Foundation of the State) was founded by Baron Hiranuma to combat the spread of communism. Using a mixture of patriotism, racism and strong-arm tactics the Society spread rapidly. The *Dai Ajia Kyokai* (Great Asia Society) which had already been mentioned earlier was an offshoot of and a front for the *Kokuhonsha*. Another offshoot the *Meirikai* (Society of Enlightened Ethics) was founded in 1932 by, among others, Koichiro Ishihara. It grew into a powerful paramilitary organization that had almost five million members, mainly army reservists. The aim was to protect the Emperor and the nation from deviant ideology like communism.

Even this cursory survey of the tactics adopted by the remarkable men guiding Japanese espionage would show how complex the Japanese network in British Malaya was. The complexity made it hard for the Special Branch to penetrate and even harder for arrests to be effected since proof was needed when it came to this. Unless the agent actually stole military secrets, recruited or compromised a British subject, possessed and distributed seditious pamphlets or agitated openly for revolutionary change the Branch could not really do anything without a major diplomatic protest. Moreover, while *many* of these organizations were no doubt linked to the militants not all of them were engaged in nefarious activities. There were certainly individuals who acted as spies or doubled up as such. But here again not all Japanese residents in Singapore were spies. It must also be remembered that for significant periods especially during the First World War the Japanese were allies. Japanese naval intervention and marines were of much help to Singapore in the 1915 mutiny of the 5th Light Infantry. This first Japanese military engagement in Southeast Asia was, with hindsight, a harbinger of things to come. Moreover by the thirties Japanese commercial interests were well entrenched in Singapore and Malaya.

The relationship between Chinese businessmen and the Japanese they were dealing with underlined a paradox. Although many Chinese saw the Japanese as both business rivals and as aggressors out to partition China, they had gradually become dependent upon Japanese trade. Not that the overseas Chinese did nothing. Indeed, each expansionist thrust into the Chinese mainland provoked an appropriately hostile reaction in British Malaya among its Chinese. Usually this took the form of boycotts of Japanese goods and produce. However, not until 1937 when the war in China broke out did the boycott have any effect. The fishing industry is a good example of the contradictions that Japanese commercial domination brought among the Chinese. In 1932, events in northeast China resulted in an attempted boycott of the lucrative Japanese fishing fleet in British Malaya.

Since the 1920s, Japanese militants of the *Sakura* or Cherry Blossom Society as well as individuals like Colonel Dohaira Kenji had been attempting to force the Japanese hand in Manchuria. On 18 September 1931, Japanese army officers in defiance of Tokyo set off explosives that destroyed a stretch of railway line belonging to the Southern Manchurian Railway Company (SMR) outside Mukden. The SMR was notorious as the front organization for Japanese expansion in the region. This explosion provided the necessary excuse for military intervention. An outbreak of fighting with the Chinese troops guarding Mukden followed which resulted in the capture of the barracks and the city. Almost simultaneously the Kwantung Army in Korea advanced across the border cutting off the Liaoning peninsula and threatening Tianjin. By the end of the year, this carefully orchestrated incident and the lightning attack had conquered Manchuria. The Japanese military named their puppet state Manchukuo with Henry Pu Yi, the last Chinese emperor, as its titular head. The Mukden incident created very strong anti-Japanese as well as anti-foreign feelings in China. Demonstrations broke out in many cities and in both Tianjin and Shanghai. In Shanghai, troops had to be deployed to protect the foreign concessions of the International Settlement.

Overseas Chinese also joined in the demonstrations. In Malaya, enraged Chinese called for the boycott of Japanese goods including the fish landed by Japanese trawlers mentioned before. The boycott had some initial impact but soon fizzled out. The attempted boycott ran into difficulties almost from the start. As the bulk of fish sold in Singapore by this time came from Japanese boats, any boycott would be like shooting one's own foot. Fish, after all accounted for a major part of the protein consumed by the population especially those from the working class. The economics made it unlikely that the boycott could be enforced. A face-saving if hardly Solomonic solution was finally negotiated whereby the Japanese wholesalers paid an additional 5 per cent commission to the Chinese Chamber of Commerce who undertook to use this 'tax' for the war effort in China. It was truly a case of commerce winning over ideology! With this settlement, the sale of fish resumed, the boycott coming to an end by 1932. There the matter rested although one lesson that was not lost on all was the stranglehold the Japanese had managed to gain even among the Chinese traders. The event also underlined the contradictions experienced by the Chinese as well as British in their efforts to contain Japanese penetration and aggression. The Chinese realized to their discomfort how much they had gradually come to depend on the Japanese for a staple part of their diet. The British was also faced with a similar Hobson's choice: the longer the boycott dragged on, the more their own commercial profits were affected. Furthermore, they had no real interest to see the Chinese organized successfully against the Japanese as the tactic could be turned into a weapon against the British themselves. So, both commercial considerations as well as the political realities worked to strengthen the Japanese hand while weakening their enemy.

Despite the relative lack of success in this early boycott, the Chinese felt that hurting the Japanese economically remained their most potent weapon. A series of Anti Enemy Backing Up Societies and boycott movements sprang up as the Japanese incursions in China increased. In 1937, another boycott of Japanese goods was called, this time in response to the outbreak of war. On 7 July 1937, what historians regard as the first battle of World War II took place when Chinese and Japanese troops fought over the Luguoqiao (Marco Polo Bridge). The Chinese won the first round but within days the Japanese had seized the bridge and dug in around its perimeters, effectively severing rail links between Beijing and the rest of the country. The conflict widened when Japan sent 15 additional Japanese divisions to North and Central China.

In Tokyo, Prince Konoye called for a final solution to the China problem. The war soon engulfed Shanghai, Nanjing and much of the Eastern China seaboard. In British Malaya, a boycott was declared once again. This time round it was more effective. The Rape of Nanking at the end of the year aroused further widespread public anger and resolution when Japanese troops ran riot killing, raping and looting.

Japanese economic interests in Southeast Asia suffered severely from the 1937 boycott. Exports to British Malaya dropped by almost two thirds in 1938 from 67,433 million yen in 1937 to 30,696 million yen in 1938. A further decrease was recorded the following year. Japanese traders tried various means to break the boycott including repackaging and reshipping their goods. They also resorted to the use of local proxies to distribute their produce. Despite these underhand tactics, the boycott slowly began to have its required effect. The Chinese were prepared to enforce their action sometimes with violence. A number of riots broke out as gangs rampaged through shops looking for and destroying Japanese goods. In 1937, one such incident in Penang rapidly escalated into a major riot. Onraet, then Inspector General of Police and former Director of the Special Branch, recalled how he was summoned to Penang to deal with the troubles as they brought the city to a standstill. His account gives us a sense of the turbulence of that period:

> One such serious affair occurred in Penang during a visit of the Governor, Sir Shenton Thomas, who was so impressed by the violence of the outbreak that he phoned me in Singapore and ordered me to fly to Penang to direct police action. I got in touch with Air Commodore Tedder who was then in command of the RAF in Singapore and he had me flown up to Penang. The trouble had arisen from the sale of soya beans said to have been exported by the Japanese from Manchuria. The local boycott committee decided that the beans should not be sold and ordered their immediate reshipment back to the consignor. From the beans the trouble spread to other goods imported by this and other firms, and in a flash search committees invaded the Chinese shopping district; and then the fun began. Shops put up their shutters, searchers tore them down; local society feuds flamed up, and for 48 hours Penang looked like a city being sacked. Any police parties that were not sufficiently strong at any point were treated as sympathizing with the Japanese and driven off.
>
> (Onraet, n.d., p. 118)

Onraet's account reminds us that the rioters were just as ready to turn against the police as they were upon each other. The Special Branch knew that movements such as the China Relief Fund Committee and the Singapore Overseas Chinese Anti-Japanese National Salvation Association were prime targets for the Malayan Communist Party as well as the Kuomintang. These contending parties sought to extend their influence through the anti-Japanese campaign by taking over the key patriotic organizations. The British crackdowns on these movements were seen as efforts to appease the Japanese. However, the Branch tried to maintain some equilibrium by being selective in the arrest of the dissidents. They could well afford to be, as by this time they had infiltrated an agent into the Malayan Communist Party. Moreover, the British were also more restrained in their arrests of the Chinese as they recognized the Japanese threat to the security of the British possessions in South East Asia.

Even then, there continued to be a number of those in authority who had their heads buried so deeply in the sand that even Special Branch efforts to alert them to the danger were dismissed as unnecessarily alarmist. By the early 1930s, though, London had become alarmed by the continuing Japanese expansion. It was acknowledged that in the event of war in the Far East, Japan would pose the greatest danger to the Empire. Here again, the consideration was not just military as commercial competition had become increasingly fractious. By 1931, Japan's advances in Manchuria had placed her in a position to threaten Britain's vital interests, especially trade:

> Those interests stood directly in the path of Japanese expansion. Japan could not hope to operate in China without appropriating the use of British-owned railway stock, interfering with British control over Chinese maritime customs and the salt gabelle, upsetting British merchant trading monopolies, and in many other ways disturbing Britain's nearly 50 per cent share in Chinese commercial affairs, a level of investment worth perhaps 500 million pounds at 1937 prices.
>
> (Calvocoressi et. al., 1999, p. 837)

While alarm bells were going off in Whitehall awakening the bureaucrats and politicians reluctantly to the danger that had crept up on them, many senior authorities in Malaya remain strangely unperturbed.

Mervyn Llewellyn Wynne, the Deputy Inspector General of Police and previously Special Branch Director, "found his preoccupation with writing reports on Japanese subversion dismissed as paranoia in some quarters" (Elphick and Smith, 1994, p. 140). He made repeated efforts to warn his superiors but found them either complacently certain that there would not be any danger or reluctant to act upon Japanese reaction. It was literally a case of not being able to get it right either way. Indeed, the Japanese often took advantage of their knowledge of British reluctance to antagonize them to further their actions. This is illustrated by what we may describe as the grand espionage inspection tour in 1940 by top Japanese officials just before war broke out. In January 1940, the Branch became aware of a sudden and significant upsurge in the number of key Japanese officials passing through the region. At the beginning of the month, the Japanese Consul-General, Kaoru Toyoda, accompanied by the Vice-Consul, Tomogoro Hashizume, and his private secretary, Shunzo Nagayama, made a sudden visit to Malaya without the usual courtesy of first informing the authorities, thereby seriously breaching protocol. The Branch recorded, not without irony, that a brave face was finally put on the matter:

> It is usual for a Consul-General to make such a tour but in this instance it appears to have been done rather hurriedly; the first information received was from a report in the *Nanyo Nichi Nichi* that the Consul-General had gone.
>
> (item 50, PIJ, 1940)

In other words, the first the British knew of this clearly significant inspection visit, which took in a number of key strategic sites, was from a press report! This shows the disregard the Japanese had for the British lion.

It turned out that this Consul-General's visit was just the tip of a whole series of orchestrated events. In the same month, Malaya was visited by Rei Ori, a Secretary of the Overseas Affairs Bureau of the Department of Overseas Affairs; Koun Takeda, Vice-President of the Economic Investigation Committee of the Southern Manchurian Railway Company (SMR); and Ichiro Inamine of the East Asiatic Investigation Bureau. British Intelligence was aware that both these entities were intelligence arms of the Japanese Secret Service. The SMR was entrusted with the collection of information (*chosa*) for the whole of Asia, and the East Asiatic Investigation Bureau headed by Shumei Okawa, who was among those who arranged the "incident" on 15 May 1932 when Ki Inuka, the Prime Minister, was assassinated. Given this context, there could be no doubt what the tour group was doing; it was inspecting the future battleground as well as prospecting the future colony they were so sure would be theirs within months.

The SMR was often used to create what the communists called "semi colonies", areas that were under the economic control of the Japanese military. The SMR or *Mantetsu* was, in fact, a typical example of the intertwining of government, military and private business that characterized Japan's expansion at the time. It was to all purposes a semi-government corporation, which monopolized the development and management of economic and political matters in Manchuria. The SMR was in many ways indistinguishable from the military since the Imperial Japanese Army was ever ready to back up its actions. The Railway Company was but part of the Imperial War Machine of Japan. Established in 1906, it soon grew to a giant consortium of 80 companies that carried on its espionage work through the war until the Soviet invasion of Manchuria in August 1945. The *Mantetsu* did not confine its activities to Northeast China; it also engaged in extensive research in South Seas affairs.

As if this was not bad enough, hard on their heels, another bunch of—from the British point of view highly unwelcome—visitors turned up in Singapore on 25 January aboard the *S.S. Brazil Maru*. These included Shinichi Sato of the MBK who was believed to be connected with the Japanese Navy; Tamoh Ikeda, technical expert of the Ministry of Welfare; Eiji Hanamizu, Secretary of the Exchange Bureau of the Finance Ministry; Takesaburo Kazuma, Director, Mitsubishi Shoji; and last but not least Peter Hashimoto, adviser to the Yamanken Shoten. The British believed Peter Hashimoto to be a high-level courier and also a controller in charge of field agents. The team on board the *S.S. Brazil Maru* spelt out starkly the Japanese motives. A more complete train of officials inspecting a colony—or, in this case, an intended colony—could not be imagined. At the same time and seemingly by chance, Murata Senda, proprietor of Senda and Company who had been deported from Malaya for spreading propaganda inciting anti-British feelings among the Indians, was compelled to stay in Singapore on 6 and 7 February. His excuse to the authorities was that he had to be in the British colony while waiting to catch a connecting flight on KLM to Palembang in Sumatra. Senda flew off on 7 February in the company of Peter Hashimoto. The Japanese were not only playing mind games, but showing their contempt for the helplessness of the British authorities. They clearly knew that the broad policy of appeasement would ensure that the Special Branch could not crack down on them and was testing the limits. They were not unhappy if an incident arose from the friction and provided excuse for official grievance.

All these members of the great espionage tour, as we may call the occasion, chose to stay while in Singapore at the Toyo Hotel. The hotel, known as a notorious centre of espionage, was the permanent residence of Shinzo Nagayama of the Japanese Consulate. Nagayama was known to be more than a consular functionary. He was, in fact, a major specializing in intelligence in the Japanese Army. Later that year, in October 1940, he fled Singapore when things got too hot, returning to Japan by way of Surabaya on the *S.S. Nitiran (Nichiran) Maru* in the company of Ichizo Kobayashi, leader of the Japanese economic mission to the Netherlands East Indies. Dutch sources confirmed that Nagayama entered Java under an assumed name, Shigekazy Tanaka, although he proffered a diplomatic passport. The incident highlights the persistent abuse of consular privileges by Japanese intelligence agencies using diplomatic cover to conceal the identities of their field agents.

***

There was no doubt what this sudden flurry of Japanese interest in the region signalled. It was no less than an inspection tour of their projected colony to further their knowledge as well as rectify their intelligence shortcomings at first hand. It was also deliberately cocking a snook at the British, given the circumstance and the composition of the meeting. It was certainly provocation and if not all the military authorities in Japan approved or condoned this, the actions certainly had the support of top officials. The Japanese came, provoked and waited for the roar. Nothing happened—not even a squeak in protest. At the very least, the lack of reaction must have further emboldened those who wanted war. In addition, sympathizers to the Japanese cause would also have drawn the conclusion that the colonial decline was clear. The Special Branch recorded its frustration in not being able to deal with this and other incidents in its usual vigorous manner. The Branch was helpless in the face of the general reluctance to offend the Japanese. The evidence was there for all to see:

> The movements recorded are too convenient and fit too well to be mere coincidence.
>
> (item 6, PIJ, 1941)

The intelligence evaluator ended by pointing out:

> It would be *hardly correct* to assume that the whole of the above is one huge conference though it may have been. The Cabinet just changed in Japan, and the new Overseas Minister must want first hand information on all Japanese goods, the China incident is boiling up for settlement: and the *Brazil Maru* is a brand new super-boat, on which everyone would like to travel.

All these must have been factors which brought these people together in Singapore at this time. Nothing more should, *it is considered*, be read into this.

(item 50, PIJ, 1940)

The frustration was quite obvious. Wherever that considered view came from, the Branch's suspicions were forcefully clear. On the other hand, there was really nothing the Branch could do given the general policy of the colonial government. Internal security had to give way to the larger needs of the Empire. So although from its monitoring the Branch knew that such provocation always had a larger meaning, its views were subordinate. Japanese subversion went beyond the political domain to the active gathering of intelligence material for an invasion.

It can be argued that often the British as well as the Americans went to extraordinary lengths not to provide the Japanese with an excuse to extend hostilities. In December 1937, Japanese air force and navy planes attacked and sank the *USS Panay*. Later that day similar attacks were also carried out on the British ships; the *HMS Bee* and *HMS Ladybird* being 'only' damaged, as the reports went. Then there was the strafing of the British Ambassador Hughe Knatchbull-Hugesson as he was travelling from Shanghai to Nanjing. How the times had indeed changed! One could not have imagined a deliberate attack on and wounding of a British Ambassador in the near past that would not have brought a spirited response from the Royal Navy. In the following year, Japanese soldiers in Shanghai, once again without strong British reaction, killed two British policemen. What happened in Malaya was, therefore, a relatively minor bearding of the British lion. These events increasingly convinced and assured the more militant of the Japanese that the fighting spirit of the British was absent. To others, these events showed that the bankruptcy of white colonial rule was at hand and soon they would be able to realize their nationalist aspirations.

So, at this stage when decisiveness was most needed from the British, their hesitations merely confirmed the views of those who argued that continued provocation would not meet any strong response. Hence, the Japanese Army occupied Indo-China without expecting the Americans to retaliate with a full-scale economic boycott. Intelligence officials had indeed believed that embargo was the wrong move, as it would push Japan into war. Thus, both Allies and the Japanese appeared to be caught in a mutual embrace as they plunged unthinkingly towards a conflict that would bring death and destruction to so many innocent people. One great injustice was that political intelligence was rarely given the credit it deserved. Such intelligence was marginalized for the more immediate expediency of other aims.

Whatever intelligence was gathered went to naught as the defence chiefs vacillated and the politicians sought to placate Japan. Within Southeast Asia, intelligence was often not collated despite the presence of many agencies. It was a case of too many cooks spoiling the broth. All matters regarding Malayan intelligence were, in theory, sent to the Far East Combined Bureau (FECB) and from there to MI5 and the British Secret Service.

In turn the FECB supposedly reported to the Committee for Imperial Defence (CID) at least until 1939 after which the War Cabinet replaced it in the war years. Unfortunately, the CID itself was less of a decision-making body than a structure to filter and refine (Calvocoressi, 1999, p. 828) such information as came in from the various parts of the Empire. Burdened as it was by the sheer amount of information it had to handle as well as the various actions expected of it, the CID often left the day-to-day decisions to the military command. Moreover, the CID was a complex network of unwieldy units that often worked at cross-purposes. There were nearly 100 inter-departmental sub-committees that often did not consult with each other. Hence, the top often made decisions without really being able to consult the relevant departments. It was really as some have put it, Churchill's war!

Such conflicting priorities and aims were seen in the British intelligence coverage of Southeast Asia. In Malaya itself, intelligence was coordinated through the Defence Security Office (DSO) of the Singapore Government. However, the DSO itself reported to the Malayan Intelligence Committee that also included the armed forces and the civil police. While this Intelligence Committee was supposed to have an overview of all the threats, it did not have an intelligence gathering capacity for which it was dependent on the goodwill of the military or police agencies. The authorities apparently did not heed the lesson of the Political Intelligence Bureau that had a short and ineffective history. The Bureau proposed in 1921 by Sir Lawrence Guillemard to Churchill never did anything more spectacular than arrange for the collating and publishing of abstracts of intelligence for the peninsula that came out as the *Political Intelligence Journal*. In essence, the Bureau could not really do anything since it had no agents, no expertise and none of the police powers to intervene and investigate civilian affairs.

There was also at this time a proliferation of intelligence outfits. The military ran its various intelligence outfits that often kept findings to themselves. There was, for instance, the Military Intelligence Department that had direct control of the military side of things. In addition, each of the armed services had in place or were developing their own intelligence units such as the 300 Air Intelligence Liaison unit that Patrick Heenan was assigned to. The Far East Combined Bureau, for instance, attempted its own surveillance of anti-British activities through the Far Eastern Security Service. This must not be confused with the British Secret Intelligence Service (SIS) or MI6 as it was renamed after 1942. SIS often operated through the Foreign Office with station chiefs attached to various countries. MI5 also had an agent housed in the Special Branch headquarters in Singapore who passed himself off as the Defence Security Officer. Underlining the importance of the island was a Special Liaison Unit from Bletchley Park that carried out the interception and deciphering of enemy communications. This was the highly classified Ultra unit that broke and read Japanese as well as German codes. In Singapore the Ultra unit of three officers, Captain P Marr-Johnston, Captain G G Stevens and Lieutenant N F Webb, was innocuously named the military special intelligence party (Elphick, 1998, pp. 174–175). Since Ultra was hardly deployed outside England, the presence of this unit in Singapore suggests the intelligence planners' growing certainty that Japan was about to go to war. How much the unit managed to find out about the actual Japanese plans for the invasion of Malaya is not yet known but the suspicion is bound to be that the full details when they are finally known may substantially rewrite the whole history of the British defence of her colonies in the East.

While the armed forces covered the external approaches, the Government largely depended for their ground intelligence of Malaya and the neighbouring countries on the civil police. This meant, of course, the Special Branch, which had to face up to the increasing presence of the senior services like the MI5 and the SIS from London. As part of the contingency planning for a future war, MI5 had suggested that a Civilian Security Officer (CSO) be appointed to work with its station chief then known as the Defence Security Officer. In 1939, Arthur Dickinson, who by then had replaced Onraet as the Inspector General of Police, was appointed the first CSO. Dickinson suggested, in 1939, the setting up of the Malayan Security Service (MSS) that would merge the Special Branch and the Defence Security Office. At the same time, a Security Officer was appointed for each of the states, the forerunner of the present Malaysian Special Branch setup. The MSS that was set up on the eve of the war came too late to have much of an impact. Besides, one feels that it merely expanded on and often duplicated the work of the Special Branch without really adding to the value of the intelligence.

One major consequence though was that existing agents handled by the Branch were now passed on to other agencies. In this way, Loi Teck, the Secretary General of the Malayan Communist Party and by then a British agent, was handed first to MI5 and then to MI6. Unfortunately, these different agencies were sometimes at odds with one another making not only for confusion but also inter-departmental rivalry. The Special Branch was, for example, often felt to be too tough in its methods, too much of the secret-CID police type and not sufficiently mindful of the larger political game to be played. Of course, that this game of appeasement and reproachment that British politicians emphasized backfired and did not have much value, was conveniently overlooked.

The Special Branch was seen as basically a political unit carrying out what were essentially thought of as police duties. Larger matters of international diplomacy and war were not regarded as being within its purview. The Branch reflected the political doctrine as well as the ideological persuasions of its age. This was brought home with force in the monitoring, or rather lack of monitoring, of Malay subversion. While the colonial authorities had always been alert to the threats from the Indians (since the mutiny of 1915) and the Chinese (as a result of their triads, nationalism and communist activities) these suspicions reflected colonial prejudices. On the other hand, despite their status as subject population, the Malays, for a variety of reasons, never received the same intensity of coverage from the Special Branch. Perhaps the constructed image of the Malays as a happy-go-lucky and docilely gentle race deceived the British into thinking that the natives were happy to accept their colonial role. Perhaps it was also essential to the framework of colonial ideology to dismiss any possibility of the Malays as likely dissidents since British writings often represented and justified the British as the defenders of Malay freedom and their liberators from slavery. In other words, colonial ideology was caught within its own contradictions; it could not carry on the pretence of being the well-received saviour of the country if it was to admit that there was any hint of resentment towards it. With the Chinese and the Indians, the colonial response was simpler; they were not regarded as natives or locals, merely immigrants who had little stake in the country. This myth was perpetuated and formed the basis of an essentially racial justification of colonial exclusion towards a large part of the population. The Malays, on the other hand, were people who recognized the advantages of colonial rule. When the time came, the vehemence and intensity of Malay nationalist dissidence surprised both the military authorities and the Special Branch.

With the first shots of the invading troops pouring across the beaches at Kota Bahru and as the first bombs were exploding, the British awakened to the bitter truth. There was a fair amount of substantial sympathy for the Japanese calling for pan-Asianism and the throwing off the white colonial yoke. By then as we shall see it was far too late to contain the damage. The date 8 December 1941 ended more than the myth of British military prowess. It also showed up the falsity of colonial propaganda that its rule was welcome.

The Branch swung around to the other extreme, noting with a despondent alarmism that:

> The reaction of Malay nationalism to Japanese aggression has been at once spectacular, and the most dangerous feature in the conditions created in the country by the invasion. The speed and initial success of the Japanese stroke which has given them temporary possession of Penang and Province Wellesley, Perlis, Kedah, Trengganu and most of Perak within the first three weeks of the campaign, has had much to do with the change of sentiment against the British connection. The protected States have found themselves unprotected, and the assurance of preparedness has been disproved by events. In the East, and perhaps in the Far East, particularly nothing succeeds like success, and the strongest arm rules.
>
> (item 178, PIJ, 1941)

Again and again throughout this period we find deep shock and disbelief in the palpable sense of betrayal the British felt by a constituency they thought they had cultivated so successfully and taken for granted for so long.

Such was the prevailing mindset that the Branch could only resort to the catch-all and meaningless term of 'fifth column' to laying the fault on any convenient target. They felt dissension was everywhere and where they had once blamed the Chinese, they now blamed the Malays:

> But invasion has proved there exists a dangerous and actively hostile and treacherous side to Malay sentiment towards the British, which is the Malay Fifth Column in the country. Although reports are lacking, enough is known to divide this treasonable section of the Malays into the following categories:
>
> 1. Disaffected Malay Sultans, Chiefs and Ministers suspected of having secret quisling (sic) "understanding" with the Japanese prior to invasion.

2. A Malay nationalist organization largely composed of Malay Government servants and others of the English-educated class definitely in the service of the Japanese chiefly for propaganda work and to swing Malay sentiment in favour of the Japanese during the invasion on the pan-Asian appeal.
3. Disaffected members of the Malay armed forces forming part of the garrison of the country, viz., the various State and Settlement Voluntary units, some of which are stationed in Singapore, the Malay Regiment, the Johore Military Forces, and to a lesser extent, some members of the various Police Forces in the Peninsula.
4. An unknown number of paid enemy agents of various nationalities including Malays, active behind the invaders, in such work as signalling to aircraft, feeding information to the enemy, operating illicit wireless transmitters and the like.

(item 178, PIJ, 1941)

The report should not be accepted without questioning; the British appeared to have gone to the opposite extreme in their accusations of disloyalty. Perhaps the shock of the invasion and the loss of their stereotypical view of the natives were making them see shadows where there were none.

The list as it stands is surely too comprehensive, more a list of likely seditious activities than anything else. Whether all of these actually existed and to what extent they did will, perhaps, never be known. Certainly, panic and despondency were now prevalent and must have contributed to the increasing reports of enemy agents and fifth column activities. At one stage the RAF flew over Singapore at night while air raid alarms were sounded in an attempt to entice Japanese agents into breaking the blackout curfew. Persistent rumours also swept through Singapore of a transmitter located in the northwestern part of the island that was providing military information to the Japanese. Some of these had bases—in fact one was found Heenan's possession when he was arrested! On the other hand, many of the stories about agents, fifth columns and transmitters were planted by Japanese disinformation aiming to weaken further the morale of the defenders. In any case, the panic was so widespread that people were ready to believe anything.

Yet even if half of what the Special Branch had written is true, the security of British Malaya would have been seriously compromised. In many cases, the Branch found that there was a basis to the speculations of disloyalty. For instance, the Special Branch found out to their acute embarrassment that one of their own Malay agents had been compromised. 'Turned' by the Japanese, the agent built around him a network of agents that was prepared to work against the British. He was also in touch with the Indonesian anti-colonial agitators who viewed him as a key man in unifying opinion against the British. These were part of Major Fujiwara's *F-Kikan* efforts to penetrate and destabilize the Malayan population. The 'turned' agent was a good catch for the Japanese since he was also President of the *Kesatuan Melayu Muda* (KMM) or Malay Youth Union of Kuala Lumpur and by that time he:

> was known to the Special Branch as a paid agent of the espionage section of the Japanese Consulate in Singapore (and) associated with a political organization referred to by the Japanese as *Kame* (tortoise) and intended to aid a Japanese invasion on Fifth Column lines …
>
> (item 178, PIJ, 1941)

the damage had been done. He had also managed to buy over the Warta Malaya from Syed Hussain Alsagoff with the $18,000.00 cheque given to him by Ken Tsurumi, the Japanese Consul-General in Singapore. In his case, the Branch had been monitoring him for some time although

> caution and reticence imposed by the requirements of source-protection, prevented earlier action against Ibrahim and his activities.
>
> (item 178, PIJ, 1941)

The Special Branch had managed to penetrate into and place a source close to this group of potential enemy agents after becoming suspicious of their actions. This was a double game in which the Branch was watching a person who was supposed to be an agent in their employ. The case also illustrates the intense ambivalence on all sides.

Actually the Branch did not move against their agent until the eve of the invasion itself when he was arrested as part of a widespread crackdown during which 113 Malays were detained. At 7.30 p.m. on Sunday, 7 December 1941, the Special Branch arrested their man at his house at No. 75, Siang Lim Park, Geylang in Singapore. Moments after they completed his night-long interrogation, the Branch received the news that the Takumi Detachment, part of the 18th Division had landed at Kota Bahru at 1.30 a.m. At least the uncertainty that war had come to British Malaya was over now. Intensive interrogation of Ibrahim confirmed the close links between the KMM and the *Kame*. Following this, the Branch arrested Isahak bin Haji Mohamed, the editor of the *Warta Malaya*. Fujiwara of the *F-Kikan* wrote of how Onan Siraji, Vice-President of the KMM, told him at their meeting that in late December Ibrahim, president of the KMM, upon receiving the message from you (i.e. Fujiwara) sent from Bangkok, issued an order to his comrades-in-arms to co-operate with the Japanese troops.

(Fujiwara, 1983, p. 99)

More of the conspirators would have been arrested as the Branch soon compiled a list of more than 500 suspects. But by now the Japanese advance was sweeping all before it. Despite the rapidly disintegrating situation the Branch managed to detain 71 suspects in the Federated Malay States, 13 in Malacca, three in Johore and 26 in Singapore. Other KMM members like Mustapha Hussein, the Vice-President, evaded the dragnet and would come forward in due course to help the Japanese as guides and interpreters.

Even though arrests had been made, the Branch was forced to confess that all this effort was perhaps too little and too late. In particular, the monitoring of the Malay ground which their own circumstance as colonial rulers should have reminded them was crucial, had been shoddy. The KMM, for instance, as a platform for the expression of Malay nationalism enjoyed considerable support across a wide segment of society. The movement was popular with members of the aristocracy as well as the intellectual elite like

Raja Shariman in Perak, Datuk Hamzah bin Abdullah in Selangor, Tengku Mohammad bin Tengku Besar in Negri Sembilan, Tengku Mohammad bin Sultan Ahmad in Pahang, Datuk Onn bin Jaafar in Johore.

(Cheah, 1983)

The Branch was forced to admit that they were caught on the wrong foot as far as the monitoring of the Malay ground had been concerned. The British colonial administration did not help much in winning over the Malays. There had been no effort until late into the Japanese invasion to prepare key members of the Malay political elite for evacuation or the setting up of an alternative administration-in-exile. Fumbling British efforts to persuade the Sultans to leave did not meet with much success or approval. The Sultan of Selangor and the Raja of Perlis rejected offers to evacuate to Singapore while the Sultan of Pahang wary of being moved by force took refuge in the jungles until the issue was decided. Tunku Abdul Rahman, the future Prime Minister of an independent Malaya, took his father, the Sultan of Kedah, away to the relative safety of a detached palace at Kulim, west of Penang, when he heard rumours that the British were trying to remove him by force to Penang. Lieutenant Goro Nakajima of the *F-Kikan* met the royal family there, promising them Japanese cooperation. Major Fujiwara himself met Abdul Rahman in Alor Star. The Japanese took positive actions to assure and to win over the Malay royalty while the British were vacillating.

The flood of information often came too late for any decisive intervention by the Special Branch. This was the case with the conspiracy to restore the Rhio (Rhiau) Sultanate under Japanese protection or the equally disturbing news about the formation of the *Persatuan Partai Kebangsa'an Indonesia dan Malaya*, a pan-Malayan political party that sought to create a greater Indonesia. In fact, as the Branch realized, it was often in the dark about the nature or extent of Japanese-Malay link-ups,

> One general comment is justified at this stage, namely the complete absence of inside information from local Government or other sources, of the existence of treasonable hook-ups between the Japanese and the Malays of high and low estate, as a preparation for the invasion.
>
> (item 178, PIJ, 1941)

This is a frightening admission of the failure of British intelligence to anticipate the reaction of an important constituency of their Malayan possessions. It could hardly have expected that grave consequences would not result from such failures! To be fair though this failure comes in part from a wider myopia about its possessions, itself a reflection of the ideological and cultural paradigms that had marked its perception of the land and its people.[5]

***

The military momentum of the Japanese advance cut through hastily erected and badly prepared British defences like a hot knife through butter. The imaginative tactics of the Japanese: bypassing strong points, appearing from what the British had thought were previously impenetrable jungles, and the efficient organization of their supplies were accounted for in part by wild speculations of agent provocateurs, fifth column elements and enemy sympathizers. The obvious panic and poor behaviour of some of the troops and the colonials as they fled added to the general collapse of morale as well as the will to resist. Penang was a tragic example of the British readiness to evacuate Europeans over the locals. British troops and administrators scrambled to board the ships, leaving behind them scenes of chaos. The general population suffered as essential services and supplies dried up and became unavailable. This deprivation of public amenities and food also meant that it was pointless to talk about resistance for any length of time. Penang simply could not hold out against a Japanese siege as food, water and other utilities were not available. The lesson of Penang was that civil defence needed to be organized if a siege was to be withstood. It had become apparent by mid December that it was likely Singapore, too, would face a Japanese onslaught. Whether the island could fight off a siege would depend on the effectiveness of its civil defence. Under the circumstance, only total mobilization of all resources and manpower could stave off the approaching catastrophe.

It was at this point that the tides of war brought the Special Branch to a special place in their dealings with the Chinese whom they had been monitoring for the last 30 years. The events that followed as the Branch helped set up the anti-Japanese front under Tan Kah Kee are both an apt example as well as a fitting end to the fateful encounters that the Special Branch played in repairing the relationship between the British and their colonized subjects. Amidst the ruins of war and even as the bombs rained down, a ray of hope shone through in the genuine recognition of each for the other's strengths. If this was born out of desperation it also represented the possibility for unity in the common wish to perform public good. That, after all, was what the Special Branch had been set up to do and what it had sought to do all these years. It needed, though, the flames of war in 1941 to bring this to centre stage for all the participants. Perhaps it was also prescient of the future when the countries would be independent. It was in any case a signal pointing out that internal security was inseparable from national security.

Japanese espionage and subversion had changed the nature of Special Branch activities as the 1930s proceeded. Instead of a preoccupation with the political dimensions of communism, the Branch became aware that a common and more fearsome enemy had appeared. The Japanese were a threat both to Britain as well as the Chinese residents of their colonies. They were, by this time, well aware of events on the Chinese mainland. By 1933, the gloves were off as far as the Special Branch was concerned as Japanese intentions became ever more clearly militaristic. Onraet had formed the Japanese Section by 1933 as the Special Branch began to be more than just interested in the movements of Japanese passengers and residents in the area. In 1936, Onraet recruited Major K S Morgan of the Indian Army to be the first head of the Japanese Section of the Branch. It was Morgan who built up the very substantial information resources on Japanese intelligence organizations and the various agents they were running in Malaya and Singapore. In the same Special Branch headquarters as Morgan, Colonel Hayley Bell, the

MI5 station chief, operating under cover as the Defence Security Officer, also began building up files on the Japanese. There are indications suggesting that Morgan and Hayley did not get along—this antagonism unfortunately extended to their work. Morgan's files, for example, were strictly 'eyes only', not easily available to his Special Branch colleagues, let alone Hayley. For his part, Hayley was convinced that the authorities in Singapore knew hardly anything about Japanese infiltration. This tragic state of affairs in which the two parties kept each other in the dark meant that the full extent and real nature of the threat was not realized until it was too late.

Moreover, the authorities as well as the general population did not want to know anything. The governor, Sir Shenton Thomas, apparently told Hayley:

> Who but a fool, thinks Japan wants Singapore?
>
> (cited Elphick, 1998, p. 136)

According to Elphick, this view was strongly challenged by Dickinson, the Inspector General of Police (IGP) who insisted that it certainly did not represent the views of the security establishment:

> When A.H. Dickinson, the last pre-war Inspector-General of Police heard of this remark some years later, he commented, 'This could not have been said on the advice of the IGP. For years we have been building up our anti-Japanese section. Who in this case misled him (Thomson) so grievously?'
>
> (Elphick, 1998, p. 136)

One reason contributing to such an outlook is that these were years of plenty with the likelihood of war a remote possibility. Many in the establishment simply did not wish to see the prosperity end and certainly not be Cassandras constantly harping on about an approaching war! Historians have referred to the apathy and complacency among officials who felt that if they ignored the Japanese often enough the whole bad dream would go away. Besides, a number of these people actually thought the Japanese were reasonable, rational people who, already up to their necks in China, would not want to start additional trouble. Why, they argued, should the Japanese want to start another front? If all else failed, there were always the Russians who posed a strategic threat to the Japanese. It was more probable that their attention would be fixed on Manchukuo for a long time. So the game of drawing maps in the sand went on through the closing years of the decade. British

Malaya had its own version of Chamberlain's doctrine of appeasement. The authorities very often went out of their way not to be seen to be taking action that would annoy or provoke the Japanese. This cultivated ignorance of the militarism that by now must have been clear to even the most naive observer continued to mark the authorities' responses even as late as 1939.

In that year, Japanese naval forces seized Hainan Island, bringing Japanese naval and air power to the northern approaches to Southeast Asia. Despite the threat, the appeasement continued:

> Britain and the United States grew closer in response to Japanese expansion but still aimed to maintain friendly relations with Japan.
> (Turnbull, 1997, p. 159)

So even as events rushed towards the inevitable war, the chimera of friendly relations was still sought. In the meantime, events escalated. By 1941, Vichy France had caved in to Tokyo's demands and Japanese troops were now in southern Indo-China. From there, it was but 300 miles to the air bases in northern Malaya. Still as Turnbull notes, the spirit of self-deception went on:

> The Singapore authorities were still trying to preserve friendly relations with Japan. Representative of the Japanese-owned *Singapore Herald* were admitted to press conferences and military demonstrations as late as September 1941. Japanese businessmen remained in large numbers until their business dried up as a result of the embargo and an official evacuation ship repatriated about 600 of them in early October. The Japanese Consul-General, Tsurumi Ken, was recalled later that month, but most of the Japanese photographers, barbers and dentists remained, while the *Singapore Herald* and the Japanese language *Singapore Nippo* continued in operation until the day war broke out.
> (Turnbull, 1997, p. 164)

The authorities simply did not possess the nerve to prepare the general population for the possibility of conflict.

The Branch itself was also stretched thinly. Fixed as its attention was on the communist problem, the Special Branch did not possess the additional manpower or resources to devote necessary time and energy to the entire spectrum of the Japanese espionage machinery. Often the gaps that inevitably opened up allowed the Japanese to slip past the various devices and efforts to maintain security. As so many of the Japanese espionage operations were intertwined with commercial and other ventures, it would have demanded huge resources to monitor each and every event that could pose a likely danger. The Branch was certainly aware of the threat since they had monitored attempts to steal secrets, seized documents as well as detained spies. The question was whether they had the resources or the political will to take the necessary actions.

The Japanese had been preparing the grounds for a long time. As Onraet wrote:

> I look back at Japanese activities in Malaya with the conviction of having witnessed a patient and confident preparation for ultimate occupation, all the more easy to organize as no-one thought a military success, on which such an occupation depended, was possible.
>
> (Onraet, n.d., p. 43)

Ever since the decision to build the Singapore naval base in 1922, Japanese military planners had realized that Britain would not give up its colonial possessions and military dominance without a fight. Throughout the decade, they stepped up their efforts to penetrate and to discover the strengths of British preparations. Even as the Japanese began their incursions into China, they continued their espionage in Southeast Asia. On 29 November 1934, the Special Branch detected the entry under pretext of Lieutenant-Commander Tetsuhiko Kaseda of the Naval Intelligence Staff. Katsujiro Kizaki, a member of the *Kokusuito*, the enforcement section of the *Kokuhonsha* accompanied Kaseda. Kizaki travelled under the false name of Kashima describing himself as an author. Cover for their visit was provided by Y Nishimura, manager of the *Isihara Sangyo Koshi Company (ISK)* in Singapore. Nishimura had helped Kizaki apply for a visa in Japan and knew that he was passing himself off under the pseudonym of Kashima.

During their six days' stay in Singapore, these two men lay low in the Tokiwa Garden, a geisha guesthouse at Katong that Nishimura had booked for them. Special Branch surveillance showed that they were in touch with the Japanese Consul-General. It became clear that the two were engaged in espionage activities. Among other things, they had attempted to purchase a copy of the air force's signal code from a warrant officer of the RAF, offering him a substantial sum of money. Kaseda and Kizaki were arrested by Edmund Victor Fowler of the Special Branch at 7 p.m. on 4 December and deported on 5 December. The police found $8,000.00 and a miniature camera in their possession. The next day, Nishimura was asked to present himself at the Special Branch for questioning. Choosing suicide by taking strychnine, Nishimura without divulging any secrets dropped dead in front of the police officer questioning him. The Branch suspected that he had killed himself either out of fear of being exposed or to prevent any possible leakage about the two spies he had sponsored.

These events which might have come out of a lurid spy novel did not end with Nishimura's death. The spy ring in Singapore having been compromised, other agents soon fled. The Special Branch noted the hurried departure of Koichio Ishihara of the *Nanyo Boeki K K* as well as Kingora Miyaka and Shozo Isobe of the *Mitsui Bussan Kaisha*. All were suspected to be agents operating on behalf of Japanese secret societies. An even more explosive discovery occurred on 5 December when the Branch arrested Hiromichi Kobuko and Sjoji Ohki. It was known through surveillance that Kobuko had cultivated the friendship of four British artillerymen at Blakang Mati (Sentosa Island) that guarded the harbour entrance. A search led to the discovery of compromising evidence in his house. The Branch found, to its considerable dismay, documents on the Changi defences, one of the keys to the island's security. The two men were banished on 12 March 1935 probably adding to Japanese feelings that the Branch was helpless against them.

There can be no doubt through these alarming incidents that a sustained and determined effort was underway to conduct espionage against the British in Malaya. Japanese intelligence tried the whole range of tricks—secrets buying, front organizations, double crossings, appeals to pan-Asian pride, anti-European rhetoric, nationalism, bribery, coercion, threats and strong arm tactics when all else failed. It also had no hesitation penetrating and using criminal organizations like triad societies, newspapers or even their sworn enemies such as the Kuomintang and the Malayan Communist Party. In 1940, we are told that:

Special Branch is now in possession of evidence which shows that besides endeavouring to clamp down local anti-Japanese feeling, Japanese agencies in Malaya are trying to turn local Chinese feeling as a whole anti-British. To this end they have begun to penetrate, with what success it is not known, the most violently anti-Japanese organizations directed by the Malayan Communist Party in an attempt to turn the energy of these organizations against the British in Malaya.

(item 79, PIJ, 1940)

It was truly in dark and murky waters that the Japanese agents often worked in. The Japanese understood the corruption and desires of the frail, the arrogant pride of the brave and the fears of the bravest.

ilenameITYstod

They also understood the advantages of using wheels within wheels to mislead and to compromise all manner of people and organizations.

Gangsters were used frequently as their underground networks, providing a ready courier service as well as a means of smuggling arms. Of course, gangsters also provided a ready supply of enforcers to break up anti-Japanese trade boycotts or perform other duties. The Japanese were also known to have trained Formosans and other Chinese in their spy schools in Fujian and Shanghai specifically for undercover work in the region. It would have been surprising indeed, given what we know of Japanese tactics and their propaganda, that they did not seek to use ('co-opt', as it is called) the Chinese. This method also fitted in with the way they concealed their military advances through a close intertwining with economic and commercial interests. In Malaya, they had often to use proxies since the authorities were, from the beginning of the 1900s, uncomfortable with the speedy growth and nature of Japanese businesses, taking steps to curb some of the more obvious Japanese attempts to subvert the security. As early as 1917 Major General Ridout, General Officer Commanding Malaya, had drawn attention to the dangers of an increased Japanese presence in Singapore:

> In a report to the War Office on 18 April 1918, he raised the issue of the Japanese acquisition of properties in the vicinity of Singapore Island. He was particularly alarmed by the Japanese control of land in Pengerang, situated just across the Straits of Johore at the south eastern tip of the Malay Peninsula, and in the neighbouring islands of the Rhiau Archipelago.
>
> (Ong, 1997, p. 4)

Yet there was little the British could do. The Japanese cleverly turned the national self-interest of capitalist free trade espoused by the British into a weapon. They would often claim legitimate business reasons for their moves. In addition, the British were loath to act against the Japanese even when they clearly bought land that allowed them to pose a strategic threat. Some of these pieces of land could be acquired by the Government but there could not be seen to be a systematic denial of commercial opportunities to the Japanese. At any rate, the Japanese were experts at bypassing boycotts and other obstacles to their infiltration by the cunning use of willing proxies. For instance, efforts to limit their fishing licences, as the British were more than convinced that the fishing vessels were also engaged on spying missions, often did not work as the Japanese applied for these through other people. In 1936, as the Japanese Navy became interested in a possible conflict in the Indian Ocean, the Special Branch noticed a sudden upsurge to apply for fishing licences for the Burmese and Andaman Islands regions. To name just one case, the Branch reported that:

> There has been a rush on the part of local fishing firms to get fishing licences for the Mergui area and a local Indian woman has put up to apply for a licence for shell fishing in the Andamans.
>
> It seems to be a definite policy on the part of the Japanese to work behind local Asiatic interests.
>
> (item 59, PIJ, 1936)

It was a known fact by that time that most of the larger ocean-going fishing vessels were owned by Japanese either directly through their companies or through proxy co-operatives like the *Taichong Kongsi* which operated as far as the Pacific coast of the United States. Still neither the Navy nor the Special Branch was able to do anything against their eventually blatantly obvious use as spying vessels.

So while the Chinese took the lead in anti-Japanese activities, there were also those among them who saw the advantages of collaborating with the enemy. However, most of the time these gangsters were used for arms and people smuggling and couriers. On 27 May 1941, the Special Branch arrested E H Ong in his office at Perak Road, Penang, for subversive activities. Investigations soon revealed that he was implicated in pro-Japanese activities supporting the sale of their soy bean products. More seriously, it was found that he had attempted to smuggle into Malaya 50 dozen arms including revolvers and Mauser pistols from Siam. Based upon the evidence, the Defence Tribunal, Singapore, ordered his detention for the duration of the war.

The Japanese had carefully chosen Ong as a person they wished to cultivate. He had extensive contacts with Formosans who were frequently used by Japanese espionage as agents to penetrate the Chinese both in Malaya and China itself. In Ong's case, the Japanese knew what they wanted: a man with underworld connections who was ever ready to engage in strong-arm work as well. The Branch found that the Penang Detective Bureau had a thick file on him:

> E H Ong, Hokien, a resident of Penang, who claims local birth. Formerly in Government Service, for the past twenty years has been professional gambler, gangster and head of the secret society known as "Ji Tian Lor". He was concerned in the anti-Japanese soy bean riots in Penang of 4 July 1938, when he took the side of the soy bean growers. He was connected with gaming at the Astana, Kuala Kangsar, in 1934. Since 1934, he has

had continuous contact with Formosans, and has maintained Formosan actors in his house in Perak Road, Penang. In 1939 he kept a camp for professional boxers which included some Thais. In 1940 he and his gang "protected" a Formosan Opera Company which played at Wembley Park, Penang for three weeks.

(item 70, PIJ, 1941)

The Chinese in Penang had objected strongly to any performance by the nine Formosan artistes of the *Giok Ki Lin* Opera Company whom they felt were spreading propaganda on behalf of the Japanese. The Anti-Enemy Backing Up Society (an MCP front organization) threatened to cause trouble at Wembley Park and letters were sent to the Chinese Protectorate asking that no licence should be issued for the company's performance. In the event, Ong's gangsters 'protected' the performances and ensured that they were well attended for the two weeks they ran before political pressure from groups such as the Penang Chinese All-Circles Anti-Disturbance and Exposure of Traitors Section caused its cancellation.

This potted account of Ong's career shows why he and others like him were the perfect henchmen and were sought out by spymasters of the *F-Kikan* and the 8th Section (Intelligence) of the General Staff of the Japanese Imperial Army. Ong was the ready recruit—open to bribes and ready to risk strong-arm tactics on behalf of his Japanese employers. Moreover, he had a group of followers who were ready to lend themselves to desperate acts and even serious crimes like the smuggling of arms. Ong also had extensive contacts in Siam, an important launch point for the Japanese penetration of Southeast Asia. It would be through Siam that the Japanese would infiltrate their many Formosan propagandists into Malaya as the invasion drew near.

It is usual to condemn those who worked for Japanese espionage as traitors or people who had sold their souls for money. Perhaps that was the case in many instances but not all were like that. Some actually believed in the possibility of learning from the Japanese. Others may have subscribed to the ideals of a united Asia that the Japanese touted. Still others may have hoped to cooperate with the Japanese to realize their political objectives. In any case, these collaborators or helpers were an important part of the landscape of Japanese espionage and occupation. They should not be too readily consigned to the dustbins of history as their full stories still await telling.

As with the communists, the Special Branch soon realized that external events played a major role in the Japanese efforts in Malaya. This was certainly the case with the attempts to influence and shape the perceptions of the Chinese community in Malaya towards the events. In the 1930s, the rise of the Wang Jin-wei (Wang Ching-wei) faction in China coupled with its strong support by the Japanese who sought to use it as a propaganda platform added another element to the KMT/CCP competition for their loyalties. Wang Jin-wei was one of Sun Yat Sen's trusted lieutenants. He was one of the two persons chosen to draft the articles for the reform of the KMT (Kuomintang) in 1919. In comparison, Chiang Kai Shek was very much a junior, just emerging into prominence at this time. After Sun's death in Beijing from liver cancer in March 1925, Wang for a while had an opportunity to take over the leadership of the KMT. However, Wang mouthed but never subscribed to Sun Yat Sen's principles of national unity and his lack of sincerity soon became obvious. In 1927, he joined Chiang Kai Shek, Cai Yuan Pei and other members of the Green Gang to destroy, by force of arms, the General Labour Strike in Shanghai. In those uncertain times, loyalties often shifted and alliances were as temporary as the morning mist. This was certainly the case with the Wang Jin-wei/Chiang Kai Shek alliance. By 1930 Chiang Kai Shek had fallen out with Wang, joining Feng Luxian and Yan Xishan in their efforts to seize control of northern China. It was here in Manchuria that Wang's interests converged with those of the Japanese who were seeking to carve out a colony of their own.

After the 1931 Mukden (or Manchurian) Incident, Japan was firmly established in northeastern China even creating the puppet kingdom of Manchukuo under Pu Yi in 1932 to legitimize its military presence. Chiang Kai Shek, his prestige dented by the incident, 'retired' from politics leaving the stage to Wang Jin-wei and Sun Fo who were trying to set up a separatist regime in Kwantung. By the late 1930s Wang Jin-wei drifted more and more into the orbit of the Japanese as he depended on them for military support. In March 1940, Wang Jin-wei agreed to head the Japanese puppet regime in central China. This development was of considerable importance to the Japanese who proceeded to milk it for its propaganda value. They also used the Wang Jin-wei regime to drive a wedge among the Chinese by spreading misinformation in the hope that it would take away support from the nationalists so Wang also lent his name to various proxy companies that were fronts for Japanese espionage among the overseas Chinese. The full extent of this operation became apparent in 1940 when, acting upon its surveillance, the Special Branch in Singapore and Hong Kong raided his firms. The authorities' aim was to cripple his organization as well as sever his attempts to recruit sympathizers.

In May 1940, the Special Branch discovered that there was a Wang Jin-wei agent in Singapore sending intelligence reports to a Hong Kong firm, Chung Who Company of No. 67 Des Voeux Road, Hong Kong. The suspicions that this discovery formed but the tip of the iceberg were confirmed when, in that same month, some agents of the Chung Who Transport Company in Shanghai attempted to enter Singapore posing as a crew of a Moller Line ship. These men were detained with the Special Branch alerting its counterparts in Hong Kong that surveillance should be stepped up on the firm operating at Des Voeux Road.

In August, the Hong Kong Special Branch raided a known Wang Jin-wei front operating under the name of Chun Kee Company registered at No. 157 Wanchai Road, Hong Kong. Tse Tak Nam, the proprietor, was ordered to suspend operations but the police who continued with their surveillance soon found him operating again, this time not surprisingly at No. 67 Des Voeux Road. When the police raided this address they found that it fronted a number of Wang Jin-wei's firms including the San Chung Who Company (a variant of the Chung Who Company detected in May in Singapore) and the Wing Kee Company. A large quantity of documents was seized and Tse Tak Nam detained. Under interrogation he revealed that the real owner—and his 'controller'—was Ng Ying Pui who ran the operation from Shanghai. However, as the investigation widened, it soon became clear that the real puppet masters were the Japanese pulling the strings behind the scene. From the evidence, the Hong Kong Special Branch concluded that:

> The names "Chun Kee Co.", "San Chung Who Co." and "Wing Kee Co." are merely bogus "cover" names.
>
> (Special Branch Memorandum on the Exposure of the Chung Who Co. of Hong Kong as Japanese/Wang Jin-wei 5th Column Organization for the South Seas, PIJ, 1941)

These companies ran and funded a string of operations that was intended to infiltrate agents into Southeast Asia for subversive and espionage activities. These organizations were also actively recruiting members. It is interesting to note that the regions where these firms operated, which stretched from the Philippines to Burma, and as far south as Australia, corresponded to the Japanese idea of the South Seas or *Nanto*. These countries fell later into the operational area of the Southern Expeditionary Force that invaded Southeast Asia.

Among the documents that came to light was one that listed the broad aims and objectives of the 'New Order in East Asia' vis-à-vis the

Overseas Chinese in the South Seas and the means of attaining them. This clearly bore the stamp of the most recent strategic thinking from Tokyo as the new order in Greater Asia was only described in such terms in August 1941. Although the author is unknown, the Branch noted that "it is quite obviously the work of a highly intelligent person with a keen analytical and practical mind" (Memorandum, PIJ, 1941). The praise here is interesting for its professional acknowledgement of Japanese intelligence about Malaya as well as for what it tells us about British views. The document was praised because its conclusions were similar in a number of important ways to British thoughts about the role of—and the threat posed by—the overseas Chinese in their imperial colonies:

> The document reviews the great part played by the Overseas Chinese in the construction of Nationalist China and subscribes to the Kuomintang tenet that the Overseas are the "mother of the revolution". It states that the Overseas Chinese have contributed over 800 million dollars to the Chiang Kai Shek Government and have been largely the cause of the firm spirit of resistance shown in the war against Japan. It concluded that the Overseas Chinese must play an important part for or against the construction of the "New Order in East Asia", and that it is necessary that they be won over; this can only be done by the use of "ingenious methods".
> (Memorandum, PIJ, 1941)

Here, in effect, we have a good summary of what the British themselves think of the overseas Chinese. To the colonial authorities, the overseas Chinese were an unsettled mass similar to iron filings who would always be firmly responsive to the magnetic pull of China. Events in the mainland compelled their attention, shaped their perceptions and influenced their actions. This was the case with the triads and the anti-Manchurian forces in the 18th and 19th centuries. It was certainly so with the reform or nationalist movements and increasingly so with the communists. Since the Chinese had by now become so economically important—it was not for nothing that British Malaya was called the "Dollar Arsenal" of the Empire (Heussler, 1981, p. 252)—control of their political loyalties was crucial to the paramountcy of Britain as a colonial power. It was for precisely this reason that the Special Branch devoted, after its initial concern with Indian nationalism, consistent attention to Chinese affairs and to communism, in particular. The British were very clear-eyed about the need for control and like all good colonialists responded fundamentally to the perceived threat to their investments. Once Chinese influence (and the population) increased to such an extent that they were able to exercise considerable influence upon British commercial interests they were regarded as the main threat.

The Japanese new-order document mirrors this way of conceptualizing the position and handling of the Chinese situation in Southeast Asia. It showed a keen and analytical mind for precisely the reason that it had hit upon what the British had taken all along as the underlying aim of their security posture that security was inseparable from trade. The purpose of intelligence was first and foremost to ensure continued dominance over trade and commerce. In a sense, whatever the British did in this corner of the Empire, whether legitimizing their rule, enhancing the local aristocracy, separating the local population into ethnic enclaves, building roads or ports, extending education or administering cultural implantation and, above all, ensuring security, there was never a doubt about their position as rulers and the meaning of their presence. Not surprisingly, the Japanese thought about these issues in the same way: after all commercial competition was one of the two important reasons for their conflict with the British. The other reason was, of course, race and manifest destiny. Yet, in a way, all these showed the common concerns of the imperial powers. Japan and Britain were out to exploit as successfully as possible the colonies they had control over. In that sense, the two countries recognized from early on what they were each seeking to do.

The Japanese documents seized from the Chung Who Company confirmed the perception of the 'China hands', the experts who ran the system, that there existed a close relationship and uncomfortable link between events in China and Southeast Asia. These 'China hands' were often called upon to shape and determine the way Britain treated their extensive Chinese subjects in Southeast Asia, just as 'Malayan hands' claimed a special knowledge of the peninsula through their first hand experiences of the region. Inevitably, the political aspirations of the Chinese in the colonies were nearly always thought of in terms of developments in China. There was little incentive, given the situation, to think of the aspirations of the overseas Chinese in the context of their domicile. The impact this had on later political developments would indeed be grave. However, it suited the prevailing colonial ideology on dealings with the Chinese which always had a certain duplicity about them. Even the Chinese Protectorate created in 1877 with William Pickering as the first Protector of the Chinese was not free from this duplicity. In addition to its declared aim of helping the Chinese, the Protectorate also gave the British an effective instrument to monitor and manage Chinese actions. Taken further, the Chung Who document anticipates the mass killing of Southeast Asian Chinese. To the Japanese, the overseas Chinese were a problem that needed resolution. Either the people would be won over as the document suggested or other recourses would be looked to. The final solution was *sook ching*, the mass killing advocated by Masonobu Tsuji, a key member of the Taiwan Army Research Unit that planned the invasion of Malaya. Since the Japanese Army had to redeploy its divisions to other battlefields, extermination was to Tsuji the answer to the Chinese guerrilla activity that posed a definite security threat to the small garrison force. Tsuji had, in fact, long been obsessed with the overseas Chinese problem. In the booklet, "Read This Alone and the War can be Won", that was distributed by Tsuji's Research Unit to the invading force of the 25th Army a whole section was given over specifically to the problem of the overseas Chinese and some methods for handling it.

In the years before the invasion the Japanese aim was to win the overseas Chinese away from their support of the two main existing political movements, the KMT and the CCP. This could be brought about through a combination of propaganda designed to strengthen the new faction of Wang Jin-wei as well as the active destruction of the competing factions.[6] Propaganda and disinformation coupled with bribery of various kinds were often used to gain new recruits to their cause. However, as usual, the Japanese did not hesitate to resort to threats and even violence to persuade those who were less compliant. Whatever the methods used there could be no doubt that the real aim remained the destruction of the KMT and the CCP. The Chung Who document advocated the following courses of action:

1. To use both propaganda and agents to win over the Overseas Chinese.
2. To contact Overseas Chinese and induce them to return to occupied China and invest money there so as to restore its prosperity.
3. To attack the Communist Party and the Kuomintang.
4. To discredit the aid given by Third Powers to the Chungking Government.
5. To use propaganda in favour of peace between China and Japan.
6. To break the unity and moral support of Overseas Chinese for the national Government of China and cut off the financial and well being given to Chiang Kai Shek by them.
7. To establish branches in Singapore, Batavia, Cholon, Manila and Bangkok and to start clubs there as secret organizations under which to conduct Party affairs.
8. To buy over cultural elements and thus control the newspapers.
9. To subsidize the anti-Chen Yi (Governor of Fukien) movements started by Tan Kah Kee; to foment anti-Chen Yi demonstrations and concurrently to incite Aw Boon Haw's clique to support Chen.

(Memorandum, PIJ, 1941)

Japan was equally prepared to employ these methods against other targets and other groups. The basic thrust of what its field agents were asked to do is clear enough as the description provides a bird's-eye view of the major characteristics of its espionage strategy. Unfortunately, by the time the British obtained this clear map of their enemy's intentions it was really too late to counter the Japanese intention. The military strike was already around the corner.

Among the documents, the Special Branch found an organizational chart that divided the various parts of the South Seas into spheres of espionage activity. In addition, the chart listed the various objectives the Japanese hoped to achieve. The chart shows clearly that Japanese infiltration and subversion were well advanced by 1940 and that these were meticulously planned. The argument advanced by Fujiwara and Tsuji, among others, that the decision to go to war was unexpectedly thrust upon them, is contradicted by the carefully worked-out plans to carry out subversion using their agents and various sympathizers. The organizational chart reveals both the extent and range of the Japanese espionage effort:

Overseas Work of the East Asiatic Chain of Co-Prosperity

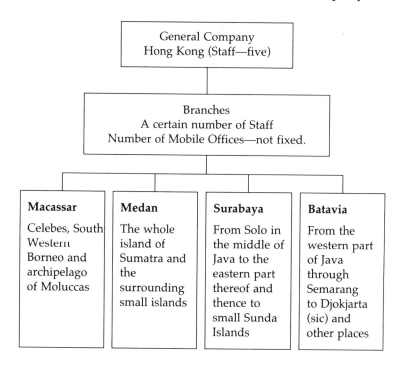

General Company Hong Kong (Staff—five)			
Branches A certain number of Staff Number of Mobile Offices—not fixed.			
Macassar	**Medan**	**Surabaya**	**Batavia**
Celebes, South Western Borneo and archipelago of Moluccas	The whole island of Sumatra and the surrounding small islands	From Solo in the middle of Java to the eastern part thereof and thence to small Sunda Islands	From the western part of Java through Semarang to Djokjarta (sic) and other places

Centre of Work			
Macassar	**Medan**	**Surabaya**	**Batavia**
To cultivate friendly relations with the overseas Chinese to offer resistance against the NEI; and to support Sino-Japanese peace and construction of New Order in both the Orient and the West.	To instigate the natives to (a) claim for independence; (b) sabotage by force, if necessary, military defence works in the NEI; (c) attack the military and the police forces in the NEI; and (d) disturb peace and good order there.	To obtain information regarding military, political and economic affairs there.	To spread propaganda of an inciting nature.

(Memorandum, PIJ, 1941)

Ambitious as all this may seem the Japanese had used similar tactics with marked success in China. Wang Jin-wei, who lent his name to the scheme, was himself a good endorsement of the likely advantages that could result from such plans. The list of members that had already signed on with the venture must have given the British a shock even if they did find the membership list useful in their arrests of suspects. The number of members included 62 in Singapore, 19 in Penang, two in Malacca, 45 in the FMS and UMS, 82 in the NEI, 35 in the Philippines, 10 in Thailand, 35 in French Indo-China and, ever the good bookkeeper the Japanese were, one in Sydney, Australia. The chart reveal that there was certainly an extensive web of agents in place that the Japanese could build on rapidly should hostilities break out in Southeast Asia. In British Malaya soon after the Japanese occupation, Wang Jin-wei agents helped to form the Overseas Chinese Association (OCA) that forced many prominent Chinese into working for the Japanese occupation forces. A number of the OCA members were killed by the Malayan People's Anti-Japanese Army on the grounds that they were collaborators. The Japanese agents had also been busy compiling lists of anti-Japanese activists. Lists of names of people in Singapore to be arrested (or more likely shot) were handed to the *Kempeitai* the moment the invading troops reached Ipoh. In fact, even while he was in Formosa planning the invasion of Malaya, Tsuji had asked the Japanese network of spies in Singapore to collect names of prominent anti-Japanese Chinese. The intention was to take action against them when the troops reached the island. Lieutenant-Colonel Ichiji Sugita, who was in charge of Intelligence in the 25th Army was to admit later that the

> highly effective spoiling actions undertaken by the anti-Japanese Chinese units during the invasion of Malaya had constituted a serious threat to the 25th Army.
>
> (Ward, 1996, p. 139)

These views appeared in a statement defending the punishment of the Chinese that Sugita argued was appropriate at that time!

While there were always those who could be tempted or coerced into joining an anti-British, anti-colonial platform, the brutalities of the Japanese soon stiffened resistance. The Chinese paid a bitter price for their resistance to the Japanese invaders. Once the initial shock of the landings was over, the British made efforts to form irregular units that could add on to the military effort. Many of these units were organized and led by the Special Branch or other police officers who had knowledge of the terrain and who knew the population. Colonel J D Dalley who was in charge of the counter-intelligence section of the Special Branch (by now, the Malayan Security Services) organized Chinese volunteers, known as the Dalley Column (abbreviated to Dalco although subsequently this was called Dalforce), who were attached to the Third Indian Corps. These poorly armed men fought resolutely on the frontline against the advancing Japanese, causing many casualties. The subsequent *sook ching* (translated as "purification by elimination") massacre of the Chinese was partly in revenge for the losses inflicted by Dalco and partly to forestall the possibility of further resistance by eliminating anti-Japanese elements:

> The campaign was planned by Lieutenant-Colonel Tsuji who proposed the idea of the *sook ching* aimed at the "suppression of hostile Chinese" in retaliation for the tenacity of the Chinese volunteers in Dalforce.
>
> (Cheah, 1983, p. 21)

Through Dalco and other mobilization efforts, Chinese from the whole spectrum of political opinions were brought into a common cause. Even the Malayan Communist Party and the British authorities came to an understanding in their fight against the common foe.

In this matrix of events, the Special Branch can claim an almost unique role. Within a few days of 8 December, it was apparent that things were going badly for the British. Both the KMT and the MCP had offered to work together with the British in forming a common resistance to the Japanese by mobilizing the people. Initially the British had been suspicious of the offer especially from the MCP, feeling that the communists were merely seeking to take political advantage of the situation. However, the rapid series of British reversals convinced them that the situation was truly desperate and that extraordinary measures were needed. Within three days of the Japanese landing, the British had lost their main strike force of the two battleships *Prince of Wales* and *Repulse*. On 12 December, the Japanese 5th and the Imperial Guards Division entered Alor Star, Kedah. Penang, one of the first British possession in the peninsula, was lost a week after that.

The fall of Penang was a sobering experience of what was to come as panic broke out among the fleeing English seeking evacuation from the harbour. The locals who were brushed aside as irrelevant felt justly outraged. Of greater concern, essential supplies and services broke down and insufficient workers, mobilized to restore these causing even greater suffering. The Japanese bombing of Penang with the casualties that resulted and the difficulty of restoring essential supplies confirmed that general mobilization of the population was necessary if the war effort was to be enhanced. If the civil defences in Singapore were as poor, the island would similarly not be able to withstand a prolonged siege. Under the circumstance, the government began to take note of the increasing call from the public for general mobilization of all resources and personnel. Various Chinese groups and in particular Mr Tan Kah Kee had been calling for such a unified resistance. One apparently insurmountable obstacle was that the various Chinese groups remained wary of each other while the government remained suspicious of the intentions of the MCP, not convinced that the communists were prepared to put aside their political objectives.

Interestingly, only the Special Branch was in a position to talk to all these parties playing the mediator among all of them. This gave the Special Branch a unique place in the history of Malayan resistance to the Japanese. Circumstances had made them the only party which these disparate groups were prepared to speak to and even trust. The Special Branch could in a sense guarantee a certain amount of neutrality and disinterestedness in bringing adversaries like the KMT and the MCP to the negotiating table. The Branch already knew that the local KMT was prepared to put aside differences and had, in fact, been told by Chung Jing to cooperate with the British. That left only the MCP and here the British were in a unique position to influence events since the MCP Secretary-General, Loi Teck, was a British agent!

The events over the following week confirmed the central role of the Branch. On 15 December, the Branch had released some political prisoners mainly from the MCP as a sign of its goodwill. They followed this olive branch with feelers about the formation of a united organization among the Chinese to strengthen resistance and for civilian defence. On 18 December, the Central Executive Committee of the MCP passed a resolution to go ahead and rely on the people's efforts for mobilization. In the complicated jargon of communism, this meant that the Party had, for the time being, suspended their ideological anti-British line. The Branch was well aware of the MCP's every move. Not surprisingly, the very next day they contacted the MCP and accepted its offer to work together. One cannot help but wonder how much of a role Loi Teck had in speeding up these negotiations not least of all because the British must have been briefing him all along.

On 19 December, the MCP formed the broad-based Malayan Overseas Chinese Anti-Japanese Mobilization Society which attempted to include the KMT and the Chinese Chamber of Commerce. This nearly threw a spanner in the efforts to bring the different parties together as, quite naturally, these were reluctant to join what was a united front with the communists. Once again the Branch had to mediate. It needed strenuous efforts before the Society could finally get going. In the end, a Chinese Mobilization Council was formed after all parties met at the Special Branch headquarters in Singapore. Mr Tan Kah Kee was prevailed upon to be its President ensuring unity and trust since he was widely accepted by all concerned. The Branch's record of this extraordinary event hardly does justice to the high drama that must have gone on behind doors even if it is worth quoting:

> The Chinese section of the Special Branch put out feelers on 16 December 1941 for the formation of a united organization to mobilize Chinese activities to resist the effects of bombing, and profit from the lessons of Penang. A surprisingly unanimous result followed. The Kuomintang, the China Relief Fund, the Chinese Chamber of Commerce and the Communists all came to the Special Branch with what almost amounted to demands that a Mobilization Committee should be set up, and that all party and clique differences should be sunk in a common purpose. All parties however—and this point is most significant—insisted that

Tan Kah Kee was the only person who could successfully command the support of the broad masses of the Chinese people in the fulfillment of the project.

Mr Tan Kah Kee, who had already made arrangements to leave the country, was most reluctant to accept leadership, and it looked for a time as if the whole idea might fail, but after strenuous efforts, between 18 and 24 December, by the Special Branch, supplemented by the Chinese Consul-General, Mr Kao Lao Pai, Mr George K C Yeh, representative of the China International Publicity Bureau, and Mr Heah Wing Choo, the President of the Chinese Chamber of Commerce, Mr Tan Kah Kee was persuaded to accept the leadership of the "Mobilization Council" for Singapore upon which all shades of Chinese opinion agreed to serve.

(item 174, PIJ, 1941)

The Council comprised 95 members with the Chinese Chamber of Commerce being allocated 31 seats while the Kuomintang and the Malayan Communist Party had 10 seats each. The rest of the seats were made up as follows: the Straits-born Chinese had 10 seats, Chinese women had four seats, culturists, 10 seats, the newspapers had 10 seats and labour, 10 seats. The final seats were distributed among prominent people. The Standing Committee was to be the key executive and policy body of the Council with the following representatives:

President:
Mr Tan Kah Kee

Members:

The Hon. Mr. Tay Lian Teck	Member of the S.S. Legislative Council
Mr Heah Wing Choo	President of the Chinese Chamber of Commerce
Mr Ong Kiat Soon	Leader of the Malayan Kuomintang
Mr Ng Ia Lo	Representing the Malayan Communist Party
Madame Wong Tian Han	Sister of Mr S Q Wong
Mr Hu I Tse	Chief editor of the *Nanyang Siang Pau*
Mr Chong Quek Cheong	Principal of the Chinese Normal School

The allocation of seats and the members of the Standing Committee represented the reality of the Chinese political structure in Singapore at this time.

The formation of the Mobilization Council was a significant moment in the history of the overseas Chinese as it brought the hitherto divided

Chinese together. Not only did it give shape to their political aspirations but it also led to the recognition that a civilian force should be armed. Soon after this, the first batch of MCP members began training at the 101 Special Training School (STS) at Pulau Ubin, Singapore. Many of the volunteers who were trained at these camps went on to join the British irregular columns such as Dalco. In due course after the British surrender, those members who managed to escape the Japanese round-up of suspects went on to form the first units of the Malayan People's Anti-Japanese Army (MPAJA), the Overseas Chinese Anti-Japanese Army (OCAJA) or other resistance groups. Without overstressing the importance of the 101 STS, it is still possible to see that the roots of armed resistance began with these men. The 101 STS provided a very basic crash course in guerrilla warfare including wireless communication, bomb-making and basic shooting skills. In a sense, the Branch also had a hand in the history of these units as it actively intervened in the formation of the Mobilization Council that was responsible for all these volunteers.

The Japanese occupation brought to an end one phase of the Special Branch work in British Malaya. From 1940 onwards till the onset of the Emergency in 1948, it was the military dimension of security that preoccupied the police. This was reflected in the formation of the Malayan Security Service headed by a military man, in this case Colonel Dalley. During the war years, it was organizations like the Secret Intelligence Service (SIS) or the Special Operations Executive (SOE) formed in 1940 that became the prominent players. The Special Branch, which had been formed to maintain British paramountcy, could obviously no longer perform the same function until such time as the Union Jack flew again in Malaya. Yet before it retired from the scene and became reconstituted as part of different war intelligence activities during the Japanese interregnum, the pre-war Special Branch had, on the eve of the war, cobbled together the various strands that made up the anti-Japanese resistance movement. Even in this last assignment, many felt that only the Branch was, paradoxically, uniquely placed to effect it successfully for it involved securing the trust of those very forces which had been its most worthwhile adversaries for most of the last two decades; old adversaries know each other best.

Notes

1. The Japanese plans to take over and colonize may be traced through the deliberate ambiguity in the term *Nanyo*, or South Seas. They divided their area of influence into:

(1) The 'rear' South Seas (*Ura Nanyo*)—the Mandated Islands and

(2) The 'front' South Seas (*Omote Nanyo*)—Formosa, Philippine Islands, Siam, Borneo, Netherlands East Indies and Malaya. They developed two main umbrella organizations to look after their development of these areas, the South Seas Development Company for the 'rear' and the Formosa Development Company for the 'front' South Seas. Of course this did not preclude interference by other well-known Japanese fronts as the SMR, the South Manchuria Railway, to set up base in Southeast Asia.

2. "Japanese Secret Intelligence Services Part 1", General Staff (Intelligence), Australian Military Force. AL1341, Imperial War Museum, London.

3. Abu Talib Ahmad, "The Impact of the Japanese Occupation on the Malay-Muslim Population" in *Journal of Southeast Asian Studies*, Special Publication No. 3, 1995, p. 8.

4. P Lim Pui Huen, "Memoirs of War in Malaya", *Journal of South East Asian Studies*, Special Publication No. 3, 1995, p. 139.

5. This is not the place to discuss this extremely complex issue that characterized the whole nature of British administration and, in particular, the paradigm of the 'Malayan' sensibility that enabled their colonial expansion. I will raise these in my book on ideological history, *Racial Imaginations and the Malayan Sensibility*.

6. Okakura Tenshin (Kakuzo) declared that "Asia should be one" while touring countries including China, India and European countries. He was well known as a scholar and advocate of Japanese culture, served as director of the Oriental Division of the Boston Museum and was a friend of Rabindranath Tagore.

Photograph courtesy of the Internal Security Department

"An enormous crowd, reliably estimated to number more than 15,000 people..." saw the execution of the mutineers outside the walls of the Singapore prison.

Photograph courtesy of the Internal Security Department

The memorial tablet at the Victoria Memorial Hall dedicated to the memory of the victims of the 1915 mutiny.

235

Sir David Petrie was appointed Indian Intelligence Officer for the Far East in 1915. His recommendations led to the founding of the Special Branch.

Petrie in 1920.

Rene Onraet, the second Director of the Special Branch from 1925 until his appointment as the Inspector General of Police of the Straits Settlements.

R. H de S ONRAET. C.M.G
INSPECTOR GENERAL OF POLICE
STRAITS SETTLEMENTS
1935 TO 1939

Photograph courtesy of Yap Hong Kuan

Photograph courtesy of Yap Hong Kuan

Senior Police Officers of British Malaya in 1939, among them a number of Special Branch members.

A E G Blades who became Director of the Special Branch in post-war British Malaya and Singapore.

Photograph courtesy of the Internal Security Department

Blades with Mr Linsell.

Photograph courtesy of the Internal Security Department

Conf

GD
62/
1916

CONFIDENTIAL.

Col Sec off
Conf 13/16

4 May, 1916.

Sir,

I have the honour to apply for your approval of
the creation of Criminal Intelligence, and Criminal Investigation, Departments in the Straits Settlements Police
Force in the manner set forth below.

2. It is proposed to follow the system in force in
India, and to arrange that the Criminal Intelligence Department shall devote itself mainly to work in connection
with sedition, with the operations of spies and political
agents and with political information generally, whilst
also specializing (as in India) to a certain extent upon
organised crime, such as the activities of a gang of coiners.
Criminal Investigation, on the other hand, is concerned only
with the ordinary offences against the law.

3. The only thing corresponding in any way to a
Criminal Investigation Department has been the detective
branch of the force. The proposal to create a Criminal Investigation Department first came under consideration in
September 1914 in connection with the promotion (approved
in Mr. Harcourt's Despatch No.295 of the 8th August 1914)
of Mr. W. H. Taylor, Chief Detective Inspector, to be Head
of the Preventive Service, Government Monopolies Department.

The

The Right Honourable,
A. Bonar Law, M.P.,
&c., &c., &c.,
COLONIAL OFFICE.-

Photograph courtesy of The National Archives of Singapore

The Governor of the Straits Settlements, Sir Arthur Young's letter to London in 1916 recommending
the setting up of the Special Branch. We may regard this as the founding charter of the organization.

239

The events which followed the outbreak of war showed that
not only was a Criminal Investigation Department needed,
but that a Criminal Intelligence Department (which was
wholly wanting) was also essential. The present proposals
have been drawn up by Captain A. R. Chancellor, Inspector
General of Police, and are made in the light of the experience of the past year in dealing with the activities of
enemy agents: they have been referred to, and concurred in,
by Mr. D. Petrie, C.I.E., a Deputy Director of Criminal Intelligence in the Indian Police Service, who has been visiting
the Colony upon duty.

4. I recommend the appointment of a Director of Criminal Intelligence on a salary of £720 per annum rising by annual increments of £20 to £840 per annum, with a Duty Allowance of £150 per annum. This is the salary of a Superintendent of Police under the scheme. It is proposed that the appointment of Second Superintendent of Police, Singapore be
abolished, and replaced by the appointment of an Assistant
Superintendent of Police. (It will be possible to do this in
connection with the changes of appointments which will result
from the retirement on pension of Major de Hamel, Chief Police
Officer, Penang).

5. I also recommend the appointment of an Assistant
Superintendent of Criminal Investigation on the same salary
as that of an Assistant Superintendent of Police, namely, £600
per annum rising to £660 per annum, with a duty allowance at
first of £100, and later of £125, per annum.

6. If these appointments are approved, I propose to
create three appointments in the Criminal Intelligence Department for Indians (who will probably be selected from Northern
India) on salaries of £1365 per annum,- £195 A - £2280 per annum, with a consolidated allowance of £655 per annum. For the
Japanese

Photograph courtesy of The National Archives of Singapore

240

Japanese side of the Department, I consider it best to add a lump sum of $4,500 to the provision for secret service in the Estimates. On the Chinese side, the department will, as in the past, work in close touch with the Chinese Protectorate, whose staff it is proposed to increase by two clerks, and six detectives. It is also proposed to increase the annual secret service vote from $1,500 to $5,000.

7. It is also proposed to regrade the salaries and allowances of the European and native staff of the detective Department. The expenditure will not be increased, but certain allowances, which do not always work out satisfactorily, will be abolished. The vacant post of Chief Detective Inspector, Singapore, will be abolished.

8. If these recommendations are approved, I submit the names of Messrs. G. G. Seth and W. H. Taylor to be Director of Criminal Intelligence and Superintendent of Criminal Investigation respectively. Mr. Seth is an officer in Class IV of the Cadet Service, and is at present acting as Deputy Public Prosecutor. He is particularly well qualified for the post. Mr. Taylor was formerly Chief Detective Inspector, and (as mentioned above) was transferred to be Head of the Preventive Service in the Government Monopolies Department. His present appointment can well be filled by a less able officer. In my despatch No.386 of the 31st August 1915, I referred to the consideration which was being given to the subject of Criminal Investigation, and mentioned Mr. Taylor's name in this connection.

I have the honour to be,

Sir,

Your most obedient, humble servant,

298 Arthur Young

Photograph courtesy of The National Archives of Singapore

S ofs 335
1916

Downing Street,

15 June, 1916.

Sir,

I have the honour to acknowledge the receipt of your despatch Confidential of the 4th May; and to convey to you my approval of your proposals for the creation of Criminal Intelligence, and Criminal Investigation Departments in the Straits Settlements Police Force; and of the appointment of Messrs G.C. Seth and W. H. Taylor to be Director of Criminal Intelligence and Superintendent of Criminal Investigation respectively.

I have the honour to be,

Sir,

Your most obedient,

humble Servant,

A. Bonar Law

GOVERNOR

SIR A. H. YOUNG, G.C.M.G.

&c., &c., &c.

Photograph courtesy of The National Archives of Singapore

Bonar Law's approval for the new department.

Kreta Ayer Police Station where the 1927 shootings and subsequent riots in Chinatown took place.

Tanjong Pagar Police Station near Happy Valley where a supposedly peaceful observance turned into a riot through deliberate provocation and orchestration.

243

Photograph courtesy of the Internal Security Department

The Special Branch headquarters in Robinson Road.

Appendix

Chapter 3 of *Spring in the South*, the history of the Malayan Communist Party issued by the MCP (1946). This pamphlet is clearly propaganda, pushing a certain position on the doctrines and development of the Malayan Communist Party. However, it does show something of the political tactics and persuasive efforts of the MCP at a crucial stage of its development. In addition, I am almost certain that the volume was written by Loi Teck or, at least, through his direct instigation to counter suspicions and rumours about his activities during the Japanese Occupation.

Ban Kah Choon

Translated by Grant Shen and Ban Kah Choon

Chapter 3
A Concise History of the Malayan Communist Party

The Malayan Communist Party, a branch of the Communist International, came into being in 1925, when capitalism and imperialism intensified their oppression and exploitation in their colonies after the First World War. At the same time, the victory of the October Revolution of the Soviet Union forcefully advanced the world revolution. The proletariat of the West continually burst into heroic struggles. The toiling masses of the colonies or semi-colonies in the East also awakened. The advanced progressive Chinese comrades in Malaya established the Party organization under this circumstance. The Party then was in fact an overseas branch of the Chinese [Communist] Party. It had a very small organizational structure. The Party based its organization and activities solely on the clerks of the Chinese shops and the workers of the West rubber businesses.

In 1926, the Party established the South Seas Centre and its activities gradually spread out to every corner of the South Seas. In 1927 the Party convened the First Representative Conference of the Nanyang Communist Party and erected its Provisional Committee. As the young members of the Communist Party lacked both experience and the leadership of the Comintern, the Party organization was unable to make significant advance.

In 1929, the Nanyang Communist Party received instructions from the Central Committee of the Chinese Communist Party and, thereafter, defined the nature of Malayan revolution and the basic principles of its overall struggle. All the comrades were able to heighten their Bolshevik fighting spirit as well. As a result, the Party's weak and ordinary body was progressively transformed into a strong fighting organization.

In 1930, the Nanyang Communist Party convened the Second Representative Conference and formally elected the Central Committee of the Malayan Communist Party. It called on every level of the Party organization and all the comrades to stand in the forefront to fight heroically to defend the interests of the working class and toiling masses. This call further awakened the class-consciousness of the Malayan proletarians and masses, heightened their fighting attitude against the bourgeoisie and imperialism, and advanced the tidal waves of Malayan revolution.

In the first half of 1932, a critical event took place within the Party, that is the emergence of the opposition that organized the Great League of the Malayan Communist Party. It openly carried out anti-Party activities, surrendering to enemies and betraying the revolution. However our comrades kept their heroic spirit of fighting for the Party and sacrificing for the revolution. They followed the correct political direction and took the initiatives. They finally purged the opposition members. The Malayan Communist Party thus more firmly took the true Bolshevik path.

In the same year, the Malayan Communist Party convened the Third Representative Conference, during which it re-elected the Central Committee, determined the direction for its future work, and issued 12 revolutionary guiding principles for Malaya in the current stage:

I   Drive out British Imperialism from the Straits colonies and states of Malaya. Overthrow the puppet regimes of British imperialism— raja, sultan, landlords, and comprador bourgeois.

II   Confiscate all the banks and enterprises of the imperialism. Confiscate all properties of counterrevolutionaries.

III Seize and expropriate the land and farms owned by the imperialism, raja, sultan, landlords, bureaucrats, and temples. Distribute the land and farms to peasants, plantation workers, and soldiers who partake the revolution.

IV   Strive for the national and social liberation of Malaya. Establish the Malayan Soviet Republic of Workers and Peasants.

V   Abolish the bourgeois system. Develop the national economy of Malaya. Take the socialist road.

VI   Institute eight-hour working day. Eight hours for young workers, six for women. Increase wages. Issue labour laws to protect workers. Give workers the right to organize labour unions. Provide unemployment insurance. Improve the living conditions of labouring masses. Abolish contract labour and apprentice system.

VII   Ensure the absolute freedom of assembly, association, speech, publication, strike, demonstration, faith, and education.

VIII Oppose all reactionary religions.

IX   Strive for free education in mother tongues.

X   Abolish all the feudal modes of exploitation by imperialism, *raja*, sultan, and princes. Eliminate multifarious tax. Collect progressive tax.

XI   Oppose the war preparation in Malaya by British imperialism. Oppose militarism. Oppose imperialist wars.

XII   Defend the Soviet Union. Support the Chinese and Indian revolutions. Unite the proletariat and the oppressed small and weak nations all over the world.

From then on, the Malayan Communist Party experienced major changes in its organization. The foundation of the Party structure was fortified.

In 1935, the opposition again emerged in the Party. It ignored Party resolutions, betrayed the interests of the proletariat masses. It appealed to some younger members of the Communist Party and roped them in to carry out activities of the anti-Malayan Communist Party. They attempted to help the enemy destroy the Malayan Communist Party. They wanted the Malayan workers and suffering masses to be the obedient slaves of British imperialism and the bourgeoisie. This was the hardest period of turmoil in the history of the Malayan Communist Party. Yet the Central Committee of the Malayan Communist Party, every level of the Party organization, and all the comrades did not give up their great mission of struggle for the final liberation of the Malayan nation and people. Instead they kept their Bolshevik spirit more vigorously and persistently. They carried out the resolutions of the Enlarged Plenum of the Fifth Executive Committee of the Malayan Communist Party. Defending the interests of Malayan workers and toiling masses, they organized and led big-scale league strikes and thus gave a resounding answer to the cruelty of British imperialism and bourgeoisie, as well as to the anti-Party activities of the opposition. As a result, the opposition was purged from the Party. The Party was protected and the Party's foundation solidified.

In 1938, the Standing Committee re-evaluated the objective conditions of Malaya and reviewed the Party policies. The Standing Committee believed that the characteristic of the current international situation was an intensified conflict between the aggressive Fascist front and the peace front. The barbaric forces of international Fascism speeded up their invasions. The German Fascism madly prepared wars in continental Europe. The Japanese Fascist forces, in particular, accelerated their attacks on China. They announced and materialized their "mainland policy," which included the whole of East Asia. Such an aggressive position taken by the Japanese Fascists greatly threatened Malaya's peace and security and evoked a general anti-Fascism sentiment among the Malayan people. On the other hand, the Chinese people's heroic war of resistance enhanced the Malayan people's faith in anti-Fascism. Especially those overseas Chinese in particular, who represented nearly a half of the population, had a more indignant spirit against the Japanese invasion of their motherland, due to their direct national relations, native connections, and ideological identifications [to China]. Besides, the "mainland policy" and the southward invasion of Japanese Fascism threatened British imperialism's rule in Malaya. British imperialism was thus upset with Japanese Fascism and wished to maintain the status quo so that its interests in China and Malaya might be preserved. Apparently, this situation called for our Party to grasp people's mood and needs and to rally all the people to fight against the Fascist aggression. At the same time, such a move might enhance our Party's own force, expand our Party's influence, and make our Party a truly popular political party. For these reasons, the Party placed the improvement of the lives of the Malayan people of all nations and the fight against the Fascist invasions as the first priority in the Party's calendar of struggle during the current stage of democratic revolution of the bourgeois nature. The Party thus defined its urgent tasks as to establish a united front of all nations in Malaya, to defend peace, to fight against Fascist invasions, and to strive for sovereign rights.

The Party decided its guiding principles of struggle for that period as:

I   People of all nations in Malaya, regardless of their race, party, class, faith, and religion, join force to establish the United Front of Malayan People. Strive for a democratic system. Defend peace. Punish the Fascist bloc of aggression of Japan, Germany, and Italy.

II   Reform the political structure. Implement a democratic political system.
   A) Politics
       (1) Establish the parliament that truly represents people of all nations of Malaya so that people may have the rights to resolve the problems of national defence, economy, politics, and society. This parliament is elected in a general election by people of all nations in Malaya, regardless of their races or property. The right to vote starts at 21 years of age. The right to stand for election starts at 25 years of age.
       (2) Establish the local assembly in every state of Malaya, so that people of every state have the right to resolve local problems of politics, economy, and society. Hold a general election according to the electoral law. The right to vote starts at 21 years of age. The right to stand for election starts at 25 years of age.
   B) Administration
       (1) Purge the reactionary forces in the government and military. Hire persons of ability in political institutions.
       (2) Improve the living conditions of government employees. First, raise salary regularly and resume the previous salary for all government officials. Second, officials of all Malayan nations and those of England should enjoy the same equal remuneration.
       (3) Within a kampung, villagers elect the *penghulu*, whom the government should pay a sufficient salary. Prevent the *penghulu* from exploiting villagers.
   C) Justice
       (1) Abandon the cruel laws and cases that suppress and exploit people. Invalidate all the colonial decrees. Apply the democratic laws of England in Malaya.
       (2) Civil court should make use of local counsellors.
       (3) Implement agricultural laws. Make laws to mediate the disputes between landlords and peasants.
       (4) Prosecute those who arrest people without a warrant.
       (5) Public trial for all the political prisoners. Grant defendants the right of hiring lawyers.

(6) Abolish the Alien Residential Acts. Eliminate import and export taxes.

(7) Release all political prisoners and improve the prison system.

D) Finance

(1) Eliminate multifarious taxes. Reduce *pasah* (market) tax and *pai-shui* ("residential" tax). Implement democratic taxation. Collect tax from interest income.

(2) Prohibit forced selling of properties to collect back taxes, back rent, or loans.

(3) Penalize loan sharks. Set limits for interest rates.

(4) Open agricultural banks everywhere. Prolong loan terms to help middle peasants, poor peasants, small merchants, and handicraftsmen.

(5) Self-determine tariff. Reform tariff policy. Develop Malayan national industries.

(6) Eliminate government subsidy of production capital to big companies. Use that money to relieve the unemployed and refugees.

(7) Reduce police agency expenditure. Use that money for hospitals and other causes that are beneficial to the people.

(8) Develop agriculture. Open up waterways. Provide disaster relief. Remove rubber quota. Discipline compradors, profiteers, and [market] manipulators. Limit the power of banks.

III   Improve people's living condition.

A) Workers

(1) Institute eight-hour working day. 15 days off per year.

(2) Abolish contract labour and apprentice system.

(3) Men and women enjoy equal pay for equal work.

(4) Implement social security. Provide unemployment relief.

(5) Two-month paid maternity leave for female workers.

(6) Increase wages. Regular raises. Sunday off with pay. Improve workers' material life.

(7) Give workers the right to organize trade unions.

B) Peasants

(1) Reduce land rent. Eliminate multifarious taxes.

(2) Assist poor peasants with seeds and tools.

(3) Provide minimum rent for land-short or landless peasants. Rent-free during natural disasters. Prolong loan terms.

        (4) Firewood rights to mountain-dwelling peasants.

        (5) Set up peasant relief funds to help peasants.

    C) Women

        (1) Equality for men and women. Forbid polygamy and mercenary marriage.

        (2) Annul the system of slave-girls.

        (3) Prohibit arrest during pregnancy. Prohibit "bao-liang-ju" (rehabilitation-bureau) retention.

    D) Social Welfare

        (1) Expand, build, and sponsor hospitals.

        (2) Set up and maintain orphanages.

IV   Improve military administration.

    (1) Give equal remuneration and rights to military officials of Malayan nations and those of England.

    (2) Institute volunteer military service. Reduce the service time to 18 months.

    (3) Improve the political education of anti-Fascism to soldiers.

    (4) Increase stipends. Give equal remuneration to British and Malayan soldiers. Give preferential treatment to soldiers' family members. Provide enough welfare funds for soldiers' families. Guarantee employment after [soldiers'] military service.

    (5) Abandon the cruel laws that suppress the soldiers. Grant soldiers the right of reading books and newspapers.

V   Implement universal education.

    (1) Grant the people the rights to run schools and education in mother tongues.

    (2) Establish higher education to teach all subjects of science.

    (3) Abolish admission rules. Abolish the uniform system of the entrance examination.

    (4) Free tuition for poor students. Grant local people rights to study abroad.

    (5) Set up military academy for all nations. Set up technical schools to teach handicrafts. Set up libraries everywhere for all nations.

VI   Urge the British government to impose sanctions against the aggressors immediately as required by the League of Nations and to participate in the collective security of the alliance. Effectively bar the Japanese Fascist aggressors from the ocean shipping of all the raw materials for military supplies, munitions, and food.

Disallow their mininge or purchases in Malaya. Reject their credit or borrowing.

VII   Aid the Chinese war of self-defence. Refuse to work for the Japanese Fascist aggressors in transportation, mining, rubber-collection, or anything else. Boycott Japanese products. Raise funds, collect gifts, and organize international armies of volunteers to vigorously rally round the Chinese to drive out the Japanese Fascists from China. Support the People's government of Spain. Down with Franco's rebellion forces. Drive out German and Italian Fascists.

VIII   Punish Fascist spies, infiltrators, and Trotskyian bandits. Confiscate their properties and use them for the anti-aggression expense.

IX   Grant people the absolute freedom of speech, publication, association, faith, strike, and organization.

X   Defend the true pillar of peace—the Soviet Union. Unite workers all over the world and all peace-loving countries, peoples, and nations. Support international peace. Punish Fascist aggressors for their atrocity. Thoroughly root out Fascism.

In addition, the Party has also decided on much concrete working tactics. For instance, the Party described sufficient means and ways in establishing the united front of the working class and promoting the movements of peasants, soldiers, youth, etc. During this period, Party's policies attracted wide response from the masses that have further learnt and supported Party's policies.

In July the same year, Party's Fourth Plenum of Executive Committee decided on many working tactics in even more concrete terms. To the British imperialists, the Party would urge it them to join the peace front, at least not to assist the Fascists. To the Japanese Fascists when they invaded Malaya, the Party would co-operate with all anti-Fascist forces with qualifications to defend the peace and security of Malaya. In order to consolidate and expand the united front of overseas Chinese in resistance against Japan, the Party would persist on the policy that the resistance against Japan is the priority in its dealing with labour-capital relations. On the other hand, the Party also made concrete decisions on preventing the advances from British imperialism and building up the Party's own forces.

The Party's influence became more widespread and profound because of these resolutions. The masses had a warm sympathy to the Party's proposition. These tactics also fully exposed and severely hit the British Imperialism of its lack of resolve and sincerity in the anti-Fascism struggle. As a result, the Party and mass organizations expanded.

The Party's Sixth Enlarged Plenum was the turning point in its history when the Party moved from a narrow and secret situation to a position of greater influence and wider basis. The Plenum made more concrete and clearer assessments on the current international and Malayan situations, on the relative strength of the Party and the other forces, and on the future of the united front of all nations. The Party also carried out a concrete review on its previous work.

The Party's Sixth Enlarged Plenum was held in early April 1939. The Plenum assessed the characteristics of the current situation. In the international front, a new economic panic, which was a part of the general crisis of the capitalist economy, had taken place. The new imperialist war to redivide the world had been going on in the process. Under this situation, the tidal waves of anti-Fascist aggression ran higher and higher on the one side; and the socialist Soviet Union won greater victories on the other side. In Malaya, because of the economic and political advances of British imperialism, the national bourgeoisie became more divided, while the working masses lived in greater misery on the other hand; however, the people's anti-imperialism struggle gained daily current strength on the other side. At the same time, the threat of the Japanese Fascist war of aggression heightened the people's spirit of anti-Fascism, while British imperialism actually defended Malaya with hesitation and indecision.

Under such a condition, people of all nations and the British imperialists shared the same objective of anti-Fascist aggression. Yet based on the evaluation of the forces on both sides, the forces led by our Party, i.e. the united front of all nations, were not yet in a position to negotiate a cooperation with the British imperialism, since the two sides had a great disparity in strength. The British imperialists, on the other hand, still wanted to rely on its own ruling power, but not on the people's forces. Thus our Party had to centralize its efforts to unite and consolidate all the national forces. At the same time, under the principle of "national interest first," our Party used the primary democratic rights as a weapon to quickly organize the undisciplined and backward masses. With such prerequisites and principles, the Party's urgent task was to establish the united front of all nations, strive for democracy, and struggle to defend peace. The Party also issued ten points as the concurrent objectives of struggle for the whole Party and compatriots of all nations.

I   All nations in Malaya, regardless of race, class, party, faith (religion), establish the united front of all nations. Strive for a democratic system. Defend the peace and security of Malaya.

II   Establish the All-Malaya Parliament and an assembly in each state. Elected by the people of all nations, they have the right to resolve the problems of economy, politics, national defence, etc.

III Grant the people the freedom of speech, publication, assembly, organization, faith, strike, and leaving the country.

IV   Oppose reactionary policies. Punish Fascists and traitors.

V   Increase salaries and wages. Provide disaster and unemployment relief. Implement labour laws. Institute an eight-hour working day.

VI   Reduce all rent, tax, and usury. Revitalize industry and commerce. Implement tariff self-determination.

VII Equality for men and women. Annul the systems of bond slave, slave-girl, and "bao-liang-ju" (rehabilitation-bureau).

VIII Use the mother tongue to implement universal education. Free tuition for poor students.

IX   Urge the British government to immediately join the collective security, to directly impose sanctions against Fascist aggression, and to help the national war of self-defence of the Republic of China.

X   Unite the peace-loving countries and people all over the world. Support the united movement of international peace.

A Select Bibliography

Andaya, Barbara Watson and Andaya, Leonard Y., 1982, **A History of Malaysia**, London, Macmillan.

Baker, Jim, 1991, **Crossroads: A Popular History of Malaysia and Singapore**, Singapore, Times Books International.

Barlow, H S, 1995, **Swettenham**, Kuala Lumpur, Southdene Sdn. Bhd.

Beaseley, W G, 1987, **Japanese Imperialism, 1894–1945**, Oxford, Clarendon Press.

Carruthers, Susan L, 1995, **Winning Hearts and Minds: British Government, the Media and Colonial Counter-Insurgency 1944–1960**, London, Leicester University Press.

Cheah Boon Kheng, 1983, **Red Star Over Malaya: Resistance and Social Conflict During and After the Japanese Occupation, 1941–1946**, Singapore, Singapore University Press.
— ed, 1992, **From PKI to the Comintern, 1924–1941: The Apprenticeship of the Malayan Communist Party**, Ithaca, Cornell Southeast Asia Programme.

Chew, Ernest and Lee, Edwin, eds, 1991, **A History of Singapore**, Oxford, Oxford University Press.

Chin, Aloysius, 1995, **The Communist Party of Malaya: The Inside Story**, Kuala Lumpur, Vinpress Sdn. Bhd.

Clutterbuck, Richard, 1967, **The Long Long War: The Emergency in Malaya 1948–1960**, London, Cassell and Company Ltd.
— 1984, **Conflict and Violence in Singapore and Malaya 1945–1983**, Singapore, Graham Brash (Pte) Ltd.

Colonial Office Records Series 273, 1914–1936.

Colonial Office Records Series 717, 1920–1940.

Crowley, James, 1966, **Japan's Quest for Autonomy, National Security and Foreign Policy 1930–1938**, Princeton, Princeton University Press.

Deacon, Richard, 1963, **A History of the British Secret Service**, London, Granada.

— 1983, **Kempeitai: A History of the Japanese Secret Service**, New York, Beaufort Books, Inc.

Deakin, Frederick W and Storry, G R 1966, **The Case of Richard Sorge**, London, Chato and Windus.

Degras, Jane, ed, 1960, **The Communist International 1919–1943 Documents Vols. II and III**, London, Oxford University Press.

Dixon, Alec, 1935, **Singapore Patrol**, London, George G Harrap and Co Ltd.

Elphick, Peter and Smith, Michael, 1994, **Odd Man Out: The Story of a Singapore Traitor**, London, Hodder and Stoughton Ltd.

Elphick, Peter, 1998, **Far Eastern File: The Intelligence War in the Far East 1930–1945**, London, Hodder and Stoughton Ltd.

Emerson, Rupert, 1964, **Malaysia: A Study in Direct and Indirect Rule**, Kuala Lumpur, University of Malaya Press.

Faligot, Roger and Kauffer, Remi, 1968, **The Chinese Secret Service**, New York, William Morrow and Company, Inc. (translated by Christine Donoghue).

Fielding, Xan, 1954, **Hide and Seek**, London, Martin Secker and Warburg.

Fujiwara, Iwaichi, 1983, **F Kikan**, Hong Kong, Heinemann Educational Books (Asia) Ltd. (translated by Akashi Yoji).

Gamba, Charles, 1962, **The Origins of Trade Unionism in Malaya: A Study of Colonial Labour Unrest**, Singapore, Eastern Universities Press.

Gough, Richard, 1987, **Special Operations Singapore 1941–42**, Singapore, Heinemann Publishers (Asia) Ltd.

Hanrahan, Gene Z, 1971, **The Communist Struggle in Malaya**, Kuala Lumpur, University of Malaya Press.

Heussler, Robert, 1981, **British Rule in Malaya: The Malayan Civil Service and its Predecessors, 1867–1942**, Oxford, Clio.

Hicks, George L, ed, 1993, **Chinese Remittances from Southeast Asia 1910–1940**, Singapore, Select Books.

James, Lawrence, 1996, **The Rise and fall of the British Empire**, London, Little Brown and Company (UK).

Jones, Alun, 1970, **Internal Security in British Malaya, 1895–1946**, PhD dissertation, Yale University, Ann Arbor, University microfilms.

Josh, Sohan Singh, 1977, **Hindustan Ghadr Party—A Short History**, New Delhi.

Khoo, Kay Kim, 1973, **The Beginnings of Political Extremism in Malaya 1915–1935**, PhD dissertation, Department of History, University of Malaya.

Kratoska, Paul, ed, 1983, **Honourable Intentions: Talks on the British Empire in Southeast Asia**, Singapore. Oxford University Press.

Kuwajima, Sho, 1988, **First World War and Asia: Indian Mutiny in Singapore (1915)**, Osaka, Sho Kuwajima (Department of India and Pakistan), Osaka University.
— 1991, **Indian Mutiny in Singapore 1915**, Calcutta, Ratna Publishers.

Lamont-Brown, Raymond, 1998, **Kempeitai: Japan's Dreaded Military Police**, Phoenix Mill, Sutton Publishing.

Lee, Edwin, 1991, **The British as Rulers: Governing Multiracial Singapore 1867–1914**. Singapore, Singapore University Press.

Long, Roger D, 1995, **The Man on the Spot: Essays on British Empire History**, Westport, Greenwood Press.

Makepeace, Walter et al, eds, 1991, **One Hundred Years of Singapore**, Singapore, Oxford University Press.

McDermott, Kevin and Agnew, Jeremy, 1996, **The Comintern: A History of International Communism from Lenin to Stalin**, London, Macmillan Press Ltd.

Moore, Donald and Moore, Joanna, 1969, **The First 150 years of Singapore**, Singapore, Donald Moore Press.

Miller, Harry, 1954, **Menace in Malaya**, London, George G Harrap.

Onraet, Rene, n.d., **Singapore—A Police Background**, London, Dorothy Crisp and Co Ltd.

Purcell, Victor, 1948, **The Chinese in Malaya**, Kuala Lumpur, Oxford University Press.

Riddell, John, ed, 1986, **Lenin's Struggle for a Revolutionary International, Documents 1907–1916**, New York, Monad Press.

Robertson, Eric, 1979, **The Japanese File**, Hong Kong: Heinemann Educational Books (Asia) Ltd.

Roff, William R, 1967, **The Origins of Malay Nationalism**, Kuala Lumpur, University of Malaya Press.

Rubin, Alfred P, 1974, **Piracy, Paramountcy and Protectorates**, Kuala Lumpur, Penerbit Universiti Malaya.

Sadka, Emily, 1968, **The Protected Malay States 1874–1895**, Kuala Lumpur, University of Malaya Press.

Sareen, T H, 1995, **Secret Documents on Singapore Mutiny 1915 Volumes 1 and 2**, New Delhi, Mounto Publishing House.

Schwarz, Bill, 1996, **The Expansion of England: Race, Ethnicity and Cultural History**. London, Routledge.

Sheenan, Margaret, 2000, **Out In the Midday Sun: The British in Malaya 1880–1960**, London, John Murray (Publishers) Ltd.

Shirer, William L, 1992, **The Rise and Fall of the Third Reich**, New York, Ballantine Books.

Smith, Michael, 2000, **The Emperor's Code**, New York, Bantam Press.

Song Ong Siong, 1985, **One Hundred Years of the Chinese in Singapore**, Singapore, Oxford University Press.

Stenson, M R, 1970, **Industrial Conflict in Malaya: Prelude to the Communist Revolt of 1948**, London, Oxford University Press.

Straits Settlements Police Journal—abbreviated as **SSPJ**.

Swettenham, Frank, 1948, **British Malaya**, London, Allen and Unwin.

Tarling, Nicholas, 1998, **Britain, Southeast Asia and the Onset of the Cold War, 1945–1950**, Cambridge, Cambridge University Press.

Tate, D M, comp, 1989, **Straits Affairs: The Malay World and Singapore**, Hong Kong, John Nicholson Ltd.

Tay, Seow Huah, 1956, **The History of the Singapore Police Force 1817–1889**, Honours thesis, Singapore, University of Singapore History Department.

Thio, Eunice, 1969, **British Policy in the Malay Peninsula 1880–1910**, Singapore, University of Malaya Press.

Turnbull, C M, 1972, **The Straits Settlements 1826–1867**, London, The Athlone Press.
— 1997, **A History of Singapore 1819–1988**, Singapore, Oxford University Press.

Wakeman, Frederic, 1995, **Policing Shanghai, 1927–1937**, Berkeley, University of California Press.

West, Nigel, 1982, **A Matter of Trust MI5 1945 to 1972**, London, Weidenfeld and Nicolson.

Winstedt, Richard, 1958, **Malaya and its History**, London, Hutchinson University Library.

Yong, C F and McKenna, R B, 1990, **The Kuomintang Movement in British Malaya 1912–1949**, Singapore, Singapore University Press.

Yong, C F, 1992, **Chinese Leadership and Power in Colonial Singapore**, Singapore, Times Academic Press.
— 1997, **The Origins of Malayan Communism**, Singapore, South Seas Society.

Index